DEEMED SUSPECT

Other books by Eric Koch

The French Kiss
The Leisure Riots, published in German as *Die Freizeit-Revoluzzer*
The Last Thing You'd Want to Know, published in German as *Die Spanne Leben*
Good Night, Little Spy

DEEMED SUSPECT

A Wartime Blunder

Eric Koch

〈n〉 METHUEN

Toronto   New York   London   Sydney

Canadian Cataloguing in Publication Data

Koch, Eric, 1919–
    Deemed suspect

Includes index.

ISBN 0-458-94490-4

1. Concentration camps – Canada.   2. World
War, 1939–1945 – Austria – Refugees.
3. World War, 1939–1945 – Germany –
Refugees.   4. World War, 1939–1945 –
Canada – Refugees.   I. Title.

D805.C2K62   940.54′72′71   C80-094588-3

Composition: Video Text Inc.

All reasonable attempts have been made to
trace "the unknown artists" whose drawings
have been included in this book.

Printed and bound in Canada
1 2 3 4 5   80   84 83 82 81

Contents

Acknowledgments

I wish to thank the ninety ex-internees who patiently put up with me and my tape-recorder. They have provided the main sources for this book, together with the Canadian and British men and women who were involved in our story and allowed me to interview them. I also owe a debt of gratitude to Paula Draper and John Joseph Kelly who, while doing pioneering work for their respective M.A. theses, excavated much useful material. Moreover, it was my good fortune that at a crucial stage of my research Bernard Wasserstein's book *Britain and the Jews of Europe, 1939–1945* was published by the Institute of Jewish Affairs, London; Clarendon Press, Oxford; it supplied me with many clues to my English chapters. I also am grateful to Walter Laqueur for opening the doors of the Wiener Library in London and allowing me to examine some excellent material. To Dr. Werner Röder of the Institut für Zeitgeschichte in Munich who answered a number of important questions, many thanks.

I would like to acknowledge the help I received, far beyond the call of duty, from Glenn Wright at the Public Archives in Ottawa, as well as the exchanges of information with my two colleagues in England who recently published the internment story from the British point of view (Peter Gillman's book *Collar the Lot!* (Quartet Books, London) and Ronald Stent's *This Bespattered Page?* (André Deutsch, London)).

Also, I am grateful to David Rome of the Canadian Jewish Congress in Montreal who opened his archives and told me many stories; to Karl Schatzky for his assistance and to Karl D. Renner. For the translations from German into English I wish to give credit to my daughter Monica. And—to my wife Sonia thanks are due for the many invaluable extra-marital services she performed to make this work possible.

Finally, I would like to express my gratitude to the Explorations Program of the Canada Council and to the Multiculturalism Directorate of the Department of the Secretary of State for their generous assistance.

Preface

On September 4, 1936, the former British Prime Minister David Lloyd George paid a visit to Adolf Hitler in his mountain retreat in Berchtesgaden. The two men had conversations about the state of the world. At the end of their meeting Herr Hitler presented Lloyd George with a photograph of himself in a silver frame, with a personal inscription to the great leader of the First World War. "Would you mind," Lloyd George asked the Fuehrer, "if I place this picture on my desk side by side with those of Foch, Clemenceau, and other allied leaders of the Great War?" "Not at all," replied Hitler. "Germany does not hate its former enemies. We all realize they had simply done their duties as soldiers fighting for their countries." The Allied victory in 1918, he went on, had been primarily due to Lloyd George "who had galvanized the people into a will to victory." The fact that Germany lost the war did not matter, he said; what mattered was the manner in which defeat had been accepted by what Hitler called "the worst elements of the German nation."

Lloyd George was deeply touched by the Fuehrer's words and gesture. He did not conceal his pride to have heard them *"from the greatest German of the age."*[1]

A year later, the Canadian Prime Minister Mackenzie King came to see Hitler.[2] He said he found him "a simple sort of peasant, not very intelligent, and no serious danger to anyone." However, King did point out to him that, although Canada was an independent country, if the freedom of the Commonwealth were threatened the Dominions would rally to Britain's defense. In 1939 he kept his word.

According to the 1939 German census more than half the Jewish population—280,000 confessional Jews—had left Germany since Adolf Hitler's accession to power in 1933. After the

Anschluss 130,000 left Austria. The same census also observed that 12,000 Jews were in concentration camps.[3]

Where did they go, these Germans and Austrians? Here are some approximate figures: 22,000 to Argentina; 10,000 to Australia (which was prepared to take another 15,000 when war broke out); 20,000 to Brazil; 4,000 to Canada; 20,000 to China; 20,000 to Colombia; 20,000 to Mexico; 100,000 to Palestine; 73,500 to the United Kingdom; 140,000 to the United States.[4]

Relative to size and absorption capacity, England was more open in its immigration policies towards German and Austrian refugees than the United States which, except in the year 1939, did not fill its annual quotas; after the Crystal Night in November 1938—the worst of the Nazi pogroms—when the 1939 quotas should have been extended, the Administration refused to do so.

Early that year the Wagner–Rogers Bill was drafted. It contained a proposal to admit 20,000 refugee children, but it failed to reach the floor of Congress. At around the same time 10,000 such children were admitted to the United Kingdom.

During the Depression years, the North American equivalent to appeasement was isolationism. Neither Canadians nor Americans had any wish to become involved again in Europe's quarrels. Canadians in particular did not regard themselves as custodians of the world's conscience. When in 1935 in the wake of Italy's attack on Ethiopia, the League of Nations discussed sanctions against that country, Ernest Lapointe, the Canadian minister of justice, succinctly summed up his government's attitude: "No interest in Ethiopia, of any nature whatsoever, is worth the life of a single Canadian citizen. No consideration could justify participation in such a war."

The 4,000 Jewish refugees who were admitted to Canada during the Hitler years either had to demonstrate that they had capital, or access to capital, or that they could be employed in agriculture. A few got in because they had connections or could make a special case.

On May 13, 1939, 930 refugees boarded the German ship *S.S. St. Louis* in Hamburg bound for Cuba.[5] Each one of them had paid a high price for an official landing certificate signed by Cuba's director-general of immigration. Seven hundred and thirty-four of the passengers had valid immigration papers for the United States, effective from three months to three years after arrival in Cuba.

Without exception, the refugees had suffered various kinds of hell in Germany. But on board the luxury liner they were treated like ordinary passengers. (The ship's captain, Gustav Schroeder, was decorated many years later by the post-war German government for his humane conduct throughout the voyage.) A number of them had asked relatives and friends in the United States to meet them in Havana at the dockside.

Eight days before the *St. Louis* sailed, the president of Cuba, Federico Loreda Bru, notified her owners, the Hamburg–Amerika Line, that the landing certificates, which they had bought from the Cubans on behalf of the passengers, had been declared invalid. (For unexplained reasons, the passengers were not informed of this development.) Therefore, the Cubans refused permission to land. The relatives and friends standing on the Havana pier could merely wave to those on board. One of them, a lawyer from Breslau, slashed his wrists in desperation and jumped overboard. He was fished out and brought to a Havana hospital, where he recovered. Captain Schroeder had to organize an anti-suicide squad to prevent further attempts. Negotiators arrived from New York to offer more money. But the Cubans— including their president—were so extortionist in their demands that negotiations soon broke down. Appeals were sent to several other countries, without success. Canada was not approached; a negative reply was considered a foregone conclusion. The *St. Louis* had no choice but to leave Havana. The distraught passengers formed a committee and sent a wire to President Roosevelt, but they received no reply. Instead, a U.S. coast guard cutter followed the ship, with instructions to make sure that not a single refugee could reach the shore.

The story received a good deal of publicity. The *New York Times* editorialized: "We can only hope that some hearts will soften somewhere and some refuge can be found. The cruise of the *St. Louis* cries to high heaven of man's inhumanity to man. . . ."

In Canada, even though the front pages were filled with stories and pictures of the royal visit, Professor George M. Wrong of the University of Toronto sent a message signed by forty-four prominent Torontonians to his former student Mackenzie King:

> As a mark of gratitude to Almighty God for the pleasure and gratification which has been vouchsafed to the Canadian people through the visit of Their Gracious Majesties King George and Queen Elizabeth, and as evidence of the true Christian charity of the people of this most fortunate and blessed country, Canada, we respectfully suggest that, under the powers vested in you as premier of our country, you forthwith offer to the homeless exiles on board the Hamburg–Amerika Line ship *St. Louis* sanctuary in Canada.

The prime minister was on board the royal train in Washington when he received the message. He telegraphed his advisers in Ottawa, asking them to notify Professor Wrong that the matter was under consideration. On June 19 a letter was sent to Professor Wrong:

> While every sympathy was felt for the unfortunate position in which the refugees in question found themselves, it was most regretted it was not possible to recommend their admission en bloc into Canada. . . .
>
> None of the passengers on the *St. Louis*, so far as our authorities were aware, had previously indicated a desire to enter Canada, and no request for permission to land here was received from the ship or passengers. . . . The immediate difficulties in which they found themselves were due to the working of the United States quota system in conjunction with the revision of the Cuban system of temporary admission.

That letter was based in part on a memorandum written on June 8, 1939 by F. C. Blair, Director of Immigration.

> I understand that most of the refugees are hoping to get into the United States. I suppose if they were admitted to Canada a number of them would smuggle themselves across to the U.S. shortly.

He went on to say that Canada owed them nothing. Moreover, he argued that if they subsequently went to the United States, this would not be appreciated by Canada's neighbor.

> The readiness with which a German liner took these people on board in the hope of landing them in some other country,

creates the impression that this is but another of Germany's methods to get rid of unwanted refugees, and if this is successful it is likely to be followed by other shiploads.

Captain Schroeder sailed the *St. Louis* back toward Germany. He moved his ship slowly across the Atlantic to give Jewish organizations sufficient time to appeal to West European countries for help. If they failed, he secretly considered beaching the ship on England's south coast.

At long last, Great Britain, France, Holland and Belgium agreed to accept the passengers. Many, and it is impossible to know exactly how many, of those who went to France, Holland and Belgium were seized by the Nazis less than a year later and subsequently died in extermination camps. Only those who had the good fortune to land in England survived.

In August 1939 the Berlin publication *Weltkampf* made this comment:

> We are saying openly that we do not want the Jews while the democracies keep on claiming that they are willing to receive them—then leave the guests out in the cold. Aren't we savages better men after all?

Introduction

In the spring of 1940, during the Nazi assault on Holland, Belgium and France, the British government interned close to thirty thousand refugees from Nazi Germany and Austria as "enemy aliens." In July, 2,290 were sent to Canada. The stories of their internment, their reception in Canada, the description of life in the various camps, and how they finally made it to freedom, is the subject of this book.

More than half of the internees returned to England, but almost one thousand became Canadian citizens after the war. A chapter, followed by a *Who's Who* at the end of the book, will describe what has happened to us since our release.

Most of us accepted our arrest and internment as a reasonable precaution to be taken by a country threatened with invasion. British newspapers at the time were full of stories of how Hitler's fifth column had undermined Holland's resistance, and there was no reason to assume that England had not been similarly infiltrated. England panicked.

Therefore, we quietly accepted the injustice that was being done to us. As refugees, we were grateful to England for having given us a haven at a time when other countries were making every effort to keep us out. Besides, we felt it was infinitely better to sit behind British barbed wire than to be exposed to mortal danger in Nazi Europe. After all, refugees usually don't tell their hosts how to behave in times of extreme peril.

Our situation was fundamentally different from the internment of Japanese Canadians after Pearl Harbor. That action was the culmination of decades of prejudice and suspicion of the Japanese minority living on the Pacific Coast. Three-quarters of the twenty-one thousand people incarcerated were Canadian citizens, their property was confiscated and sold, and they were threatened with "deportation" unless they dispersed across Canada.[6] Few, if any, would have accepted such treatment as not unreasonable in wartime, as we did. They were the victims of racism, clearly demonstrated by the restrictive measures taken against them for nearly four years after the end of the war which denied them the right to live and work where they chose.

Undoubtedly, there was also an element of prejudice in our treatment. It was a mixture of anti-Jewish and anti-German sentiment, but perhaps it would be fairest to call it anti-alien. About 75 percent of us had Jewish or half-Jewish backgrounds. Even in peacetime the British are somewhat ambivalent on the subject of foreigners. In a crisis their latent suspicions come to the fore. Yet, while the bombs were falling on Britain, long and soul-searching debates continued in the House of Commons on the status of refugees. The story of the government's retreat, and how the best side of the British tradition prevailed after the short aberration, is a memorable chapter in the history of Western democracy.

Somewhat different, however, is the actual account of how the British authorities persuaded the Canadian government to accept custody of seven thousand dangerous Nazis, while they had only managed to round up two and a half thousand suspect German civilians and had taken three thousand German prisoners of war. Rather than admit that they did not have enough "subversives" to make up the numbers, it was decided to fill the vacant spaces on the prison boats with refugees. It was a prime example of bureaucratic bungling.

The arrangements made with the Canadian and Australian governments specifically had referred to dangerous men. No wonder the Canadians were flabbergasted when they watched a column of Catholic priests, rabbinical students and chubby faced teenagers come ashore; thirty-five percent of our Canadian contingent was between sixteen and twenty years old! . . .

Yet this book is one of the few Second World War stories with a happy ending.

Part One

ONE

Panic

In the afternoon of Whit-Sunday, May 12, 1940, I was sitting in my digs at Cambridge. The "phony war" was over: on May 10 the Germans had invaded Holland. I had almost completed my third year as a law student and was preparing for my final exams. There was a knock on my door. I said "come in," and two policemen stood before me. "You're under arrest," said one of them.

"You'll be away for only a few days, Sir," the second bobby told me. Ironically, my main concern was whether or not I would be able to take my notes along. I decided to play it safe and throw a few papers into a small suitcase. What I remember best about this whole encounter is that my bobbies were singularly unimpressed by the behavior of my landlady. Naturally worried about her rent, and convinced that she had been harboring a dangerous German spy these past months, she created a violent scene. The policemen calmed her down while helping me to pack my toothbrush and sundry belongings. They also graciously allowed me to scribble a brief note to my mother who was living in London at the time. But they would not permit me to mail it; they kindly did it for me.

In Cambridge students and professors were rounded up, including those who had been evacuated there from the London School of Economics. The gathering point was in front of King's College Chapel. From there we were sent by bus to Bury St. Edmunds, less than one hour's ride away.

I left my native Frankfurt in 1935 to go to an English public school in Kent. I was fifteen at the time. Had there not been a war I would have become a naturalized British subject at the end of 1940. Two months before my arrest I had appeared before the Cambridge University Joint Recruiting Board which had recommended that, regulations permitting, I be trained as an officer in a British infantry regiment.

I wasn't particularly upset when I was arrested. I realized that the military threat was so serious that neither my friends nor I had the right to challenge the wisdom of the authorities. It seemed perfectly plausible that I would be detained only for a few days. We were treated with punctilious politeness, and there was no hostility during the whole procedure.

This did not happen everywhere. In other parts of England men were woken in the middle of the night, allowed only minimum time to settle their personal affairs, and were then transported in police vans accompanied by truck-loads of soldiers to various rallying points. But that kind of harsh treatment was not typical of the operation, as courtesy and kindness usually prevailed.

To be arrested by people considered to be friends was a traumatic experience for the thousands of those who had suffered cruelty at the hands of the Nazis. A family friend, a man of sixty-two, had been tortured in a concentration camp. In 1939–1940 he was engaged in chemical research work in London and his firm applied for exemption from internment. This was ignored by the police when they came to intern him. He told them he could not endure another internment, but they remained adamant. He took a quick poison. According to Eleanor Rathbone, M.P., who mentioned this case in the House of Commons on July 10, "he had escaped the stupidity and malice of others."

Noel Baker, M.P. mentioned the case of a man aged 53.

Refugee from Nazi oppression; . . . three months in a Nazi concentration camp where he contracted diabetes. Now living on daily insulin. Only child in English sanatorium with chest disease; offer to serve Britain three times refused. Had this morning been detained by C. I. D. men for immediate internment. Fainted; carried away semi-conscious. Here's to victory.

On July 27, 1940, this story about scientist Dr. Martin Freud, son of Sigmund Freud, the founder of psychoanalysis, appeared in the London *Daily Herald*. "Four weeks ago police officers came to Dr. Freud's house in Hampstead at seven in the morning, a friend of the family told the paper. He was given half an hour to prepare, and was removed unshaven and without breakfast. We later learned that he had been taken to internment near Liverpool." His son Walter was arrested at his school.

But many of us recounted the stories of our arrest with resigned amusement. Emil Fackenheim, who had been in a German concentration camp from 1938 to 1939, was impressed by the good manners displayed by the policeman who had come to arrest him in Aberdeen, where he was studying. He said he was grateful that he was being detained with such respect, if not with deference. How different from the situation from which he had so recently barely managed to escape alive, he told me. The policeman also had informed him that it was only a matter of a few days. But Fackenheim didn't believe him. He had become an expert on the subject of arrests and felt he knew more about it than the nice man who had come to detain him. So he calmly picked about forty books from his bookshelf and put them in his suitcase. "You won't need all those, Sir," the policeman said. So Fackenheim proceeded to give him a little lecture: "You know your business, officer, and I know mine."

Walter Nussbaum published this story of his arrest in an Israeli newspaper many years later:

> The first time I was addressed as Mister was in May 1940, when the British Secret Service called at the hostel for Jewish refugee children in London and asked to see me.
> The minister of our small community of youngsters, all cared for by the Jewish Refugee Committee at Bloomsbury House, told the agents that "Mister Nussbaum was saying his morning prayers just now," adding, "You won't have to wait too long as he usually finishes before he even starts."
> The moment I heard that someone had called me "Mister" my curiosity rose. I stepped out into the hall holding my head straight up as a "Mister" should, especially as I had just turned sixteen, and faced the two gentlemen.
> "We are sorry to inform you, Sir" (What a day—first

Mister, now Sir!) "that under the Emergency Regulations . . . we have to arrest you."

"A rest? What for a rest? I am not tired. I don't need a vacation."

The gentlemen looked at each other and a faint smile passed over their faces.

"Detain you, Sir."

After packing a few belongings and receiving a crown from the minister, I was led to a waiting car and thus I had my first car ride through this great city of London.

Many of John Newmark's friends had already been arrested, so when they came to pick him up on his birthday, June 12, he had already packed his things in a little brown bag. When the bobbie who came to his rented room in Hampstead suggested he get his things together, Newmark said, "I'm all packed, Officer. I'm at your disposal." So, as they had time to spare, the two of them went off to the corner pub to have a beer. Then they drove together to Bow Street Police Station. "I had nothing to lose," Newmark observed. "I was a musician, without a work permit."

William Heckscher recalls, "I was intensely interested what kind of psychological impact all this would have on me. . . . I was utterly optimistic, which shows how foolish I was at the time. I lived from one day to the next."

Gregory Baum had been working on a farm in Wales. "I thought that some invisible power had rescued me from shovelling manure. . . . I had not realized how unhappy I had been."

Ernest Borneman had been working in films and writing about folk music. He had just recorded his first broadcast for the B.B.C., "Folk Songs from Three Continents." While sitting in the bus on the way to the police station, the radio was on and coincidentally his talk was being broadcast. Chuckling to himself, he asked the policeman, "Do you recognize the voice on the radio?" He answered, "The man has an accent." "Yes, that's me," Borneman replied. The policeman was astounded. "Why are you here?" he asked. "That's what I would like to know," Borneman replied.

While Borneman had been specializing in folk music, Freddy Grant was making a name for himself as a writer of songs and film music. He had been working with Gracie Fields and Jessie

Matthews who at the time were the big stars in London's West End.

> I remember reading a headline in the papers, "Intern all Aliens!" It was the day before I was to sign a contract for twenty pounds a week for two years. But when the news about the internment got around, the publisher said, "I'm sorry, I don't think you can sign that right now." Gradually some of the people I had been friendly with wouldn't talk to me any more in the street. They thought I was Hitler or something: I don't know what they thought.

Anderson's Prisoners, by "Judex," a book published late in 1940 by Victor Gollancz, contains the following paragraph:

> What did Hitler say to this? He said to his people: "The enemies of Germany are now the enemies of Britain, too. The British have detained in concentration camps the very people we found it necessary to detain. Where are those much-vaunted democratic liberties of which the English like to boast?"

Britain and the Refugees

The British, opening their doors to us, had saved our lives and, generally speaking, were kind and hospitable toward us. We, in turn, thought it prudent to keep a low profile. The Jewish organization, encouraging such behavior, handed out a pamphlet entitled *Helpful Information and Guidance for Every Refugee* which adjured us to refrain from speaking German or reading German-language newspapers in public, and indeed from speaking in a loud voice. The pamphlet also urged us not to criticize existing government regulations or the way things were done in Britain. "Englishmen attach very great importance to modesty, understatement in speech, and quietness of dress and manner. They value good manners far more than the evidence of wealth."

It was not difficult to follow this last piece of advice, as most of us had neither money nor permission to work. Jewish organizations supported the Jews, and non-Jews were helped by other associations, such as the Quakers. Many of us were appalled by the apparent British complacency vis-à-vis the Nazi danger. We had all been previously awed by brutal German efficiency, but to hear the British blithely singing "We're going to hang out the washing on the Siegfried Line . . ." was aptly described by the Austrian writer Stefan Zweig as "an obtuse form of courage."

Thirty-five hundred refugees were in the Richborough Camp near Sandwich in Kent, more popularly known as the Kitchener Camp. This was a "City of Refuge" maintained by the "Council for German Jewry." Launched at the end of 1938 after the horror of the Crystal Night, it accommodated the men who had been thrown in concentration camps such as Sachsenhausen during the pogrom only to be released if they could prove that they had an English visa, as well as those who were in acute danger of being arrested unless they left Germany or Austria immediately. The camp, designed to house transients, who waited for visas to the United States or other countries, was a self-governing enterprise, and hundreds received agricultural and technical training there. Few of the inmates spoke English; the camp was facetiously named "ANGLO-Sachsenhausen." It attracted the attention of many politicians and journalists and was visited by the Archbishop of Canterbury who told the men that "it is a great thing that this country can look upon you not only as refugees whom we have been glad to welcome, but also as fellow workers in a common cause in which we may all join."[7]

When war broke out more than half the residents of the Kitchener Camp volunteered for service in the non-combatant alien companies of the Pioneer Corps. Having sworn their oath of allegiance to King George VI, and having received the King's Shilling, they called themselves the "King's Own Enemy Aliens." As soon as the first five companies, each containing about three hundred men, had finished their training, they were sent to France in the first months of 1940. When France collapsed they were given arms, and together with the British Expeditionary Force they were evacuated from Dunkirk and came back to England. According to Colonel Arthur Evans, M.P., they had acquitted themselves "in a manner worthy of the best traditions of the British Army."

As was to be expected, as increasing numbers of refugees arrived in the United Kingdom they aroused some antipathy, on two grounds: they had the advantage of private—and later publicly subsidized—assistance; and they were labelled "carriers of Marxism and other forms of decadence." However, until the spring of 1940 anti-refugee sentiment was restrained, even though organs like *The Fascist* and *Fascist Weekly* did their best to fan it. More serious, however, was the line taken by pro-appeasement newspapers such as the *Daily Express* and the *Daily Mail* which regarded the influx of these people as a needless irritant in Anglo-German relations. It must be said that it was very much to the credit of the British public that their innate sense of decency prevented any major outbursts of opposition. Yet, there was enough resentment to cause concern to the government, strengthening its determination not to issue work permits to refugees unless it was sure that no native Britisher could, or would, do the work.

By the time war broke out 73,500 Jewish refugees had arrived in England, but many people assumed there were far more. In April 1940, the public opinion poll *Mass Observation* reported that "one middle class man put the number at a couple of million, and another at four million. The tone of voice did not indicate that these persons were being facetious."

Another element that colored British attitudes towards Jews at the time was the policy restricting immigration to Palestine. Just before the war the Arabs had been given a veto over all long-term Jewish settlements. Not only the Jews but also men like Winston Churchill considered this an unforgivable retreat from the pledge made in 1917 by the Balfour Declaration which promised "the establishment of a national home for the Jewish people," at the same time assuring the Arabs that nothing would be done to prejudice the civil and religious rights of existing non-Jewish communities. These contradictory pledges had been made in the context of the First World War; since then Palestine had become England's second Ireland, an intractable problem which made enemies for her not only in the Middle East but also everywhere else. Throughout the thirties the British government increasingly had subordinated the pledge given to the Jews to that given to the Arabs, because it seemed England needed Arab loyalty more, in case of war, than Jewish loyalty, which it felt could be taken for granted. There is, however, plenty of evidence that some policy-makers in Whitehall—not Winston Churchill—may have agreed with Anthony Eden when he "murmured" in 1941 to his private secretary that he preferred the Arabs to the Jews.

As Max Beloff remarked: "Since the Jews got in the way of

the policy of a Great Power which was perfectly rational from its point of view, is it surprising that they were disliked?"[8]

However, there would have been an outcry in Great Britain if in 1939, when war broke out, all enemy aliens had been interned, as they had been in 1914. The presence of so many of Hitler's victims would have made such a policy unacceptable when cool minds still prevailed. There was no similarity between the Kaiser and Hitler. Yet some of the language used in connection with our later internment was reminiscent of 1914: "Will my Right Honourable Friend bear in mind," Lieutenant-Colonel Acland-Troyte, C.M.G., D.S.O., Tory member for Tiverton, shouted across the House of Commons to Anthony Eden, "that you cannot trust any Boche any time?"

Tribunals

The day after England declared war on Germany, the Home Secretary, Sir John Anderson, announced to the House of Commons that "an immediate review of all Germans and Austrians in the country would be made." One hundred and twenty one-man tribunals were established, usually comprising one King's Counsel, or one county court judge, with a police secretary in attendance. On the basis of dossiers made available by the Home Office, and containing information supplied by refugee organizations, their duty was to decide whether or not the enemy alien who appeared before them was a threat to national security. They also could determine who was "a Refugee from Nazi Oppression" and who was not a refugee at all.

Three categories were established:

1. Men and women in Category A: deemed suspect—to be interned immediately. There were six hundred of them.

2. Those in Category B to remain at liberty subject to certain restrictions, such as a five-mile travelling limit and the surrender of cameras and bicycles. Six thousand eight hundred fell into that group.

3. The 64,200 in Category C to be exempt from internment and all restrictions.

Altogether 51,200 were declared "Refugees from Nazi Oppression."

At first there was little criticism of the work done by the

tribunals, although certain inconsistencies soon became evident. Why were some thirteen thousand "friendly enemy aliens" in Category C not stamped "Refugees from Nazi Oppression"? Who were they? Why was a sizeable number of genuine refugees in Category A? And who precisely qualified for a B?

Different judges had different criteria. They did their work conscientiously and with dispatch, and no doubt accurately reflected the state of public opinion—or at least the state of opinion of the social class from which King's Counsels were drawn. By virtue of the fact that the tribunals had large discretionary powers, some allowed, for example, their anti-bolshevik bias to prevail, by declaring suspect all veterans of the International Brigade which had fought the fascists in Spain. They were interned forthwith. A husband and wife, when asked about their political affiliations, stated they had been supporters of the Weimar Republic; they were classified as communists, and the judge ruled they be interned.

Other judges scented something "fishy" about those anti-Nazis who had fought Hitler from inside Germany, in underground trade union movements or in whatever political opposition they could muster. Many of the judges had no concept of the plight of men and women who, because they possessed one Jewish grandmother, had been declared "non-Aryans" according to the Nuremberg Laws. Some refugees who had overstayed the period allowed by their visitor's visa were interned immediately, and certain people were incarcerated because they were in trouble with their employers.

The tribunals can be described as a symptom of the phony war; psychologically they were closer to peacetime. Smacking of amateurism, they had something gentlemanly about them. Nevertheless, the categories they had placed us in stuck with us for a long time.

As early as March 1940 a change in atmosphere became discernible. The Home Secretary, Sir John Anderson, wrote to his father: "The newspapers are working up feelings about aliens. I shall have to do something about it or we will be stampeded into an unnecessarily oppressive policy. It is very easy in wartime to start a scare."

On April 9, 1940 the Germans invaded Denmark and Norway, and on April 20, 1940 the *Daily Mail* demanded that "the police round up every doubtful alien in the country." The *Daily Sketch* and the *Sunday Express* then began denouncing the tribunals for being half-hearted, interning only a few hundred of these "dangerous men." Allegedly, Scotland Yard now was gravely concerned about the leniency shown by the Aliens' Tribunals, and by April 23, 1940 Colonel Henry Burton, Conservative M.P. for Sudbury, could not help suggesting in the House: "Would it not be far better to intern the lot and then pick out the few good ones?"

On May 10, 1940 Hitler invaded Holland and Belgium. That same evening Winston Churchill became prime minister of Great Britain, and one of the first things his new government did was to declare certain areas along the south and east coasts of the British Isles "protected areas," decreeing that all male German and Austrian nationals between the ages of sixteen and sixty living in that region be interned forthwith. When Hitler's armies swept into France, the British had every reason to fear that they would be next.

The Enemy Within

During the French Revolution, on the night before the September massacres of 1792, it was said that Paris was full of aristocrats disguised as ecclesiastics.[9] During the Franco–Prussian war of 1870–71, Parisians thought they saw Prussian spies "about everywhere," sending light signals to the enemy. Early in August 1914, the Germans had no doubt about activities by French and Russian agents, some in German uniform, others disguised as priests or nuns. In Paris it was rumored that German officers in French uniforms were destroying bridges. The Swiss firm Maggi (partly owned by Germans) was charged with delivering poisonous milk. It was said that "a band of itinerant musicians, who, though they played mournful airs in the street, were really a group of German officers" considered to be spies. In the Scottish Highlands, Germans were supposed to have assembled fuel for their zeppelins. When America entered the war in 1917, every German immigrant since 1914 was assumed to have occupied himself with nothing but subversive plots. In the Second World War, Canadians and Americans of Japanese descent were supposed to have sent light signals to

Japanese submarines in the Pacific, not to mention the secret transmitters which they allegedly were using to perform this task. The *Nisei,* apparently were also poisoning the vegetables they sold to American and Canadian housewives.

This universal phenomenon is known as "war hysteria." It is caused by fear of an enemy, thought to have immense power and capable of unleashing a catastrophe of unimaginable proportions. The symptoms of war hysteria are particularly virulent when hostilities begin. After people get used to living under the tensions of war, these symptoms normally diminish. At the end of April 1940 the polling organization *Mass Observation* had reported that anti-alien sentiment was very pronounced among "the middle and upper classes."

> There is as yet no sign that the press campaign for internment has fully registered on the masses, but there is every sign that the situation is developing.

On May 14, four days after the invasion of Holland and Belgium, *Mass Observation* had noted a changed atmosphere:

> Nearly everyone, as previous research has shown, is latently somewhat anti-Semitic and somewhat anti-alien. But ordinarily it is not the done thing to express such sentiments publicly. The news from Holland made it quite the done thing, all of a sudden.

Two months later *Mass Observation* conducted a third poll. Fifty-five percent of the people questioned favored interning all enemy aliens, and 27 percent favored a more discriminating policy. The report pointed out that of the majority, many recognized the injustice it implied. Someone was quoted as saying, "You can't say which is good and which bad. Some of them is very nice people, but it's safest to put them all in."

The *Daily Mail*'s campaign was particularly ugly. On May 24 a columnist wrote:

> The rounding up of enemy aliens must be taken out of the fumbling hands of local tribunals. All refugees from Austria and Germany . . . women and men alike, should be drafted without delay to a remote part of the country and kept under strict supervision. . . . As the head of a Balkan state said to me last month: "In Britain you fail to realize that

every German is an agent. All of them have both the duty
and the means to communicate information to Berlin."

No wonder some employers began to fire foreigners, even men
and women who were British subjects but had foreign ancestry.

On May 30 Sir Neville Bland, who, as British Minister in
Holland, had witnessed the German invasion, said on the B.B.C.:

> Be careful at this moment how you put complete trust in
> any person of German or Austrian connection. If you know
> people of this kind who are still at large keep your eye on
> them; they may be perfectly all right, but they may not, and
> today we can't afford to take risks. . . . We may have many
> lessons to learn from Holland . . . there may still be some
> devilish surprises in store for us.

Finally, on July 12, when the anti-alien feeling had begun to
subside, the *Daily Mail* published a story by Alice Hemming
under the headline "Canada is all out to win."

> In Montreal a shopkeeper told me that he is convinced that
> Hitler drove out the Jews and political opponents with the
> express purpose of sending Gestapo agents among them in
> the Christian countries that took them in. "Where did so
> many of them get so much money to live on?" he said. "Poor
> refugees—huh! All they have to do is say Hitler was mean
> to them, and half of them are spies!"

TWO

Internment

The criteria for the internment of enemy aliens were widened in step with the crescendo of voices. It had started on May 12 with the arrest of all males between sixteen and sixty in the protected areas. From May 16 on men and *women* in Category B—that was the vague category of people about whom there was a small cloud of doubt—began to be rounded up, not only in the protected areas but across the country. How efficient the operation was depended on the competence and attitude of the various police constables. Many people were left alone. As the news from France became more desperate, plans were made to intern all male enemy aliens in Category C between the ages of sixteen and seventy, the ones who earlier had been completely cleared by the tribunals. By the end of June between three and four thousand women in Category B had been rounded up.

In the Kitchener Camp, where seven tribunals had examined 3,500 refugees in seven weeks and labelled them "Refugees from Nazi Oppression," the Army took control without changing the self-governing nature of the camp. During the Dunkirk operation, when in the first week of June 215,000 British and 120,000 French troops were evacuated, leaving almost all their equipment and 20,000 prisoners to the Nazis, those members of the camp who had not joined the Pioneer Corps were transferred as internees to camps on the Isle of Man. Manfred Wolff recalls: "From our train which took us along the south coast we saw the sky all lit up during the night of June 2. We had no idea why. We only found out later."

"Some of the soldiers returning from Dunkirk were assigned to our camps as guards. They were in a terrible state," Edgar Sarton remembers. "They were completely passive, utterly depressed. I shall never forget the picture of helplessness. Here we were, under British guard; and the British Army was in *that* state."

When on June 10 Italy entered the war, it was immediately decided to intern all Italians who had lived in England for less than twenty years—seven thousand of them. In London, there were attacks on Italian restaurants and ice cream parlors. The *Hotel Review* was gratified to note that "the extensive Italianization of our hotels would now be checked."

All this was the result of the two-months-long scare. The irony was that, all expectations notwithstanding, no significant fifth column existed in England. Churchill wrote in his memoirs: "There were known to be twenty thousand organized German Nazis in England at the time," a wild exaggeration by whoever had supplied him with this figure. In truth, the German espionage network in the United Kingdom was small and incompetent and was quickly penetrated by British security services. As for the Italians, Count Ciano noted in his diary on September 11, 1940: "It seems incredible, but we do not have a single informant in Great Britain."

This is not to say that the Germans did not use fifth columns elsewhere. But newspaper reporters and diplomatic observers never had enough time to investigate the extent of these activities: the Germans won too quickly. Once they had won, the curtain dropped. Inevitably, this led to exaggerated reports in the British press and on radio. If you didn't believe them, you were either a fool or a traitor.

In Holland, in the period immediately preceding the war, the Dutch government, in an attempt to appease the Nazis, apparently had allowed one hundred thousand Germans to immigrate. They were loyal Germans, not refugees, and many of them helped the German invaders, that is, they acted as fifth columnists. In Belgium, however, the Germans had apparently disguised some of their agents as refugees. German saboteurs also were landed in the United States. To the extent that fifth columns were observed at all, they were believed to be part of a huge and incredibly cunning scheme. In fact, their numbers were insignificant and their objectives limited. But the fact that fifth columns existed at all in the war zones had a powerful psychological effect on the population. It is therefore not surprising that, at a time of acute hysteria, the fifth column was thought to be a decisive factor in enabling the Germans to score such devastating victories during their *Blitzkrieg*.

If it was impossible for the British to know in May and June 1940 that Hitler had *not* planted a fifth column in England, it was even more impossible to establish whether he actually intended to invade Britain *at that time*.[10] British security might, after all, have uncovered some subversive activity, but it would have been rather more difficult for them to look into Hitler's mind. According to the diary of General Jodl, Chief of the *Wehrmachtführungsamt*, Hitler told him on May 20, 1940, "The English can have a special peace any time after they give us back our colonies." And Chief of General Staff General Halder quoted Hitler as saying, "We hope to get in touch with England on the basis of a division of the world." During the British evacuation at Dunkirk on June 2, Hitler was cited as expressing the expectation that the "British are ready now for a reasonable peace," because he wanted to have his hands free for "his real task," the "confrontation with Bolshevism" and the conquest of European Russia. According to Karl von Weigand, chief correspondent in Europe for the Hearst Press, on June 13 Hitler repeated to him the familiar line, "I have no intention of destroying the British Empire." And even after Churchill declared on June 4 and on June 18 that England would fight on alone, Hitler still believed that she would give in. Among many other factors he was said to have come to this conclusion as a result of conversations with Lloyd George in 1936 and the Duke of Windsor in 1937. Only in mid-July, when Grand Admiral Raeder persuaded him that no invasion of Great Britain by sea was possible without first establishing supremacy in the air, did Hitler abandon his hope for an immediate separate peace, and the Battle of Britain began in earnest.

The English Camps

The weather was lovely in Bury St. Edmunds camp, when I arrived there with other members of the Cambridge group. The food was inadequate, and whatever news leaked through—we were not allowed radios or newspapers—devastating. However, lectures started right away.

The men from the London region were sent to Kempton Park race course where they slept under the open sky in tents, or on thin mattresses on stone floors in the tote buildings and stables (some underground), often one hundred in a room. One could spend the day sitting in the grandstand, watching the sentries, or one could stroll about the enclosure. Others were sent to a camp in Seaton, Devon, where half the population was Nazi and the Gestapo was active. Consequently, some ugly violence developed there between Nazis and Jews. The worst camp, physically, I am told, was Warth Mill, a derelict cotton factory in Bury, Lancashire. It was a rat-infested place with broken windows and a broken glass-roof and one bathtub for eighteen hundred people.

From Bury St. Edmunds my group was transported to a much larger camp in Huyton, an unfinished housing estate near Liverpool. On arrival, one of us heard the adjutant say to the commandant: "I never knew so many Jews were Nazis." I remember the two young men who climbed through a hole in the fence, to do some shopping. When they came back with their groceries, they couldn't find the hole, and promptly reported to the guards at the front entrance. Of course, the guards wouldn't let them in. The two men were highly indignant: "We're enemy aliens," they cried, "we live here!"

Henry Kreisel, a Jewish boy of sixteen from Vienna, kept a diary while he was in the English camp; he wrote in his as yet halting English:

May 16, 1940. Leeds At 12:30 I am called away from work and told that I would have to be interned. Town Hall in Leeds for five hours. Then Pontefract (Yorkshire). Barracks full of dirt and dust. We sleep on the floor. Food very good. We are allowed to receive visitors. My mother comes to visit us, and I write a poem about it. For two hours we are taken out into the fresh air every day. We have variety and sometimes classical concerts. Our own people entertain us, of course. There is an excellent violinist amongst us who plays every night after lights out. We do not see him, we just hear the sound of the violin. Really marvellous. Hygienical conditions are not too good, there are only two lavatories for 150 men. Food, however, is excellent. On the 20th day of May I start to write a novel which I think I will call *Miguel Amore* when it is finished. It is going to be quite long, about 300 pages, I think. I have had the idea quite a long time, about one year.

May 30, 1940 At 13:30 we are told to be ready in half an hour as we are going to be moved. We hope it will be the Isle of Man; we land however in Huyton. We sleep in new-built but unfurnished houses on the floor. Health conditions much better than in Pontefract but food scarcely. I am often hungry. Post supply is bad as well. First we dont get letters at all, later it grows better. We make music across the barbed wire. Soldiers stand on one side, we on the other. We sing and play, they sing back. We grow very intimate with them. This is stopped after a few days by the officers. There are so many professors and lecturers among the internees that a camp university is opened. One of us has a gramophone and records, including the fifth symphonie, by Beethoven, and the "Unfinished" by Schubert.

After two weeks it is announced that all internees would be transferred to the Isle of Man. During the two weeks stay in Huyton two chapters of *Miguel Amore* are written. I feel, however, dissatisfied with them and angry I throw it aside, deciding either not to write any more at all, or at least to rewrite.

Bernhard Pfundt also kept a diary. He was older than Kreisel. An anti-Nazi Catholic from Munich, he was in Lingfield, Sussex, which like Kempton Park was a racetrack, where many Nazi sympathizers had been gathered.

May 23 . . . The Tommies have started collecting our footwear every evening after roll call, so that we would not run away. . . . It must be tough to guard a blacked-out camp. Rumors are running wild.

May 24 This morning I wrote to the Vicar-General at Westminster about my own situation. Some hope!

June 1 There was an anti-Semitic demonstration today. The Jews amongst us protest to the authorities. Seven of the Jewish youngsters are forming a group with me. They call me Pius or their sky-pilot. . . . They still have hapless memories of their arrival in the United Kingdom, when they were lined up with names and age labels around their necks, like livestock at a country fair. . . . Now they were harried by renewed Jew-baiting in the camp. . . .

June 11 The Italians arrived today, and with them, news. The Germans are already in France. We are finally taken off the grandstand. The area with the horse stables is added to the grandstand.

June 15 From the guard we learn that Paris has fallen. Incredible. Some put their ears to the ground to find out whether they would notice the rumble from across the Channel.

From Huyton we were sent to the Isle of Man after first being subjected to a humiliating trek through the winding streets of Liverpool. The inhabitants had been led to believe we were German merchant seamen, captured from enemy vessels that had been sunk by the British Navy. We were cursed by the spectators and—although I can't swear to it—spat at. Some internees remember bricks being thrown at them. For the older internees, whose bags we younger men were carrying, this was a particularly painful experience, corroborating in our minds the suspicion that we were being used to display some sort of victory by the new Churchill government.

The Isle of Man camps were much superior to those on the British mainland. Blocks of rooming houses on or near the seafront had been requisitioned, presumably for the duration of the war. There was a holiday atmosphere about the camps and we were allowed to bathe in the sea under military guard. But there was also a severe shortage of food. Whatever meagre rations we did receive were so bad that some of us trying to conserve our energies stayed in bed all day. We had no sugar, fruit or eggs, and mainly subsisted on herring, cabbage and potatoes.

We almost might have considered our conditions tolerable had it not been for the suppression of all news, the absence of letters and, above all, our anxiety about the war.

Walter Loevinsohn remembers that the commandant summoned the Camp Committee and explained to them that he understood the situation we were in. We were not there at our wish, he said, and he was not there at his wish. He was a soldier, who wanted to fight the enemy. "But in wartime you don't ask questions. You do as you're told." Loevinsohn continues:

He proposed an understanding; if we made his life easy by complying with all the regulations, he would try to make our life as pleasant as he could. He stepped back, very pleased with himself. Then an impressive-looking white-haired gentleman got up. He introduced himself as the Reverend Somerville. He said that his three sons were all officers in the R.A.F. He was born of an English father and a German mother, in Germany before the First World War, during a visit. As soon as his mother had been fit to travel, she had taken him back to England. Nobody had ever explained to him that at twenty-one he would have to opt for British citizenship. He had fought in the First World War. He had been arrested on Whit-Monday while preaching a sermon in his church. Scotland Yard had taken him directly off his pulpit. All this was not really serious, but, since the commandant had said that he respected our position and that we should respect his, he felt the commandant should know that about 90 percent of the camp was Jewish and about half had been inmates in German concentration camps. We were thus on the same side as the commandant and rather resented any implication that we were on different sides of the fence. The commandant was shaken to his roots. He got up, put his cap on, saluted the Reverend Somerville and the rest of us, and marched out. He didn't know what to say. He had been prepared for riots, for hostility and demonstrations, for anything. But not that. . . .

During the last two weeks of June we heard more and more stories about the "changing of the guards" in France, that French refugee camps were being handed over to the Nazis. I remember one particular conversation with a communist who had fought with the International Brigade in Spain. He was the grandson of Paul Ehrlich, the discoverer of *Salvarsan* and co-winner of the 1908 Nobel prize for medicine. "The logic of events will compel Churchill to make peace with Hitler, and we will suffer the same fate as the refugees in France," he told me. "I hope for some sort of miracle so that I can find my way to New York. I want to read about it in the *New York Times*," he concluded sardonically.

In one of the houses along the Promenade in Douglas, a committee was formed. Ernest Waengler (who is not Jewish) recalls:

We decided that if the Germans should invade Britain we must stage either a mass breakout and grab boats in the ports in the hope that a ship will pick us up, or send an urgent appeal to the President of the United States, the Pope, or God knows whom. . . . We couldn't just sit behind barbed wire and wait for the Germans to arrive and hang us all.

There were some people on the committee who apparently had some access to money. The group consisted not only of Jews, and it was important for us to make it clear that this was a universal action, in which non-Jewish anti-Nazis who also were in danger were participating. . . . I myself thought at the time that the Nazis *would* win the war, and if the British had not developed ENIGMA, they might have done.

Helmut Blume remembers a man in his house who, although he had lived in England for twenty years, did have Nazi sympathies.

He described graphically what would happen to us. "You'll be lined up along the beach. . . . They will go bang, bang, bang." He imitated the chatter of a machine gun very convincingly.

Others, including myself, never quite believed all the gloomy talk around us. I felt like Victor Ross who admitted that his lack of fear was not an expression of courage but a lack of imagination. "I was childishly unfeeling," he said, "singularly unaware of the political importance of what was going on, and of the quite extraordinary danger of our position." Peter Heller also remained unaffected by the doom and gloom. "This was the talk of 'experts,'" he recalls. "All the refugee-talk around me never got me down. People were showing off with all the terrible things that would happen to us. I listened with great interest, and was impressed by it. But I never believed a word of it."

The Case for the Government
One would have thought that the Anglo-Jewish community would have been up in arms about the wholesale internment of refugees. But war hysteria infects Jews and gentiles alike. On May 17 the *Jewish Chronicle* stated that the arguments in favor of internment "could not be resisted, least of all at this juncture

when the very life of the nation is at issue." A week later the paper published a front-page report from its Amsterdam correspondent which described the role of fifth columnists in the German conquest of Holland. It emphatically urged that the "most rigorous steps" be taken against refugees in Britain. The fear of fifth columnists was undoubtedly genuine.

But another motive may have been unconsciously at work in the formation of Anglo-Jewish opinion. The influx of highly visible and very audible refugees had substantially contributed to the recent rise of anti-Semitism in England. It would have been most surprising if it had been otherwise. The barrister R. T. E. Latham, a Fellow of All Souls College in Oxford, who was serving in the Refugee Section of the General Department of the Foreign Office, wrote a memorandum as early as April 4, noting that "the hatred of the Jews amongst the middle and lower strata of London's population has increased greatly since the influx of German Jewish refugees." If *he* observed it, so did much more acutely the English Jewish community.

Walter Loevinsohn remembers attending a meeting in Manchester where Nathan Laski, "the Grand Old Man of Manchester Jewry" and the father of the socialist theoretician Harold Laski, addressed a gathering of some seven hundred refugees. According to Loevinsohn, he said he would personally recommend that anybody who did not volunteer for the Pioneer Corps be interned. This did not seem to be an unreasonable position to take by a highly respected Jewish leader, but for the refugees the position was far from reasonable. The Pioneer Corps was a second-rate unit consisting of "soldiers" who weren't allowed to bear arms. One of those attending Laski's meeting got up and with firmness and possibly in inadequate English told the speaker that he had tried three times to volunteer for the British Army to fight the Nazis, but that he deeply resented any attempts to be blackmailed into enlisting in the Pioneer Corps under the threat of internment. "Give me a gun; and I'll go immediately," he cried. There was terrific applause.

Within a few weeks the *Jewish Chronicle* changed its position. By then the war hysteria was diminishing and on July 19 the paper attacked the "cruel, indiscriminate and wasteful round-ups of men whose *bona fides* had been scrutinized again and again and who had always been vindicated." Early in August Nathan

Laski wrote to his old friend Winston Churchill protesting "against the tragedies that the War Office and the Home Office have brought about to inoffensive and loyal people." By then, most of us had accepted our internment with stoicism.

Looking back calmly and unemotionally, many of us still feel the British were right to intern us, not only because of the pressure of public opinion, but also because they had no real way of knowing whether or not Nazi agents had infiltrated England in the guise of refugees.

Walter Wallich has little doubt that the Nazis did try to make use of refugees. He remembers being arrested in Berlin by the Gestapo while he was on vacation from his English school during Christmas 1936. He was closely questioned about the British Officers' Training Corps. This was, of course, absurd, since there was nothing about this organization which was in any way different from what might have been learned about it before the First World War. He was held for three or four days before being released through the intervention of Bishop Dibelius. "Had I not been let out through connections, they might have said to me, 'Well, we'll release you if you write us a letter once a month telling us what's going on in England.' No intelligence service worth its salt would have hesitated to avail itself of the opportunity to infiltrate the stream of refugees that went to Britain."

Victor Ross takes a similar view. "I suppose if I had been Churchill or one of his functionaries, I would have asked myself, 'Where do my priorities lie?' The only way to keep the island unpolluted was to neutralize all potential agents. If I had been a German, I would have infiltrated England in the guise of a refugee. . . . I knew perfectly well a Jew couldn't be an agent, but that was a calculation others couldn't make."

To Colonel Josuah F. Wedgwood, M.P., one of our great champions, and a sharp critic of the government's handling of the internment problem, the idea that Hitler might use a Jew as an agent also sounded quite absurd. Taking an active part in the great debate on the subject in the House of Commons on August 22, he stated:

> I would very much doubt whether there has been any single case in this country of proved enemy assistance from any Jew. Indeed I know there has not been, but there have been

whispers. I know that Dreyfus did not write the Bordereau, but I know that the staff of the army thought he had, and said he had. If you are to take as evidence the sort of rumors that get talked about the Jews, you will never get anywhere at all.

Nearly all these aliens, although some of them have been here for six years, speak such English that in many cases I cannot understand them. Nobody would ever mistake a refugee for anybody but an alien. Even if Hitler loved the Jews, he would not employ such incompetent spies and agents.

So much for those of us, who, like myself, had vainly tried to master the unfathomable rules of cricket during two endless summers!

Some thought that while the British decision to intern us temporarily was defensible, the fashion in which the tribunals had been conducted was not. "The incompetence and naiveté of the Chamberlain government," Emil Fackenheim commented, "is still beyond me. It was irrational, the way they wasted their time. Our internment was perfectly rational. . . . The British had every right to panic. In fact, I would go as far as to say they had a duty to panic." Sir Hermann Bondi agrees: "I think the tribunals were eyewash. By May 1940 anybody with responsibility had to tell himself 95 percent of these people will be okay. But we don't know which 95 percent."

Ernest Waengler has no particular quarrel with the way the tribunals had done their job. "But if the British believed in an imminent danger of invasion," he states, "the logical thing for them to do would have been to put us in uniform and give us a gun. From one day to the next we were suddenly treated like enemies who had to be kept behind barbed wire. We had been led to believe that the British were the one European nation that wouldn't do such a thing." Max Perutz takes a similar view. He does not think the government had any justification for interning us at all.

We have never heard of a single German agent the British caught as the result of their internment policy whom they might not have caught in any case.

François Lafitte suggested that the motives of newspapers such as the *Daily Mail* were obvious. "By taking a super-patriotic line they were making of the . . . refugees a convenient scape-goat for their own sins—their pro-Nazi past."[11] H. G. Wells even went further. "Not only was the rabble roused by the deliberate deceit of men with guilty consciences who wanted to divert attention from their own guilt," he wrote on July 28 in *Reynolds News*, "but the policy to intern refugees had been forced on the government by 'a nest of traitors' who were doing Goebbels' work."

Churchill's motive for responding to the vociferous demands for action was perfectly straightforward. Any new government might have done the same thing; he wanted to show that the Chamberlain era was definitely over.

All kinds of excuses were made for our internment. Churchill was quoted as saying at his cabinet meeting on May 15 that internment was designed for *our* protection because when air-raids developed, public temper in the country would be such that *we* would be in great danger, if at liberty. Sir John Anderson raised another point. "If the enemy appeared to be having success," he asked in the House, "might some of them not lose heart and tend to weaken the morale of the people around them and perhaps try to make terms?"

Another argument that was never publicly used, but was much talked about, was that some refugees still had families on the Continent. If there were an invasion, the Nazis might black-mail them into cooperating by threatening to act against these families who were, in a sense, held hostage.

THREE

The Canadian Connection

Before June 1940 Ottawa had never formally offered to look after civilian internees for the Mother Country, but when on February 6, 1940, a British Columbia fruit grower by the name of Tom Stodard, formerly of the King's African Rifles, wrote to the Minister of National Defence suggesting that in the interests of both England and Canada, German prisoners of war should be sent to camps in the Dominion, some discussion was triggered. Dr. E. H. Coleman, Under-Secretary of State, and a former Dean of Law at the University of Manitoba, sent a memorandum on February 28 to his colleague O. D. Skelton, in External Affairs, stating that in his opinion such an action would not be a good idea because "it might be made the pretext for reprisals against prisoners of war interned in Germany."

As to what to do with enemy aliens who were Nazi sympathizers *at home in Canada*, Ottawa was well prepared. Ian Mackenzie, Minister of Defence, had had the foresight as early as January 1937 to write to the prime minister asking for the formation of a Canadian Defense Committee which would deal with that problem. In 1939 a report was adopted which became the basis of Canadian internment policy at the outbreak of war. The power of arrest and detention was to be vested in the Commissioner of the R.C.M.P. In July the Committee on Emergency Legislation expressed the view that the War Measures Act would give the Executive ample authority to take whatever action might be deemed necessary. On August 26, 1939 the Commissioner of the R.C.M.P. submitted to the

Minister of Justice the names of individuals who should be arrested, together with a list of organizations and newspapers to be banned in case of war. By October, 358 individuals had been arrested and sent to camps at Kananaskis in Alberta, and at Centre Lake, some twelve miles from the military camp at Petawawa, Ontario. Both camps had been used for unemployment relief projects in 1935, and the internees were to be engaged in forestry work. Throughout the war, leaving aside the Japanese Canadians, Ottawa detained altogether 2,241 civilians (mostly Germans and Italians, but also some native Canadians like Mayor Houde of Montreal), as well as 174 enemy merchant seamen. German and Austrian nationals who could demonstrate that they were fugitives from Hitler had no difficulty being exempt.

The first official reference to our transfer to Canada that I was able to find on the English side of the Atlantic was contained in a statement by Winston Churchill as early as May 24: "I am strongly in favour of removing all internees out of the United Kingdom." Later three reasons were given for this: in case of an invasion, there was the possible danger of fifth columnists; there would be less mouths to feed on the beleaguered island; and less military personnel would be required to guard internment camps and could be deployed for activities more useful to the war effort.

Although the British evacuation of Dunkirk was in full swing, evidently the matter was so important to Churchill that he followed up his statement on June 3 with a note to his cabinet secretary, Sir Edward Bridges.

> Has anything been done about shipping 20,000 internees to Newfoundland or St. Helena? Is this one of the matters that the Lord President has in hand? If so, would you please ask him about it. I should like to get them on the high seas as soon as possible, but I suppose considerable arrangements have to be made at the other end. Is it all going forward?

The Lord President of the Council was Churchill's predecessor, Neville Chamberlain; according to his biographer Keith Feiling, the relationship between the two men was excellent, and Chamberlain's records "abounded in admiration for the Prime Minister."[12] Chamberlain was charged with the responsibility of organizing the overseas transfers.

Winston Churchill followed up his earlier note to Sir Edward with the following statement in the House of Commons:

> We have found it necessary to take measures of increasing stringency, not only against enemy aliens and suspicious characters of other nationalities, but also against British subjects who may become a danger or a nuisance should the war be transported to the United Kingdom. I know there are a great many people affected by the orders which we have made who are the passionate enemies of Nazi Germany. I am very sorry for them, but we cannot, at the present time and under the present stress, draw all the distinctions which we should like to do. If parachute landings were attempted and fierce fighting attendant upon them followed, these unfortunate people would be far better out of the way, for their own sakes as well as for ours. There is, however, another class, for which I feel not the slightest sympathy. Parliament has given us the powers to put down Fifth Column activities with a strong hand, and we shall use the powers subject to the supervision and correction of the House, without the slightest hesitation until we are satisfied, and more than satisfied, that this malignancy in our midst has been effectively stamped out.

The reason why Churchill's figure of 20,000 who were to be exiled to Newfoundland and/or St. Helena was not to be taken seriously was that by June 3 only 2,500 German civilians in Category A had been interned and no more than 3,000 prisoners of war captured. Civilian internees in Categories B and C had not reached anywhere near that number.

The first request by the British government asking Ottawa whether *in principle* the Canadian government would be prepared to accommodate interned enemy aliens was sent on May 30. This was the day when the danger of encirclement of the British Expeditionary Force in Dunkirk was so grave that it was feared it might be lost entirely. But the Canadian war cabinet did not get around to discussing this request until June 5 and, in the meantime, Churchill—or rather actor Norman Shelley impersonating him on the B.B.C.'s North American Service—had vowed to fight on the beaches, on the landing grounds, in the fields, in the streets, and in the hills: "We shall never surrender!"

The pro-British members of the Canadian cabinet made a

strong plea for accepting the request, stating that these enemy aliens obviously constituted a much greater danger in the United Kingdom than in Canada, especially in case of an invasion. They suggested several locations where internment camps could be set up: on Sable Island, on the Magdalene Islands, on Grosse Ile, and possibly in other locations in northern Canada. These proposals were received with little enthusiasm. The British, others in the cabinet countered, should ship these people to New-foundland or to the West Indies. After all, very few enemy aliens had been interned in Canada, and the reports of suspicious activities on the part of German elements in the West, particularly in Saskatchewan, were disquietening. Had there not been a good deal of talk about fifth column activities right here at home?

On June 5 the Under-Secretary for External Affairs, O. D. Skelton, sent this cable to London:

> Careful consideration has been given to proposal to accept internees. In view of circumstances in Canada, particularly as regards to large numbers of enemy aliens who have not been interned here, we do not consider it advisable at present to undertake acceptance, but we are having a survey made at once on the point as to whether adequate quarters would be available.

In reply, London decided to spell things out more clearly. That job was assumed by Chamberlain's colleague Viscount Caldecote, Under-Secretary of State for Dominion Affairs, and the Canadian government in turn acted through its High Commissioner in London, Vincent Massey, the future Governor General and brother of the actor Raymond Massey.

On June 7 Massey wired Skelton that the United Kingdom government was grateful for the consideration given to the problem of the interned enemy aliens. They regarded it as very urgent because of the pro-Nazis civilians and German prisoners of war who would be dangerous in the event of possible parachute landings or invasion by sea. If Italy entered the war, there would be more civilian internees. The possibility of sending all of them to the "islands within the Colonial Empire" had been considered, but St. Lucia could only take five hundred and the islands closer to the United Kingdom were "open to serious objection from the point of view of national security;" Newfoundland apparently did not have enough military resources to accommodate these men. (The British later changed their minds about that.)

Viscount Caldecote hoped that "by receiving as soon as possible at least four thousand internees whose presence in this country is a most serious risk," the Canadian government would come to the assistance of the United Kingdom government. The same cable mentioned twenty-five hundred pro-Nazis internees and three thousand prisoners of war; transportation and maintenance for these people was to be paid by the United Kingdom.

By the time Caldecote's cable arrived in Ottawa, the Director of Internment Operations, Brigadier-General Edouard de Bellefeuille Panet, had completed the survey requested by the cabinet. From 1926 to 1934 Panet had been aide-de-camp to the Governor General. He had been the head of the Department of Investigation for the Canadian Pacific Railway, as well as chairman for the Montreal Unemployment Relief Commission. He also had distinguished himself in the First World War. Other members of his committee were Commissioner S. T. Wood of the R.C.M.P., J. F. MacNeill of the Department of Justice, and N. A. Robertson, Associate Under-Secretary for External Affairs.

The committee, taking a highly sympathetic view of the British situation, finally agreed that these persons would create less of a danger in Canada, but "from a practical point of view it would be easier to handle male internees." (There had been no mention of females, but the committee thought it prudent to make sure.) Temporary summer quarters could be made available immediately, and World War I veterans would undertake guard duty. It was decided to leave responsibility for determining the classes and numbers of internees to the British.

To expedite matters, O. D. Skelton sent a cable on June 8 to Vincent Massey asking for more particulars, advising him that, in the meantime, the search for accommodation was proceeding.

An element which the committee had not mentioned was that transferring prisoners of war seemed less difficult than transferring civilian internees and dependents. In London's view, however, the civilians were just as dangerous.

On June 10 Massey supplied the following particulars:

> U. K. authorities state that their most immediate request concerns 2,633 German internees of A category, i.e. those

internees who have been interned because there is definite evidence of their hostility. . . . [They are also concerned about] those formerly of B category internees against whom further evidence has come to light. All internees are male. Among these Category A internees there are 350 Nazi leaders who would require to be segregated from the rest and placed in even more stringent confinement. Equally urgent, in the view of U.K. government, is the immediate transfer of 1,823 German prisoners of war, including 39 officers. The U.K. government has again urgently asked me to put before you the pressing military problem created by the presence in this country of these potentially dangerous groups. They have asked me to say that they would be most grateful if the Canadian government would take immediately 4,456 persons composed, as stated, of 2,613 German internees and 1,827 prisoners of war. . . . There is nothing to choose, in their point of view, between prisoners of war and Category A internees as regards the urgency of getting them out of the country.

On the same day the Canadian cabinet met again. By then those opposed to the acceptance of enemy aliens had swung around. The particulars Massey had cabled earlier that day containing a request to Canada to accept only 4,456 persons, not the previous number of seven thousand mentioned in the cable of June 7, had either not arrived in Ottawa, or had not been distributed to members of the cabinet. Therefore, it was agreed to accept the original number—four thousand civilians and three thousand prisoners of war.

This is a crucial point. Had the cabinet been aware of the reduced numbers, chances are that it would never have occurred to the British to make up the difference with internees in Categories B and C of whom they knew that very few, if any, were suspect. True, Category B aliens were mentioned, but the implication was that Category B Germans against whom no further information had come to light would not be shipped. At this stage Viscount Caldecote evidently had not intended to send men cleared by tribunals. When on June 10 Italy entered the war, Italian internees were added to the Germans already in custody.

A week later Charles Ritchie at the High Commissioner's office, who had just been appointed second secretary, attended a meeting at the War Office in London on behalf of Vincent Massey. There was talk of only sending six thousand to Canada, requiring escorts seven hundred strong. Forms "were to accompany the party." Birth certificates where available but no identity cards, no aliens registration cards nor ration books; the civilians were to receive the same rations as prisoners of war.

Finally, the rather important question of who was responsible for what, had to be settled.

> It was agreed that the Home Office would not divest themselves of responsibility for the Internees, nor could the War Office for the Prisoners of War. It would therefore be necessary for some permanent liaison to be set up.

This is how Charles Ritchie, then a man in his early thirties, described his work at the Canadian High Commission in London:

> At that time I was a sort of human wastepaper basket into which all sorts of oddments were thrown. . . . I was dealing with Immigration, with shipping people, and to a certain extent with British government departments and individuals. . . . I don't think the English were unduly or unnaturally xenophobic. The stories of fifth columns on the Continent, and in particular in Holland, had been in the newspapers and were very much on people's minds. I think the Home Office fought a rearguard action against xenophobia. I admired them for it. . . . As far as Canada was concerned, the Canadian government had to take more or less what it was told. . . . I, for instance, wasn't present at the interviews that decided the categories of internees. . . . We were largely just a post office. If a junior officer like myself was the representative on the committees which dealt with internees, one could see it wasn't a matter of the first priority.

On June 26 he made this entry in his diary:[13]

> My office is the door of escape from hell. Day after day the stream of people press in. Today, for example, some of the Austrian Rothschilds (escaped from a concentration camp) are trying to pass their medical examination to go to Canada. Would I arrange a financial guarantee for them? The wife of one of the wealthiest men in England is trying to get out of the country. Her husband is a Jew and a leading

anti-Nazi. Will I get her a letter to prove (on very flimsy grounds) that she is a Canadian? The Marchioness of C, in the uniform of the Women's Naval Auxiliary Unit, wants to get three children out to Canada at once. . . . Count X, the anti-fascist with a price on his head must leave for Canada at once on a mission of great importance. . . . Here we have a whole social system on the run, wave after wave after wave of refugees, and these are only the people at the top, people who can, by titles, letters of introduction . . . force their way into Government offices and oblige one to give them an interview. What of the massed misery that cannot escape?

The sense of the dissolution of civilized society is over-powering.

The question was raised on June 15 whether the Germans might retaliate against British internees and prisoners of war in their hands once they found out about the shipment of German prisoners of war and internees overseas. Would they send British prisoners and civilians to very bad quarters in Poland?

The relatively few German prisoners of war in British hands who were to accompany us to Canada had been taken mainly in Norway. Some Luftwaffe and naval personnel had been captured elsewhere, but sizeable numbers of British soldiers had been taken by the Germans in France and Belgium, two weeks after Dunkirk. To minimize any danger of reprisals, the British government asked the Swiss Legation in London to pass the following communication on to Berlin:

> The Foreign Office present their compliments to the Swiss Legation, Special Division, and have the honour to inform them that His Majesty's Government in the United Kingdom have come to the conclusion that it is desirable that German civilian internees and combatant prisoners of war should be transferred to a part of His Majesty's Dominions where they will be outside the area of hostilities. His Majesty's Government in Canada have agreed to accept them and I am authorized to state that prisoners of war will be treated in accordance with the International Convention relative to the treatment of prisoners of war, to which Canada is a party. Civilian internees will be treated in general, as at present, in accordance with the principles of the Convention.

Lists of prisoners of war and also of civilians transferred to Canada will be communicated to the Swiss Legation. In the case of civilians, lists will not include names of
those who do not wish this to be done.

Ten days later international repercussions of a somewhat
different nature occupied the minds of Canadian officialdom.
Mackenzie King's announcement in the House of Commons on
June 19 that the government had agreed to accept German
prisoners of war and internees from the United Kingdom was
the first time the Canadian public heard about the plan. There
had been talk about British children being sent for safekeeping
to Canada. The Opposition wanted to know why the prisoners
were to be given priority over British children.

This was Mackenzie King's reply:

The wishes of the British government are these . . . that in
the matter of preference . . . we should take first of all
interned aliens, secondly that we should take German prisoners in Britain, and thirdly that we should then consider
the matter of evacuated children. The reason they give in
this connection is that the interned aliens in Britian may be
in a position to help parachutists in the event of a bombard-
ment of the British Isles which they are expecting hourly.
They also feel that the German prisoners they have there
require a great deal by way of protection of the British Isles
themselves. There is great congestion, because of the
refugees which have been coming there, and they feel that
it would be in the interest of safety and security in every
way to have alien internees and German prisoners brought
to this country, and placed in different parts of the country
under protective measures.

Hardly had this statement been made when Mr. Lash of the
International News Service, which was affiliated with the Hearst
Press, sought—and received—permission from General E. de B.
Panet, the Director of Internment Operations, to take pictures
of the "dangerous" prisoners when they stepped off the boats in
Quebec. Mackenzie King's office got wind of this, and one of
his aides drafted this memo:

In my opinion the psychological effect of distributing
pictures of this nature, particularly the effect in the United
States, would be bad. We do not want to give the impression

that we are celebrating a Roman triumph. There is the additional factor, moreover, that publicity of this nature might produce a bad reaction in Europe, where the Germans, of course, have far more British prisoners than the British have German.

Whitehall was now faced with the dilemma whether to tell the Canadians and Australians that, regrettably, not enough dangerous Germans were in British hands to be sent to Canada, or whether to fill the space with "friendly enemy aliens" who had been cleared by the tribunals.

In his statement to the House on June 4 Winston Churchill had declared what everybody knew to be true, namely that it was impossible "at the present time and under the present stress" to draw all the distinctions they would have liked to have drawn. Still, the distinction between Category A and Categories B and C German civilians *had* been drawn. It would have been quite possible for Whitehall to tell the Dominion governments that it could not fill the quotas they had kindly agreed to take. But this would have been an admission of miscalculation, and one thing a bureaucrat rarely does is admit a mistake.

It was, therefore, decided to fill the vacuum on the requisitioned ships with refugees. No major effort was made to tell Ottawa about it. However, on July 8 the Home Office conveyed the following message to Ottawa through the High Commission:

> You will observe that B and C Categories of German internees are being sent on these ships. War office has not thought it necessary to distinguish between these categories which might have been treated on the same basis here.

It is doubtful whether any of the overworked officials in Ottawa understood what these categories meant.

On July 2, the day before we left England, the Lord President of the Council, Neville Chamberlain, presented a memorandum to the war cabinet stating that the Home Secretary had urged special care be taken not to mix Jews with Nazis or fascists in the contingents sent overseas. Furthermore, since not enough time was available to carry out proper selection, "internees in the categories the Home Secretary desires to exclude" might be sent. By that he meant "men interned in error," "men required for war production," and "married men with wives and children upon whom special hardship would be imposed by separation."

FOUR

The Prison Ships

On June 29, I wrote to my mother: "This *may* be my last letter from Europe. The rumor about Canada seems to be materializing. All we know is that those between twenty and thirty shall leave the Isle of Man for an unknown destination." (The next few words were blacked out by the censor.) "This letter is written on the assumption that we shall leave soon. . . . We will have to do work 'which appeals to us,' (the officer said so.) What that means we don't know. I am prepared to do anything, go anywhere. The chance to get to the States seems considerable. . . ."

Although the vague and contradictory criteria for the selection of those to be sent to Canada differed from camp to camp some not entirely successful attempts were made to pick primarily unmarried young men. The ages of the nearly one thousand who went, then stayed and in 1945 became eligible for naturalization, were as follows:

16–20	34.6%
21–25	16.3%
26–35	32.1%
36–45	15.1%
46–65	1.9%

German nationals in Category A, including 178 Jewish and non-Jewish refugees, were sent in two ships; those in Categories B and C in two other ships. The tribunals had labelled the refugees suspect for a number of reasons which had nothing to do with possible Nazi sympathies. Some were left-wing and therefore may have displeased the judges; others had been denounced for various reasons, or had infringed upon a work or visa regulation.

Fifteen hundred of the seven thousand interned Italians were assumed to be members of the Fascist Party and, according to Lord Snell's judicial inquiry in 1940, nominal members of the Fascist Party as well as ardent fascists were considered equally dangerous. The inquiry also found that "among those deported were a number of men whose sympathies were wholly with this country." Only 717 "party members" could be identified.

The authorities had strict instructions not to tell those whose names appeared on the overseas lists where they were going. A few knew because someone had told them; others had heard rumors, but most did not know.

Anyone who was on the list but did not want to leave England often could find someone who did. It was therefore possible to swap places, with the British authorities frequently assisting in making such arrangements. As an alternative, it was feasible to impersonate someone else during the pre-embarkation roll call.

Much confusion and chaos characterized those days. Lord Snell's inquiry described the selection methods as having followed "no rational criteria" by the military authorities.

Then sixteen-year-old Henry Kreisel recalls:

> The order came through that sons who were with their fathers did not have to go. But I wanted to go, and was on the list. We were gathered in a big hall. . . . When the order came through, fathers whose sons were going could go with them. So my father volunteered; he didn't want me to go alone, he said. So here he was and I was trying to get away from him at the time. Then I discovered that my name had been taken off the list, and his had been put on! In the end we both went.

Robert Langstadt describes the selection in Huyton: "It went by streets. One street went, the other stayed behind. My street was not on the list. But there was an old man whose name was on the list, but his son's wasn't. So I took the old man's place. In fact, I went to Canada out of the goodness of my heart!"

George Brandt also volunteered by standing in for somebody else because at the time he was deeply pessimistic and convinced the Germans were about to invade Britain. "Just before my internment," he told me, "I had seen a newsreel about logging operations in Canada; naturally I had a fairly romantic view of the country."

From the various commandants' points of view, the more people volunteered, the better, because they had quotas to fill. Though the overall criterion for selection was youth and being single, if older, married men volunteered, they too were accepted. Some even were prepared to pay money for being put on the list, while others paid to be taken off. Subsequent investigations and parliamentary inquiries frequently referred to the "voluntary principle." In my recollection, there was no choice. We were ordered to go, including some older, married men in certain camps who may not have had the means nor the opportunity to have their names struck off the list. Sometimes this met with strong opposition. On July 10 a group in Huyton wrote this memorandum which miraculously passed the censor:

> Again today another transport has been assembled. It leaves today. In spite of the most express promises to maintain, above all, the principle of voluntary departure, the majority were forcibly pressed into the group under the threat of the use of arms. Some were taken from their beds in the night. In a few cases where the Commandant permitted exchange, sums up to £15, and in one case even £100, were offered to people who volunteered to exchange. This barter business and this trans-shipment like cattle, without even an indication of destination, or of any of the travel arrangements, must be stopped. . . . We have just received news that two internees who had been pressed for the transport leaving today committed suicide in the night.

On August 6 a letter appeared in the *Times*, signed by an internee on the Isle of Man.

> On July 10 twenty-two married men left this camp voluntarily for overseas under a guarantee given to them in the name of the Command that their interned wives in Port Erin would accompany them in the same convoy. A week later it was admitted that the guarantee had not been kept. Furthermore, letters from Port Erin, dated July 10, say that all women there had been told on exactly the same day that

their husbands would leave for overseas and it was hoped to reunite them there at a later date. Apparently not even an attempt was made to fulfil the given guarantee. The twenty-two men left, trusting the word of the Command, as they had no possibility to communicate with their wives.

Once it became clear we were going to Canada, many of us were excited and happy. With the Nazis on England's doorstep, we felt the farther we could get away at His Majesty's expense the better. Edmund Klein remembers reading an advertisement in the *Daily Telegraph* which offered for sale "a farm in western Canada far away from Europe's trouble-spots." He looked at the whole deportation in that light: he was "going to be saved from one of the ghastliest experiences man has ever had to go through." We had been told we would be able to "do work that suited us." That sounded as though we could have the opportunity to do our bit for the war effort, which we hadn't been allowed to do in England. In other words, the future looked good.

There was only one thing that worried many of us: we knew nothing about Canada. Karl D. Renner was sure Winnipeg was on the St. Lawrence; Peter Heller knew about Canada's prowess in ice hockey, and so did Helmut Blume, who remembered a Canadian team which came to Berlin in 1929. He also knew that canoes on the lake near his old home in Tegel were called *Kanadier*. Tom Rosenmeyer had read a poem about the rugged strength of Canadians—they were people who never spoke more than they had to. Franz Kraemer had stayed with friends in Westmoreland where the English traveller, writer and conservationist Grey Owl had stayed.

> I lived in a beautiful, old eighteenth-century house. . . . On the panels were pencilled drawings of hundreds of beavers in various positions which Grey Owl had drawn. . . . I saw his jacket on a clothes-stand. . . . The lady of the house was a good friend of his. That whole family had been in Canada: they had canoed with Grey Owl. They loved the north; they were totally mad about Canada. . . . You can imagine how amazed I was when I suddenly discovered I was actually going there.

Helmut Kallmann remembers having seen a picture in a German magazine of a roadside box in the Canadian north near a place too small to have a store. "You put money into the box in exchange for cigarettes or bread, or whatever you needed." The caption underneath the picture read: "*This is how honest they are in Canada.*"

The ETTRICK

On Tuesday, July 2, at three o'clock in the afternoon I left the camp on the Isle of Man, arriving in Liverpool at nine o'clock in the evening. The next morning I stepped on the *Ettrick*. Aboard were 1,308 internees in Categories B and C, 785 German prisoners of war and 405 Italians.

When William Heckscher, who hailed from Hamburg and knew about ships, first saw her, he was pleased; she looked like a good ship. But once aboard, he realized that a difficult crossing lay ahead. His group was taken to a room deep in the hold, where signs were posted that read, "Accommodation for forty-eight troops." But a few hundred internees already were installed there. Barbed wire had been strung along the walls, and he saw machine gun nests in the corners. The German officers occupied cabins on the top deck.

The majority of us slept in hammocks, one above another. When we became seasick soon after leaving Liverpool, we were sick on one another. Some found better accommodation. Gerry Waldston followed his father's last piece of advice before they were separated in Huyton: "If you're sick, pretend to be sicker." Gerry spent the entire journey in the ship's hospital. Ralf Hoffmann was lucky. On the first night out he suffered a kidney attack and he, too, spent the entire voyage in hospital "under medical care with internees looking after me as orderlies. Never have I been so happy about a kidney attack!" Robert Langstadt found a "fixed residence on a table, and I made friends with a Jehovah's Witness who read the Bible to me throughout the voyage." The Catholic priests came aboard and first began to pray and, therefore, missed getting their hammocks. Our two Marx brothers—Karl and Ernst—found some for them. Fackenheim remembers how disgusted he was with the mad scramble for hammocks. "It was worse than anything I had seen in Sachsenhausen. They threw them through some kind of hole and people grabbed them and fought over them." Those who didn't manage to get one had to make do with any spot they could find. A few slept in the galley, in puddles of grease. There was a penetrating smell of oil throughout the entire area; a single electric fan provided the only ventilation in the hold. We had no boat drill, and none of us would have had a chance to survive had we been shipwrecked or torpedoed.

On the whole, overcrowding, seasickness and fear of U-boat attacks characterized our trip as the *Ettrick* zig-zagged her way across the Atlantic. Some of us remained reasonably cheerful and kept moving through the crowds of those who could still stand up. Heckscher met a man with a black slouch hat. They soon discovered each others' love for the works of Dante. So, leaning against a wall in a corner where there was a little light, they read *de Monarchia* together. He also remembers a priest who seemed in a state of deep depression. "He had a sort of nervous breakdown, and I helped him to regain his composure by engaging him in a discussion about the existence of God."

We still had not been told definitely where we were going. Some said we were on our way to Germany to be exchanged for the British prisoners taken at Dunkirk; others claimed to have heard we were bound for Scotland to build roads or fortifications there. Perhaps we were headed for British Guiana, or Madagascar? The most gruesome rumor was that German officers were plotting to take over command of the ship. But when somebody saw two or three of them in shackles, it was concluded the British must have got wind of the plot.

Occasionally we had encounters with the German prisoners of war. Heckscher once managed to get to the stern of the ship where he found the crew of a German U-boat that had been captured in Norwegian waters. The men spoke *Plattdeutsch*, a North German dialect closely related to Dutch which Heckscher understood. "I doubt they were Nazis," he commented. But the majority of the German prisoners were on top of the world, certain that they had virtually won the war and were going to be home soon.

Walter Loevinsohn had been made responsible for keeping the barbed wire doors open, although they were supposed to have remained padlocked throughout the voyage. "But if we had got torpedoed, we would never have had a chance to get out. This way, at least if they wanted to, they could let us out. We made an agreement with the guards: we promised that nobody would go in the passageway. If anybody did, he could be shot without challenge. . . . There was one guy who was desperately seasick. He had to go to the toilet, but the toilet was outside the permissible area. We literally knocked him out so he wouldn't run into the passageway. . . . When the German soldiers started singing their anti-Semitic songs, we got hold of their officer in charge, a paratrooper, and told him, barbed wire or not, we'd tear his people to pieces if they didn't stop. 'None of us are on this beautiful ship of our own volition,' we said. Even if we got shot in the process we were going to kill the bastards if they didn't stop. They stopped."

The following are extracts from a diary written mostly aboard the *Ettrick*:

Sunday July 7 Another day on the ship. The sea was beautifully calm. . . . People recovered from their sea-sickness and the food rations which had been divided among the few good sailors decreased appreciably. On the other hand, it became possible to keep the place reasonably clean. Nothing outstanding happened except a rather unpleasant interlude with the military. In the morning, when one shift of 300 odd people was taken on deck until the previous shift had gone downstairs, a sergeant, while trying to push people back, suddenly pulled out a long rubber truncheon and started beating ten, fifteen people right on the head as hard as he could. He had simply lost his head and temper. It was a disgusting performance in front of the eyes of the German prisoners of war . . . who stood on the other side of the partition and no doubt enjoyed this re-enactment of concentration camp scenes. The sergeant even tried to grab a rifle with bayonet from one of the sentries, but the sentry very decently refused. (He was later charged by the sergeant for disobedience). There was an uproar among the crowd of refugees. . . .

Tuesday July 9 Conditions on board have improved considerably. There is a little more food—though still not enough for most people. But at least the daily routine works smoothly. . . .

Saturday July 13 During breakfast it was announced that one whole group which had been in Huyton after us and had joined us on the ship would be sent to a separate camp and had to get ready by 9 a.m. Conditions on the decks were pretty chaotic. There was no time to wash up after breakfast; people were packing up and sorting out their belongings. . . . By 10 a.m. everyone had been taken up to the front top deck with all their luggage. The view was heavenly. We were now going slowly upstream—on both sides the banks of the river—some 500 yards apart—hilly with villages, houses, woods and fields. The weather was wonderful and we enjoyed one of the most beautiful sceneries I had ever seen. At first people were so wrapt in the view that they hardly noticed how the time passed as they were crowded together on the front deck, unable to get down again and waiting for our arrival. Soon it became necessary for some to go to the lavatory. I spent the next three hours at first trying to get permission for them which was terribly difficult, and then letting groups of five tortured individuals go down at intervals after hours of waiting. This had been one of our worst troubles during the whole voyage. We were locked up in our decks by night and were unable to go to the lavatory. For two nights we had an epidemic of diarrhoea which affected practically everyone. It took us hours of argument with the sergeants—no officers were visible—until they allowed at first buckets to be put inside the barbed wire, and when they proved wholly inadequate permitted people to go one after the other to the lavatories. The scenes that happened then do not suffer description. It was simply ghastly.

I had little chance of watching the scenery until about 1.30 p.m. By then people had waited for three hours and a half on the deck in the sun. The Colonel who was in command of the transport was getting more and more nervous, being unable to cope with the disembarkation proceedings: he raged about, shouting at everyone. One of our internees, a little Jewish boy, was kicked by him and beaten with his stick, accompanied by the words: "Get back, you lousy lot." Later he ordered the sentries at one point to use their bayonets against us (which they did not do). . . .

Celebrity Passengers

The attack of dysentery during the final days on the *Ettrick* marked the emergence of Prince Friedrich Georg Wilhelm Christoph von Preussen. He was the youngest son of the Crown Prince of Germany, and the grandson of the Kaiser who, at eighty-one, was still living in exile in Holland. The prince travelled under the name of Count Fritz Lingen.

He organized a "bucket brigade" to clean up the mess caused by dysentery and seasickness—*noblesse oblige!* He had been with me in Cambridge, then in Bury St. Edmunds, in Huyton, and later on the Isle of Man. But I never noticed him until he emerged as "Mr. Clean"—or rather, Prinz *von* Clean—on the *Ettrick*.

Good-looking, polite, elegant though a little aloof—a young man with true royal glamor, he had an impressive personality. Wherever he went, he became the center of attraction. Many thought he bore a marked resemblance to King George VI whose grandfather, Edward VII, was the Kaiser's detested uncle. I always thought he looked more like a youthful Frederick the Great.

At the time, he was twenty-nine years old and unquestionably anti-Nazi. Nevertheless, he was a good German and certainly not a "Refugee from Nazi Oppression." In fact, the Nazis would have been delighted had he become one of Hitler's followers, as some of his brothers had. In the thirties he had played a role in Berlin's diplomatic society. When in October 1933 the daughter of the American Ambassador William E. Dodd gave a birthday party, the prince was invited. She described him in her memoirs.[14]

> Young Prince Friedrich, the youngest son of the Crown Prince, came exactly on time, with a precise little bouquet of carnations in his hand and a polite bow from the waist. I considered him charming, with his almost perfect "Arrow-collar ad" features, the blonde hair and air of shy innocence and guilelessness. He certainly, in the time I knew him, never said a word out of order or did an unconventional thing. If he had a mind at all unique or interesting, I was never privileged to see it—and I think my experience was not uncommon. But I had never seen a Prince before, and certainly never a handsome, blushing one.

Prior to wading through rivers of filth as commander-in-chief of the *Ettrick*'s bucket brigade, the prince had lived in London where in 1937 he was granted a permit of brief residency by the Home Secretary, Sir Samuel Hoare, so that he could study banking at the House of Schröder. But banking was not to his taste and he decided to abandon his studies. As part of a compulsory stint in the German Army, he was conscripted in the *Wehrmacht's* Tank Corps and participated in its actions during the *Anschluss* of Austria in 1938. He then returned to England to be tutored in Cambridge by the great historian George M. Trevelyan. I've heard it said that he stayed in England at the prompting of his grandfather, who wanted him to re-establish good relations between the Houses of Hohenzollern and Windsor. At Cambridge, he was not a great student, but actually was marking time there while trying to decide what to do in that period of impending calamity. Whereas he had responded to the conscription call in 1938, in 1939 when other loyal Germans flocked home to join Hitler's war, he remained in Cambridge.

On the *Ettrick* he emerged as a natural leader. Victor Ross ascribes this to a pair of Wellington boots.

> I first became aware of Lingen . . . because he borrowed a pair of Wellingtons which impressed me very much. Then everybody else said, "We must have Wellingtons." . . . Suddenly everybody wanted to clean latrines.

Emil Fackenheim, too, was much impressed with the prince because of "the absence of any kind of self-pity and all the nonsense which demoralizes people. He did not put on any airs."

Walter Wallich was a member of the "royal brigade."

> We formed a gang: we flushed the place down. We caused a great deal of resentment among the older folk who felt rightly that we were a brash lot of youngsters trying to lord it over them, but we created some sort of order out of chaos and kept the place reasonably clean. But we did it in a very roughshod and callow manner.

There was another man on board the *Ettrick* whom I would not mention in this context at all were it not for the fact that a scene taking place on the ship had been included in a play about him. His name was Klaus Fuchs, who became world-famous nine years later when, at the height of the Cold War, he was arrested in England and subsequently jailed for espionage. As head of theoretical physics at Harwell, he had disclosed nuclear secrets to the Russians. On his release after nine years he left for East Germany to continue his work in nuclear research. He is now considered one of their top experts in the field.

The play, *Das Kalte Licht* (The Cold Light), written by Carl Zuckmayer, author of *The Captain of Köpenick* and *The Devil's General*, deals with the dilemma of Walters, a young German scientist with a Quaker background and pacifist convictions who is persuaded by a communist agent to cooperate with the Soviets in order to preserve world peace and create a better world. It describes how the young physicist becomes enmeshed in a web of lies and deceit. The opening scene of the play takes place in London in September 1939 where Walters is first accosted by the agent. The second scene is set on the *Ettrick* where the two are engaged in a highly political chess-game. . . .

Fuchs was a pale, bespectacled young man in his late twenties who had become a communist in 1932. The personal data on Walters in Zuckmayer's play match those of Klaus Fuchs, who was born in Rüsselsheim near Frankfurt in 1911 into a Quaker family and was educated at the universities of Leipzig and Kiel, following in the footsteps of his father who was also a scientist. In 1933 he fled to France and subsequently arrived in the United Kingdom where he continued his studies in Bristol and Edinburgh.

No one really noticed Fuchs on the *Ettrick*. Having kept away from the bucket brigade, there really is no record whether he and Lingen ever exchanged a single word on the *Ettrick*, in the Canadian camps, or on the *Thysville*, the ship on which they both returned to the Old World five and a half months later.

The SOBIESKI

Those who travelled on the *Sobieski*—a Polish ship with a Polish crew—had an easier time. Walter Hitschfeld developed a particularly warm feeling for the ship because he remembered who Sobieski was. As John the Third, King of Poland, he had defeated the Turks in 1683 at the second siege of Vienna, thereby saving Western civilization from the Muslim menace.

The *Sobieski* left Greenock, Scotland, on July 4, 1940 with 982 Category B and C internees and 548 prisoners of war on board.

Kaspar Naegele was seventeen at the time of embarkation and very much an English public school boy. His group had assembled somewhere near their boarding house in Douglas camp on the Isle of Man. This is how he described the departure in his diary:

> Suddenly there came the order to leave. . . . From the camp we had brought cups with us. Many handed them in. . . . We marched on . . . past the camp. They all stood there, waving, shouting. Then the harbor. The ship was there, half occupied with Ramsay (camp) people, some of them had also been in Huyton. We went aboard, tired and nervous. Our luggage was thrown in. And soon we left—northwards. Scotland? Yes, we were going to Glasgow. Ireland came into sight. The Northumbrian Hills, the Firth of Clyde. It was nine o'clock. We had been virtually fighting to get some bread and cheese. I had been talking to Mayer about Gordonstoun when ships came in sight, and a harbor. We waited. Small boats came in. . . . We saw troopships. . . . At last we steered towards a Polish liner called *Sobieski*. Half of us were slowly disembarking, and the rest was asked whether they would like to stay behind. *What was I to do?* No, said the others. So I took the risk, too. Afterwards I learned that the ship was full and two hundred *had* to stay behind in England, they were told. But Australia it was to be. In groups we moved in; I got separated from the others and had to ask one of the guards to let me step over. We stepped on board along a corridor into the mess room. . . . We were searched. I had to hand over my knife, never to see it again. (In Canada we were allowed to buy knives.) Then down small steps and under deck we came to our dormitory. Bed on bed, two-storied. Red blankets!!! White sheets!!! But next to my bed gaped a terrific luggage hole right to the bottom of the ship. . . . On the deck below—another big dormitory. . . . Above, the ship was being filled. . . . I went to sleep and I was not awake when we left Good Old England.

Henry Kreisel senior and Henry Kreisel junior also boarded the *Sobieski*, anchored near the coast, directly from the little ship which had taken them to Greenock.

> We were about to board. Everybody thought you would board from the top. Very few of us had been in a situation where you transfer from one ship to another. Everybody was pressing upwards to try and get on the *Sobieski*. But I had forgotten some manuscript on which I was working down below. So I said to my father, "I've got to go down and get the manuscript." He was cursing and screaming. . . . So

we made our way down through the throng of people pressing upwards. It was impossible to go up again because the gangplanks were completely filled up, when suddenly the little boat came alongside. . . . So we were the first on the *Sobieski*! All the rest had to go down! There wasn't room for all. The next lot went to Australia. Had we been up there with the others, we might not have got on the *Sobieski*. . . . That's how Fate operates.

Captain Frank Staff, who was a British liaison officer in charge of escorting the internees and POWs and who later became intelligence officer in the Canadian camps, had this to say:

The *Sobieski* is a wonderful memory for me. . . . I went up to Glasgow where, to my dismay, there was a Polish boat. We had had terrible reports of these shiploads of prisoners going over—how truculent they were. Our guards were not going to stand any nonsense. The Germans were arrogant and thought they had won the war. . . . I got there early, before the prisoners arrived, and I found it was a luxury liner that had been converted. There were about nine of us officers. Colonel Riddell was in charge. . . .

I discovered a room containing a gramophone and a whole library of records—Strauss waltzes, Léhar, and so on. I had lived with Germans and I know how they feel about things when they're in trouble. I told the colonel I wanted to relay these records all over the ship—all day long. The colonel said, "That's a good idea." We did that, and we had a wonderful crossing. Everybody was humming songs and whistling tunes. The German prisoners asked permission to give a ship's concert at the end of the trip.

We were heavily escorted going over, because our ship was carrying a mint of gold and money. . . . We had daily boat drills. No provision had been made to save the British officers; if there had been trouble, the prisoners would have been saved, not we.

Captain Godfrey Barrass, another British officer who also functioned as intelligence officer later on, described Captain Staff's reference to "the mint of gold and money" in greater detail. There were "something like two hundred gold bars from the British Treasury" to be stored in the vaults of the Bank of Montreal. The *Sobieski* had come from Narvik and was well stocked with liquor and cigarettes. Captain Barrass acquired a few cases of whiskey and gin. "The customs people in Quebec were very nice," he told me. "They just waved me aside, pretending they had seen nothing."

Fred Kaufman remembers:

> We were in convoy with two other ships carrying civilians, I believe, probably headed for either Montreal or New York. That was the period when children were being sent out of the country. The *Sobieski* developed engine trouble on about day four of the voyage. There was a good deal of signalling by semaphore with the other ships. There probably was no radio contact, in order not to give away our location. The other two ships then disappeared over the horizon. We felt terribly left alone. . . . Then we began dropping depth charges which made a very strange noise as they exploded. We did not know what was below . . . you get scared. A destroyer came; that was a very welcome sight. We were still making very slow speed as the destroyer was circling around. Then we stopped over in St. John's, Newfoundland for repairs.

On the *Sobieski* the internees were separated from the prisoners of war and treated better than on the *Ettrick*. They were allowed on deck for a few hours every day, while the POWs had less time allotted to them. They also had priority in the use of the washrooms. Altogether there was no particular ill-feeling between the two groups—no open hostility. Edgar Sarton even found himself standing on deck next to a German officer who had been serving on a U-boat. "We discussed what pennants the British warships were flying." Walter Nussbaum remembers "that chilling moment when the German prisoners, on their twice-a-day airing on deck, passed our queue and an airman recognized his Jewish school pal, embraced him and muttered, 'Teddy, what are you doing here?'"

On the whole, relations with the British troops on board were harmonious, although they may have found the group of orthodox Jews a little strange. One day, after a meal, when they were chanting their traditional prayer of thanks, the following incident occurred, according to Albert Pappenheim, a member of that group:

> There was one guard from Yorkshire, judging from his accent; he told us to stop singing. As a kind of ringleader I

asked him why. . . . He came over with his bayonet and punched a hole in my coat. At that point we stopped singing.

Charles Luwisch had more to say about the orthodox:

Just before we left, the leader of our group called us together and told us we were going to Canada and that we must stick together because Canada wasn't very friendly towards the Jews; it was a Catholic country, and we shouldn't lose our faith. . . .

The *Sobieski* had been in the emigrant trade before the war and had a kosher kitchen with kosher dishes. The Polish crew didn't like the Nazi prisoners, so they served them on kosher dishes! They didn't like us either because we were Jewish. So they put meat into our kosher soup to make it unkosher! Our rabbis decided that the amounts of meat were so small that we were allowed to eat it. We didn't starve at all: we had plenty of bread and butter.

The *Sobieski* landed in Quebec on July 15, two days after the *Ettrick*. There the Canadian Army treated everybody alike. There was not a trace of anti-Semitism in their behavior. To them we were all dangerous Nazis.

Hanfstaengl

By far the most famous of all the internees transported to Canada in the summer of 1940 was Dr. Ernst F. Sedgwick ("Putzi") Hanfstaengl. He was among the 2,112 Category A internees who sailed on the *Duchess of York* leaving Liverpool on June 20 and arriving in Quebec on June 29. Few will recognize his name today, but we had all heard of him as the scion of a wealthy and distinguished Bavarian family, patrons of the arts and originators of art reproductions.

But it was "Putzi" Hanfstaengl who had introduced Hitler to Munich society in the early twenties, thereby becoming a highly influential member of Hitler's inner circle. In fact, he was so well known to us that a year or so after our arrival in Canada we threatened to go on a hunger strike rather than allow him into our camp. It is extraordinary that his presence on Canadian soil from 1940 to 1942 never received any attention.

Hanfstaengl was an unusually tall man with a protruding chin and a shock of dark brown hair; although he was fifty-three in 1940, his hair did not show a trace of gray. Wherever he went, he was the life of the party. Among his many talents, the most remarkable was his musicality. He was a first-class amateur pianist with a Lisztian technique. He also talked a lot, waving his arms about, and his repertoire of witty and caustic anecdotes was seemingly limitless. His diatribes against his enemies at Hitler's court, mainly Dr. Joseph Goebbels and Alfred Rosenberg, were magnificently malicious. He showed social contempt for many of these men and considered them unspeakably vulgar, especially when they flaunted their anti-Semitism. To him, the anti-Semitism which was later enshrined in the Nuremberg Laws was utter lunacy.

There is no doubt that Hanfstaengl personally intervened with Himmler to save many Jewish lives. He was, however, opposed to what he considered excessive infiltration by Jews into German life, especially those who had recently emigrated from Eastern Europe.

Hanfstaengl's mother was a née Sedgwick-Heine, a relative of the American Civil War General John Sedgwick, whose statue at West Point graces the United States military academy. To become acquainted with her family, Putzi was sent to Harvard in 1905 to study the history of art. At the Harvard Club he made friends with the young Franklin D. Roosevelt, as well as others, including T. S. Eliot, Walter Lippman and Robert Benchley. In 1908, President Theodore Roosevelt invited him to the White House, having heard of his pianistic prowess. While in the United States, he also met Pierpont Morgan, Toscanini, Henry Ford, Enrico Caruso, Charlie Chaplin and Paderewski. Throughout the First World War he remained there, free on parole.

When he returned to Germany after the war, the misery and cynicism of his countrymen, and the "red rabble" that dominated the streets of Munich, horrified him. Then one day someone insisted he must hear an extraordinary man speak in a beer hall. "In his heavy boots, dark suit and leather waistcoat, semi-stiff white collar and odd little mustache," the man struck him more like a waiter in a station restaurant; but once he heard him speak, he became spellbound. Hanfstaengl was introduced to Hitler and soon began playing Wagner to him on the piano. Subsequently, a strong bond developed between the upper-class bohemian Hanfstaengl and the lower-class bohemian Hitler, because both men were steeped in German romanticism, determined to restore German honor following the crushing defeat of 1918.

For many years Hanfstaengl indulged in the fantasy that he could educate, guide and influence Adolf Hitler. What he considered most important was to neutralize the influence his vulgar entourage had upon him—those semi-educated, pretentious men from the Baltic who, dispossessed by the Russian Revolution, demanded a crusade against Russia, and the "petit bourgeois" who cried out for revenge against France. Again and again Hanfstaengl reminded Hitler that without the support of the Anglo-Saxon sea powers—especially the United States—Germany could never recover.

When he introduced Hitler to Munich society, he instructed him not to wear a blue suit with a purple shirt, a brown vest and a crimson tie. While he and members of that society became more and more intrigued with this curiously insecure figure, given to long silences and sudden outbursts of eloquence,[15] Hitler found Hanfstaengl's piano playing entrancing. He would listen for hours to his renditions of the prelude to *Die Meistersinger* and *Der Liebestod* by Wagner, and Hanfstaengl soon noticed that there was a direct relationship between those pieces of music and the way Hitler structured his speeches. The use of *leitmotifs*, contrasts, embellishments, and great climaxes at the end, were all there. It was therefore not surprising when Hanfstaengl became the Nazi musician *par excellence*, author of the *Hitler Song Book* (1924), and composer of the *Hitler Suite* (1934).

But after Hitler came to power in 1933 he listened less and less to that music. Hanfstaengl began to feel like a rejected lover, and it soon dawned on him that he may have been a trifle naive to hitch his wagon to the star of a potential mass-murderer. On June 30, 1934, the night of the Roehm *Putsch*, the Fuehrer emerged as an actual mass-murderer. Hanfstaengl was in the United States at the time, and when he returned to Berlin he was told by a friend that his name had been seen on the list of those to be purged. Curiously, he did not immediately leave Germany but had one or two more meetings with Hitler. But it soon became apparent that their relationship had ended; for instance, Hitler would sarcastically call him *Mister* Hanfstaengl in English. He was given the somewhat meaningless post of Chief of Foreign Press for the Nazi Party. However, this enabled him to cultivate his contacts in England and the United States and—although this is hard to believe—he continued to hope that the evil in and around Hitler could be contained.

Early in 1937, after a "hoax" that very much looked like an attempt on Hanfstaengl's life, he left Germany for London and sent his son Egon to school there. The Nazis seized his property; yet Goering made valiant attempts to woo him back to the Fatherland. Even Dr. Goebbels sent him a "lulling message," conveying to Hanfstaengl that there had been a misunderstanding, and that all that talk about trying to do away with him merely was a figment of "Putzi's" romantic imagination; or so the emissaries told him when they came to see him in London. Hitler's English "girlfriend" Unity Mitford also tried to act as go-between. It is not quite clear why all this was done—perhaps it was felt he knew too much. . . .

As Hanfstaengl saw the war clouds gather over Europe he thought that perhaps there was still time to put the brakes on Hitler. He therefore replied to one of the messages that he was prepared to return to Germany provided he received a personal apology from Hitler himself and an offer of a post as personal adviser to the Fuehrer on foreign affairs. Hanfstaengl heard much later that Hitler had told Winnifred Wagner—Richard Wagner's daughter-in-law—that he had actually sent such a letter.

Here is Hanfstaengl's own account of what happened when war broke out:[16]

> With the advent of the Polish crisis I realized my worst fears were about to crystallize. Hitler's mania to dominate his surroundings had become madness. The day after his armies marched into Poland I sent Egon to America. After a last lunch together at a little Italian restaurant in Soho, I saw him off on the boat-train. I intended to follow him as soon as I could. Then I returned feeling helpless, bewildered and miserable, back to my little flat in Kensington. That evening a peremptory ring came on the bell. Two plain-clothes men stood at the door: "Mr. Hanfstaengl? We have orders to take you into custody as an enemy alien!"

Internment is not a desirable condition. The British authorities had spread their net wide. There were political and Jewish refugees, Nazi functionaries from Bohle's organization of Germans abroad, the staff of the German hospital, the crews from ships seized at the ports. I could not feel I belonged to any of these categories. After a couple of nights at London's Olympia we were removed to a compound at Claxton-on-Sea and the leaden hand of camp discipline started to descend on us. Could the British not realize how I had fought against what had come to pass? What further use was I in a hut stuck behind barbed wire? I was allowed to get in touch with Kenneth Brown, my solicitor, who had helped in my London libel cases, and prepared a petition to the Crown for my release. My letters of recommendation should have been enough. They came from Sir Robert Vansittart, Sir Horace Rumbold and Sir Eric Phipps, the British ambassadors I had tried to help in Berlin, the Earl of Munster, Lord Fermoy, Vernon Bartlett. . . ."

Hanfstaengl's case came before an advisory committee which had been appointed to guide the Home Office during the winter of 1939–40, under the chairmanship of Sir Norman Birkett. What doomed him in spite of his powerful connections was his willingness to return to Germany in exchange for requisite assurances. The committee told him he would be able to "write himself free" if he helped British propaganda activities against the Nazis. But he declined on the grounds that Dr. Goebbels would be able to claim that anything he wrote was untrue because it was written under duress. "There are other ways I could help," he said, "but not as your prisoner."

The British rightly sensed that, while Hanfstaengl's estrangement from the Third Reich was genuine, he was far from committed to the Allied cause. They must have observed that Hanfstaengl thought it was by no means impossible that his mad, murderous, musical friend from the old Munich days might actually win the war, in which case he considered it prudent, for the moment, to keep all his options open.

He was sent back to the camp at Lingfield which, as he later reported in his memoirs, was completely in the hands of militant Nazis who "carried on a terror campaign against anyone they suspected of not being of their turn in mind." From Lingfield he went to Liverpool where the *Duchess of York* was waiting in the harbor.

The DUCHESS OF YORK

The voyage of the *Duchess of York* is well documented in a book by Eugen Spier,[17] an observant Jew who had left Germany in 1921, disgusted that the German revolution of 1918 had not crushed Prussian militarism, and convinced that the Weimar Republic was built on sand. Spier settled in London and in 1936 became active in an organization called "Focus for the Defence of Freedom and Peace" in which Winston Churchill, the Archbishop of Canterbury, Lady Violet Bonham-Carter and Sir Walter Citrine were fellow-members.

He does not mention having contact with Hanfstaengl on the *Duchess of York*, but Bernhard Pfundt remembers talking to him a few times. He told me that it was difficult to know exactly what he was thinking, because Hanfstaengl was always clowning.

To Spier and the other refugees on board the *Duchess*, the voyage was sheer agony. He described his utter helplessness having to leave his wife and child behind.

> From the railway station we were marched to the quayside at the harbour. There we saw, anchored in front of us, a large steamer painted all over in grey. We soon ascertained that she was the 20,000-ton ship of the Canadian Pacific Steamship Company, *The Duchess of York*. . . . It was obvious that if we embarked upon this huge vessel our destination could not possibly be the Isle of Man, but probably was to be some country thousands of miles away. This, however, I could not and I would not believe. Whilst I was gazing with astonished eyes at the grey monster which might be our destiny and drag us off to some unknown far away land, one of the Nazi seaman internees approached me and said: "Spier, there is no doubt we are not going to the Isle of Man; your English friends carry us off far away like kidnappers. Already twenty of us have received their berth tickets bearing the stamp of the Canadian Pacific Steamship Company and have been put aboard the ship."

The ship was unbelievably overcrowded, and no attempt was made to separate prisoners of war from civilians. For the refugees to be surrounded by a majority of Nazis was an extremely painful experience.

On the records of the Oral History Program of the Imperial War Museum in London is an interview by Margaret Brooks with Clive Teddern, a youngster of sixteen in 1940:

It was very traumatic with German uniforms and so on, although the strange thing is the German civilians were far worse than the German servicemen. Of course, the moment we went through the Irish Sea it became apparent that we were not going to the Isle of Man. And a large number of the Germans were, of course, naval personnel who had no difficulty in finding out which way we were going. Soon there was a terrific outcry: "Britain has been invaded, so that we can't be liberated—they are sending us to Canada. But we won't go to Canada. Halfway across, the war will be over and then the ship will go back to Germany. And then we'll throw you overboard."

A shooting took place on the *Duchess of York*. There are three versions of the incident. Karl Kruger, then sixteen, was present:

The killing occurred not long after we left port. By then we had got used to the procedure that at dusk we had to go below deck. On this occasion, the interpreter, Captain Savage, was on the upper deck, above where I was standing. He got rather excited about getting everybody to go down below. One of the prisoners of war turned around and touched his temple with his finger, suggesting that the captain was an idiot. The next thing I knew was that the prisoner was lying dead on deck. I never found out what exactly had happened. Probably one of the guards from above had shot him—clean through the temple. He was dead immediately. Someone said that the guard was going to shoot above everybody's head, and that the captain had pushed the rifle down. Whoever did it was either a very good shot, or it was an accident.

There was tremendous panic. Everybody rushed frantically down the gangways which were very narrow. Captain Savage lost his head, and was standing at the top of the gangway with a machine gun. The prisoner of war was buried at sea with full military honors.

Clive Teddern was also there.

I remember being on deck. And on one deck higher up a British officer came and told everybody to go below. And people started moving slowly. And suddenly there was a bang. And I turned round. There was somebody lying behind me shot through the head because this officer, just to speed things up, took a rifle and just shot somebody. And, of course, we moved a little bit more quickly then. And again the usual outcry that he shot somebody and officers and NCOs would take the bridge and the engine room and then they would take the ship back to Hamburg and then they'd throw . . . you know. And it was very traumatic because we certainly didn't feel safe. And we kept out of the way as much as we could, but you couldn't just disappear on a ship like that.

Eugen Spier heard about the killing from a group of Luftwaffe officers who were on the upper deck when the guards opened fire on the prisoners of war.

When orders were given that everybody should leave the deck at once, the crowd could only move very slowly as the deck was rather packed with prisoners. There was some defiance, and orders were given to the bodyguard to open fire, as a result of which one man was killed and many wounded. The excitement was terrific. Passions ran high, and some demanded immediate action such as to throw the officer in charge overboard, to burn or to sink the whole ship. This and similar reprisals were thrown into this heated discussion when another man entered our cabin with a bandage round his head. He had just come from the dressing-station and ascertained that the name of the killed man was Marquart, and that his other comrades were only slightly wounded. Nevertheless, revenge, satisfaction and severe punishment were insisted upon, and curses and threats were wildly expressed. After discussing the various and fantastic suggestions, as for instance, to immediately consign the body of the officer in charge to the bottom of the ocean, a plan of action was unanimously agreed upon, namely, to attack and storm the ship's bridge, take over the ship, and bring her to Hamburg.

These demands of some zealous bravadoes were, however, in the end abandoned, as well as the whole enterprise of attack. Finally they agreed upon electing a committee of senior Luftwaffe officers who should formulate their demands and put them before Major Ayres.

The appointed delegation was duly received by Major Ayres who, as usual, succeeded in calming the excited Nazis. He agreed to a dignified funeral for the shot man. It was further said that Major Ayres had telegraphed the whole incident to London. The Nazis were greatly satisfied with the action of the Major and congratulated themselves on having scored another great victory, the story of which they recorded at once in the report to the Swiss Legation who should convey it to the Government of the Third Reich.

All reports agree that the British soldiers on board did not have the means to control the Germans—especially after the killing. But as long as the nerve centers of the ship—the bridge and the engine room—remained safely in British hands, the Germans were left alone. The killing may have had the unexpectedly positive result of preventing the take-over of the *Duchess.*

A triumvirate of those who considered themselves good non-Nazis was formed. It consisted of Dr. Gustav Lachmann, one of the world's leading aeronautical engineers who had helped design the Messerschmidt fighter plane; Commodore Oskar Scharf, former commander of the *Europa;* and "Putzi" Hanfstaengl. The three were hoping to act as conciliators among various factions. Dr. Lachmann, who had been working as principal engineer for Handley Page in London, was friendly with Spier and when Spier needed a corner to sleep in, he offered him "part of a berth" in his cabin. Spier regularly read his prayer book and reported that he was greatly comforted by the verse, "*Refrain thy voice from weeping and thine eyes from tears, for thy work shall be rewarded, saith the Lord*" (Jeremiah XXXI). It gave him the strength to endure the boasts of the Nazis who were regaling each other with intoxicating stories about the impending liquidation of the British Empire, the acclamation of Hitler's triumph from every corner of the world, and the ever-increasing pro-Nazi attitude in the United States and the Arab world. They told each other that Churchill was likely to have the *Duchess* torpedoed, sending thousands of Germans to the bottom of the sea in order to score a victory. "After all," they gloated, "have there been any other British victories?"

On January 27, 1941 British intelligence officer Captain J. A. Milne wrote the following report to the Director of Internment Operations in Ottawa based on information obtained from an internee called Schmitt.

> During the voyage to Canada last July on the *Duchess of York*, Internee von Pilar drew up with some Internee Captains a detailed scheme for seizing the ship and navigating it

back to Germany. They were helped in formulating their scheme by the deck and cabin plans which he says were framed and hung in various cabins accessible to the Internees, and they also banked on the unfortunate conditions which, as is known, obtained among the Officers and Men of the British Escort troops. The shooting episode which occurred on the ship caused the schemers to desist from the plan. Schmitt claims to have actually overheard the discussions on the scheme, which he says was cut and dried within 30 hours of leaving port.

Schmitt states that on one occasion eight British soldiers laid down their rifles (presumably loaded) and bayonets on the deck of the ship in a row, and left them unattended for a considerable period where they were accessible to Internees. Schmitt and two other non-Nazi Internees stood unofficial guard over the rifles until the soldiers returned.

Internee von Pilar's full name was Baron Constant von Pilar von Pilchau. Born in Russia, he was what the Germans called a "Baltic Baron." A cultured, shrewd man of the world, he had been a shipping agent in the United Kingdom for the North German Lloyd Line.

From other sources, I gathered that it was Commodore Scharf and not the killing that made the baron and his conspirators desist from their plan to seize the *Duchess of York.*

As to Hanfstaengl, one wonders what he felt during that voyage. What were his thoughts when he sat at the table in the officers' mess listening to the communist adventurer Don Manuelo Fischer, who having recently returned from fighting with the International Brigade in Spain at one point stood up and cried, "Now I feel like a big general; not a German general but a general in the Red Army"?

Alas, after Hitler's former court jester walked ashore in Quebec, he was totally ignored by the North American public; soon he would be playing Wagner's music in the Canadian wilds.

The ARANDORA STAR

The *Duchess of York* docked in Quebec City on June 29, 1940. With 2,112 Category A internees and 535 prisoners of war on board, the Canadian authorities expecting dangerous men were not disappointed when a huge contingent of diehard Nazis came ashore.

Two days later the *Arandora Star* left Liverpool with a contingent of 473 Category A internees and 717 Italians. Under the heading "Britain's Prisoners," the *New York Times* carried this editorial in its July 7 edition:

> In last Tuesday's early dawn the British liner *Arandora Star*, built in 1927 to serve the luxury trade between the United Kingdom and Latin America, was steaming westward off the Irish coast. An explosion suddenly staggered the 15,501-ton vessel from stem to stern. A U-boat's torpedo had found its mark. On the stricken ship pandemonium broke loose. Voices cried out in German and Italian as well as English, for the liner, converted into a prison ship, was bound for Canada with hundreds of enemy aliens from Britain on broad.
>
> The prisoners, most of them German and Italian merchants, long resident in England, were hurled from bunks and hammocks. In darkness, for the ship's lighting plant was wrecked by the blast, they clambered toward the deck. Men killed as they sought safety. Germans beat down Italians in a mad rush for the rails. British seamen met death while trying to keep order and lower boats. Prisoners and guards alike were plunged into the cold, calm sea, then struggled for a grip on its life rafts and floating wreckage.
>
> For over half the ship's company there was no escape. Some were landed at a Scottish port by a rescue ship. More than a thousand men went down with the *Arandora Star*. Several British officers were thought to have perished with their ship. In Berlin, Germans asserted that Britain had broken international law by sending prisoners of war through a "dangerous war zone."

Here is a survivor's account:[18]

On July 2 at six in the morning (most of us were still asleep) a hollow explosion was heard in the engine-room. I tried to switch the light on—in vain. I thought we had run upon a mine. Cries, steps and running started in the corridors. I dressed scantily and went on with a lifebelt. I wanted to go to the lifeboats. The armed guard prevented me from doing so. I went to the other side to a small half-open deck. There many men were already busy throwing pieces of wood into the water. I could not see any officer nor any sailor; nobody could give any advice. Most of the rafts were left on board and were tied down with wire, which could not be loosened in the hurry, and without implements. Many could not believe that the ship was sinking. Some became hysterical. I saw lifeboats and wanted to go on deck again, where the boats were. Suddenly, two shots were fired. Later on I heard that internees were shot at, who wanted to go to the lifeboats which were reserved for English soldiers only. But as the soldiers were no seamen, they cut the ropes with an axe when the boat was only halfway down to the water and were drowned.

The Nazis went at once on deck in files of two under the leader of Captain Burfend; they had access to the lifeboats. They had many seamen and brought down about seven lifeboats. Captain Burfend stayed on board (eight lifeboats were in the water altogether) and was drowned. I came to the upper deck; no lifeboats were left. Scenes of distress. A man hanged himself; a 62-year-old Jew sat in despair on his suitcase and could not be persuaded to put on his lifebelt. The old and ill people in the decks below had no chance. Among them there was the 75-year old Julius Weiss who had been in England for fifty years.

I advised two soldiers who were still standing guard with drawn bayonets to throw away their bayonets and to spring into the water. They said they were not allowed to because they had not had an order, but I persuaded them. I did not see an officer, military officer or sailor, who would have helped us or the privates. As the boat keeled over I climbed down a rope ladder with a plank in my hand into the water. The decision to do so was very difficult for me. I swam away from the ship and saw it sink.

It took thirty-five minutes from the explosion to the sinking of the ship. The water was full of oil; hundreds of planks and pieces of wood with barbed wire threatened us. The first hours in the Atlantic Ocean were dreadful. The water was terribly cold, with fog and slight rain. Cries, praying, shouts of "Mother!" by old and young in every language (Italian, German, English, Hebrew) depressed us terribly. Old people got heart attacks and died. Bodies swollen by water floated beside me.

After about three hours a coastal aeroplane sighted us. It cruised about for hours over our heads, as if it wanted to tell us that rescue was coming. We took fresh heart. After six-and-a-half hours I sighted one of our lifeboats. I swam to it. An English sailor (first mate) was at the helm. I spoke to him in English, told him that I was quite exhausted, and asked him to take me into the boat. He said, "Full up." I held on the helm and implored the others in the boat, who drew me, quite exhausted as I was, into the boat.

After an hour the destroyer H 83 *St. Laurent* from Canada came. Behind her was a British one. On board the Canadian destroyer rum, hot chocolate, food were awaiting us. The sailors gave us their raincoats, trousers, etc., to dress those of us who were almost naked. We sailed shortly after 4 o'clock in the afternoon with about 600 survivors. Of our Seaton group of 182 persons, about 101 were drowned, among them Olbrich and Kirste.

We learned on the destroyer that we had been torpe-doed, that the *Arandora Star* had sent out no SOS, that the destroyer at the time of the torpedoing was only one and a half hours' distance from our position, and that many could have been rescued if an SOS had been sent out. Only at 11 o'clock in the morning did the destroyer get the order from London to sail to our rescue (after a report by the coastal aeroplane). In Greenock (Glasgow) an escort awaited, which led the healthy ones of us half naked and barefoot through the piers. We who were destined for the hospital waited for ambulances on the pier for over four hours, standing in the streets.

Most of us aboard the *Ettrick* heard about the sinking of the *Arandora Star* a day or two after it happened, but to avoid general panic, we were sworn to secrecy. We had left Liverpool on July 3, and I remember one of my seasick colleagues mumbling sardonically that he was afraid we were *not* going to be sunk.

Nearly six hundred internees drowned as a result of this disaster; among the Category A internees at least fifty-three anti-Nazi, Jewish and non-Jewish refugees lost their lives. One of them was Karl Olbrich, a former member of the Reichstag who had been arrested by the Gestapo in 1933 and had spent three years in a German penitentiary and one year in a concentration camp. Another was Louis Weber, a member of the International Transport Workers Federation and of the German Seamen's Union. Kurt Regner was miraculously saved from drowning. A former leader of the Austrian Socialist Movement who had been beaten up by the Nazis after participating in an anti-Nazi demonstration the day before Hitler invaded Austria, he had escaped to Czechoslovakia. A week after the sinking of the ship, Regner was shipped to Australia without being able to get in touch with his mother and sister, who were half-crazed with anxiety.

Being left-wing, Olbrich, Weber and Regner probably had aroused displeasure at their tribunal hearings. Among the Italian anti-fascists drowned was D. Anzani, a tailor who had lived in England for thirty-one years, having devoted his life to assisting refugees to escape Mussolini's terror. Many of the Italians on the *Arandora Star* were owners of or waiters in small London restaurants, specifically in the Soho district.

On July 8 a letter written by Mrs. Theresa Steuer appeared in the *Times of London*.

> Out of the chaos of Nazi Austria, my husband and I saved only each other. Country, home, family, friends, career, books, income, everything was lost, but my husband and I clung to each other resolutely, through grave dangers, and together finally reached this country and refuge. . . . We refugee wives were proud and satisfied when our men volunteered for admission into the army. These applications were rejected. . . . On June 25 my husband, an Austrian of Polish birth and parentage, was arrested. I have heard nothing of him since, have still, after two long weeks, no idea where he is. All I definitely know is that German and Austrian refugees of Category C were drowned in the Atlantic.

Many of our families and friends were in the same position as Mrs. Steuer. For at least two days my mother had no assurances that I was not one of those lost on the *Arandora Star*. Then the Home Office, via the Jewish refugee organization at Bloomsbury House, advised her that it was unlikely I was among those who had drowned. But not until she received a cable from my sister in New York more than five weeks later could she be 100 percent certain.

Anthony Eden was secretary of state for war at the time of the sinking, and on July 9 his colleague, the minister of shipping, had this to say in response to a question raised in the British House of Commons:

I am informed by my Right Hon. Friend the Secretary of State for War that all the Germans on board were Nazi sympathizers and that none came to this country as refugees. None had category B or C certificates or were recognized as friendly aliens. The Protecting Powers have been given lists of the missing passengers in order that the next of kin may be informed.

On July 16 Anthony Eden confirmed:

It was understood by my Department that none of these Germans were refugees, but I am making further inquiries on this point. . . . I can give the House the assurance that it is not the intention to send abroad anti-Nazis in contact with Nazis.

Three weeks later, Lord Farington spoke in the House of Lords about the anti-Nazis and anti-fascists lost on the *Arandora Star*: "I consider that whoever was responsible for these men . . . is answerable for their deaths."

Soon after the sinking, Dr. Goebbels' Ministry of Propaganda and Enlightenment instructed the German press not to make any mention of the incident until the government had received details through the Swiss Foreign Office. Once they had the information, the next of kin in Germany were advised as follows:

During an attempt to remove German civilian prisoners by force to Canada . . . has sacrificed his life for the glory of the Greater Germany. The ship was sunk as a result of the war at sea.

It is unlikely that the Germans knew who was on the *Arandora Star* when the order to torpedo her was given. After the sinking, the Red Cross suggested to the British government that they advise the Germans of any future sailings with internees and prisoners of war on board. The Foreign Office was sympathetic to this, but the War Office was opposed to giving the Germans any information whatsoever. There were more inconclusive exchanges between the two ministries on whether or not the ships should fly special flags. But after July 10, largely as a result of the outcry caused by the sinking of the *Arandora Star*, all transfers of civilian internees to the Dominions were discontinued.

The DUNERA

Our story of the ships that carried the refugees would not be complete without an account of the transport that went to Australia.

Approximately two hundred and fifty German and two hundred Italian survivors of the *Arandora Star*, and the two hundred men who had been scheduled to sail on the *Sobieski* but were left behind for lack of space, were among the 2,550 passengers who on July 10 left Liverpool aboard the *Dunera* headed for Sydney, Australia.

The treatment they received from the British officers and men was such that the *Dunera* soon was called the "pick-pocket-battleship." Many of the British troops on board had been evacuated from Dunkirk and as a result were embittered and demoralized. However, the main reason for their bad conduct was that at least some of the officers were accessories to thefts and merciless bullying.

For some of the interned youngsters, the voyage had elements of adventure. But it was the older men, and those who had suffered in Nazi Germany and Austria, who found the trip unbearable. Moreover, most of the passengers assumed the *Dunera* also was sailing to Canada and were deeply frustrated and angry when they discovered otherwise. Helmut Gernsheim had been particularly looking forward to going to Canada because he had previously met Vincent and Mrs. Massey socially in London and they had "sponsored" him.

A man from the Home Office had come to the British camp to tell the internees that a ship was leaving for Canada two or three days hence and that two thousand volunteers were needed. "If we can't get them, then we will appoint people. You would be wise to volunteer. We are already sending our own children to Canada, and quite a lot of their mothers are going too." He warned them of a possible German invasion, stressing that "should the situation get much worse . . . the British government would go to Canada as well."

"When we begin to evacuate this country on a large scale," he continued, "we will think of ourselves first. We won't be able to think of you. You would be wise to volunteer now." Gernsheim thought it was "eminently sensible" to do so immediately.

While in the Irish Sea, close to the spot where the *Arandora Star* was sunk, the *Dunera*, too, was attacked. But thanks to luck and to the captain's skillful maneuvering of the ship, the torpedo glanced off the hull and a disaster was avoided. There was a tremendous noise; many prisoners banged on the locked doors in panic, and even the troops guarding them were afraid. The experience must have been particularly terrible for the survivors of the *Arandora Star*. Some witnesses claim they saw British destroyers hunt down a U-boat; later, rumors were heard that the Germans had claimed to have sunk the *Dunera*.

Helmut Gernsheim believes that as a result of the torpedo attack the ship must have changed course.

> We were beginning to realize we were not going to Canada. After a few days we arrived in Freetown in Sierra Leone.... However, we couldn't get into the harbor because many British warships were blocking the way. From there we went to Takoradi [now Ghana] and stayed for two days, taking on board masses of food, toilet paper and so on. When we reached Capetown we assumed that was our destination. We asked the intelligence officer where we were going; was it India? He said he himself didn't know, sorry. We proceeded around the Cape into the Indian Ocean. There one man committed suicide by jumping overboard. His visa to the Argentine, where his mother lived, had recently expired.... We looked for him for about half an hour without finding him, and then steamed on....

Two other internees died during the *Dunera* voyage, in addition to the one who had jumped overboard. The British guards were constantly engaged in provocation. For example, they would claim that a knife had been stolen, and unless it was found, all sorts of horrible things would happen to the internees. Of course, no knife had been stolen.

No daylight or fresh air ever reached the quarters below deck where the internees slept in stifling heat. There was only one ship's doctor and hardly any medical supplies. Benjamin Patkin reports: "One internee who became ill . . . said that he noticed the same liquid from the same bottle was the only 'medicine' given to every sick man. The spoon was not washed or wiped after each patient."[19] "We weren't allowed any razor blades," Gernsheim recalls, "so none of us could shave. In any case, all our belongings had been stolen so we had no means of washing, other than using kitchen soap. . . . When we arrived in Australia we were all in rags. We had been wearing the same clothes for fifty-eight days."

The robberies had started even before the internees boarded the ship. The soldiers had subjected everyone to a rough search and "soon rows of empty wallets were lying on the floor, hundreds of gold rings and 1,200 watches were taken. Documents were torn up and thrown away," Benjamin Patkin wrote. As to the theft of the luggage, I have been told that the British troops were not the only villains; a few pieces appear to have been stolen by internees. However, there is no doubt that some of the troops committed specific brutalities which have been documented. In spite of, or because of, these horrors, a large number of internees carried on a lively intellectual life on board. Father Walter König, S.J., spoke on Goethe's *Faust*; another scholar lectured on Spengler's *Decline of the West* and Felix Werder, with his father's help, put down on toilet paper whatever he could remember of Handel's *Judas Maccabaeus* and Mozart's G-Major Mass so that these works could be performed by the ship's choir. Werder also made the first sketches for a tone poem that was later performed by the Sydney Symphony Orchestra, conducted by Sir Eugene Goossens.

On May 15, 1941 Captain H. David R. Margesson, who had succeeded Anthony Eden as British Secretary of State for War, ordered two court martials. The one found R.S.M. Charles Bowles guilty on ten charges out of twenty-one. He was given one year in prison and dismissed from the force. Sergeant Arthur Helliwell was found guilty on one out of three charges and was severely reprimanded for disobeying a superior officer "by not providing an alien with blankets and water." The second court-martial concerned charges against W. P. Scott, the officer commanding the troops on the *Dunera*. Having been given the rank of acting lieutenant-colonel on his transfer to the Pioneer Corps, he reverted to his substantive rank of major on relinquishing his command on October 8, 1940. Scott was acquitted on the first charge which had accused him of condoning thefts, but was found guilty of failure to conduct a proper inquiry into an act of violence against an interned alien.

On September 30, 1941, the matter again came up. On this occasion, Captain Margesson told the House of Commons that, where practicable, members of the escort were searched on their return to England and various articles which were believed to be the property of internees were confiscated. "Strict instructions have since been issued to commanding officers with regard to the handling of property of internees on board ship, and I have no reason to anticipate any repetition of the incidents that took place on the *Dunera*," he concluded. Since the *Dunera*, which had left Liverpool more than fourteen months before Captain Margesson made this statement, was the last of the transports carrying civilian internees to one of the Dominions, it can be stated with certainty that his instructions were followed to the letter.

Public opinion and constant questioning by three eloquent M.P. s—Eleanor Rathbone, Colonel Josuah Wedgwood and Victor Cazalet—had forced the British government to take a second look at its internment policies and practices. Viscount Cecil called them "the most ridiculous nonsense ever devised" and a number of other voices, by no means only those coming from the Left, wondered whether the military necessity plea was being used to condone totalitarian measures that easily could have been turned against other sections of the population. But Conservative M.P. Mrs. Mavis Tate took the view that if the government had erred at all it had been on the side of leniency. "This is not the time," she said, "to take a sentimental view of the matter. Have M.P.'s such short memories?" she asked in the House. "Have there not been so-called victims of Nazi and Fascist aggression who have been useful tools in other countries?"

On July 16, Charles Ritchie, at the Canadian High Commission in London, made this entry in his diary:

> I now hear that the ferocious internees whom the British government begged us on bended knees to take to Canada to save this country from their nefarious activities are mostly entirely inoffensive anti-Nazi refugees who have been shovelled out to Canada at a moment's notice where they may have a disagreeable time, as our authorities have no files about them and will not know whom or what to believe.

Part Two

FIVE

The "Enemy Paratroopers" Arrive

Our voyage up the St. Lawrence River had been gorgeous. The magnificent river, the picturesque little villages along its banks with their silvery church steeples and, finally, the sight of the dramatic cliffs of Quebec cheered us tremendously. Everyone, with the exception of a few cynics, felt optimistic and in a good mood. The weather was perfect.

Canadian Navy vessels escorted the *Ettrick* as she steamed into the harbor, and we were much impressed by the display of military might along the shoreline of Wolfe's Cove. We saw large numbers of armed soldiers, all wearing sun helmets and shorts, which made some of us think we had come to India.

Weakened by hunger and/or dysentery, we stood on deck for hours in the hot sun, until we were taken ashore at eight o'clock in the evening. Having had nothing to drink for many hours, a few people fainted and keeled over. Heavily guarded and accompanied by motorcycle escorts, buses took us from Wolfe's Cove up the Rock of Quebec to the Plains of Abraham. Some curious Quebeckers lining our route called to us *"sales boches,"* "Nazis," and similar words of welcome, but once we stepped off the buses, Canadian officers took over. They all eyed us with suspicion and some were perplexed by the ingenuity of these enemy prisoners who had donned the guises of Catholic priests, bearded rabbis and pale-faced rabbinical students complete with traditional earlocks.

Father Anton Ummenhofer, who now lives in Germany, wrote to me that there was no doubt the Canadian military personnel suspected the priests and the others to be German parachutists who had been captured in Holland. Walter Loevinsohn recounts the following story:

We had three rabbis on board. The district chaplain from M.D.5 wanted to see the prisoners coming in. So when the rabbis saw his clerical collar they marched right up to him and introduced themselves. The chaplain thought they were dangerous men in disguise, so he decided to test them.

He addressed one of them in Latin. He received an answer in Latin. The chaplain tried again, addressing the second rabbi in Greek. He got a perfect answer in Greek. He was beginning to think these must be very strange parachutists. So he tried the third rabbi; he put a question to him in Hebrew. Naturally he got a flawless reply. The poor, confused chaplain just shook his head, shrugged his shoulders and walked away.

Loevinsohn, who was among the volunteers who helped unload the luggage, observed one soldier who had been listening to the internees talking among themselves. "He marched off to one of the officers and, smartly saluting, he said, 'Beg to report, sir, most of these prisoners seem to speak English quite well.' The captain replied, 'Yes, yes, I know. Those are the most dangerous ones.'"

Some attempt had been made by the British officers who had accompanied us to explain to the Canadians that we were not dangerous Nazis. But this was not always done in the most flattering terms. Loevinsohn recalls:

A Canadian major or colonel had boarded the ship downriver from Quebec, and the English intelligence officer introduced the passengers to him. "Over there, there are a thousand prisoners of war: soldiers, sailors, airmen: very good troops. In the stern, there are 800 Italian civilian internees: they're no trouble at all. Over there"—and he pointed to us—"these people, they're the scum of Europe."

Some soldiers of the Régiment de Trois Rivières then engaged in the time-honored practice of robbing the conquered enemy of his possessions. Most of the pilfering—I prefer to use that word to the more ambitious "looting"—occurred during the first night on Canadian soil. Our luggage had been taken to the Plains of Abraham by truck and was "dealt with" separately.

We were thoroughly searched by the N.C.O.'s of the regiment until three o'clock in the morning, ten men at a time. Ernest Borneman kept a detailed record of the event:

> We had to strip and everything except our handkerchiefs was impounded. All these articles, with money listed on separate forms, were to have been entered on official impounding sheets, all to be signed by the N.C.O. responsible for the search and countersigned by the internees. In many cases the articles were not entered at all, or the impounding sheets were torn up and thrown away. I cannot recall having seen on any impounding sheet the signature of an N.C.O. When the impounded articles were to be returned, two days later, it was found that money and valuables, (watches, fountain pens, cigarette cases, rings, etc.) in the value of nearly £900 were missing. In most cases, however, the loss could not be proved, since the impounding sheets were either lost or the articles missing had not been entered. (In some cases they had been entered correctly, but subsequently erased.) Items were also found to be missing from suitcases and other luggage taken from us when we disembarked. A typewriter had disappeared. Evidence concerning its loss was given by the owner to the court of enquiry which had been set up almost immediately. A number of internees were detailed to keep the official records of the proceedings of this court. Some time later the missing typewriter was returned to its owner by one of the officers on the camp staff, on condition that no questions were to be asked in connection with its disappearance. The officer also directed the internees to strike the evidence concerning it off the official records.

A series of court-martials of the suspected soldiers followed much later. Subsequent correspondence between Ottawa and London shows that there was some doubt as to the legality of the procedure. Nine men were charged with fourteen offenses. However, all charges, except one, were dismissed.

During our first night we were also subjected to a curious V.D. inspection. Stripped, we were lined up in front of the medical officer who, using his swagger stick as a diagnostic tool, performed a somewhat cursory examination, which may have been an uplifting experience for us, though it could not have contributed much to the storehouse of medical knowledge. Some claim what it really did was further enrich certain soldiers who still found treasures, such as combs and playing cards, in the pockets of our discarded clothes that were lying on the benches. E. M. Oppenheimer lost a bottle of aspirin, which he didn't mind too much because he had been told at the dockside, "In Canada you won't get any headaches."

When the *Sobieski* docked two days later, the procedure was slightly different. Erwin Schild who belonged to the orthodox group remembers a Jewish second-lieutenant whose job it apparently was to confiscate everything they had. "Take out all your money!" he said loudly in English, adding in less audible Yiddish, "What you keep in your pockets nobody will find."

Edgar Sarton remembers the same nice officer saying to his group, "Kids, you're going to be all right. Just take it easy." According to Charles Luwisch, he then playfully checked everyone in the orthodox group to make sure they had their *talliths* (prayer shawls), jokingly reprimanding those who were without them.

It slowly became evident, at least to some of the Canadian authorities, that there had been some horrendous mistake. The overwhelming presence among the new arrivals of high school boys, students, professors, priests and rabbis was not what London had promised to deliver.

One of the most pathetic tales is told by Walter Wallich:

Mr. F. was the son of a German father and a Spanish mother. The boy had Spanish nationality and at the outbreak of war was returning to Spain from South America where he had been selling second-hand textile machinery. He was travelling on a Levantine steamer which had been intercepted by the British blockade. From his passport it could be ascertained that his father was German. So, having started out with five cabin trunks packed with all his worldly possessions, one was lost on the way to Spain. He was taken to Gibraltar, from there to Britain on the next convenient steamer—minus two of his trunks. We met him in Huyton; he spoke no German and in Spanish asked to see the Spanish consul. Nobody paid any attention to him. . . . When we were transferred to Douglas on the Isle of Man,

Mr. F. had to leave behind another one of his cabin trunks.

Being in his late twenties or early thirties and unmarried he now was a candidate for going to Canada. His last cabin trunk weighed more than the forty pounds allowed by way of luggage. I interceded with the camp adjutant on his behalf, saying that he had already lost four out of his five trunks; could he please be allowed a little extra weight? Yes, that was allowed.

On arrival in Quebec, our luggage was taken to the camp by truck. A few days later, we were paraded to an area outside the camp where the luggage was stored. Mr. F.'s fifth and last cabin trunk was conspicuously absent. So, standing there in his bathing costume, trousers and braces, instead of asking for the Spanish consul, he foamed at the mouth, threw fits and screamed. The Canadians decided he was a dangerous man and promptly sent him to a Nazi camp. I don't know what happened to him.

Bewilderment in Ottawa

No one in Ottawa was prepared for the arrival of the refugees; officials had been told to expect dangerous Nazis. Admittedly, the High Commission in London had relayed to Ottawa a last-minute telephone call from the Home Office, advising them that "civilian internees in Categories B and C" were on the high seas, but somehow that message had got lost in the shuffle. The *Duchess of York* had arrived two weeks earlier; its huge majority of Nazis had led them to expect more "dangerous men."

It took a few weeks before the Canadian press got hold of the story of the "misdirected" refugees, but if anybody had been misdirected it was the Canadian High Commissioner in London, Vincent Massey. Although he was too polite to raise his voice in indignation, he sent a letter to Viscount Caldecote, Secretary of State for Dominion Affairs, dated July 22, pointing out that if a substantial number of civilian internees who had been transferred to Canada were indeed innocent refugees, "the Canadian government would be faced with responsibilities of a character which they had certainly not contemplated when they consented to receive these internees whose presence in this country was described as being a source of most serious risk."

A week later Massey sent a copy of his letter to Ottawa, together with some explanatory notes summarizing his understanding of the negotiations with Whitehall. He pointed out that the War Office had made arrangements for the transfer of internees to Canada "on the principle that all alien internees were dangerous and that they were better out of the country." They had continually changed the categories of those sailing on the different ships, without giving due notice to the Canadian government. The sinking of the *Arandora Star* had further complicated the situation, as it was decided "that many of the dangerous internees who survived the sinking should not be shipped out to Canada again immediately, in view of the experience through which they had just passed, and that instead other categories be sent."

(I find this point difficult to follow. The *Ettrick* had left Liverpool the day after the sinking, and I cannot imagine that there was sufficient time to make any changes. Nor can I understand that it affected the contingent sent to Canada on the *Sobieski* which left a day later.)

Massey went on to explain to Ottawa that the categories finally sent on the *Ettrick* and the *Sobieski* were only "notified to us, in spite of our repeated enquiries, on July 4." (At that time the *Ettrick* had already sailed, and the *Sobieski* was to leave the same night.)

On July 30 Viscount Caldecote replied, making a valiant effort to explain why the British, without telling the Canadians in advance, had decided to send to Canada both dangerous and non-dangerous Germans and Austrians. He expressed polite regrets but made no honest effort to justify his government's actions.

It was quite true, he wrote, that the Canadian government had agreed to "relieve this country of the burden" of prisoners of war and internees "who were regarded at the time as a source of most serious risk in the event of invasion or parachute landings," but that internees in Categories B and C were persons who were not regarded as individually dangerous or even potentially dangerous. He should explain, however:

> . . . that the United Kingdom Government, after their original communication to Canada on the subject, came to

the conclusion that, in order to reduce the general danger arising from the presence of a large number of internees in this country, it was desirable to transfer overseas as many internees, whether individually dangerous or not, as the Dominion Governments were willing to accept. The fact that so many "B" and "C" category internees have been sent to Canada to fill up the quota of 7,000 prisoners of war and internees which the Canadian Government expressed willingness to accept, is due partly to the sinking of the *Arandora Star*. This ship was carrying to Canada 480 category A Germans or Austrians and 710 Italian Fascists, and also had on board tents and other equipment which were to have been landed at Newfoundland, and which, had they arrived, would have enabled the Newfoundland authorities to take, as they were prepared to do, the prisoners of war and some of the internees who were instead sent to Canada on the *Sobieski*.

The United Kingdom authorities greatly regret that the inclusion of "B" and "C" category internees among those sent to Canada was not explained to you and the Canadian Government at an earlier date, but I hope that no serious difficulties will arise in connection with their internment in Canada.

The information that Newfoundland had agreed to take custody of prisoners of war and internees may have been new to Ottawa, since on June 7 Massey had informed his colleagues at home that on the basis of information he had received, Newfoundland "did not have the military resources" to accept custody.

SIX

You'll Get Used To It

The Plains of Abraham

Having been relieved of only one rusty nail-file during my first encounter with the Canadian Army, and subsequently pronounced "clean" by the medical officer with the swagger stick, I settled down for my "Summer of 1940." In Camp L, situated on the Plains of Abraham on the very battlefield on which the English had defeated the French in 1759 and within a few hundred yards of the monuments honoring Wolfe and Montcalm, the two gallant generals who had lost their lives during the battle, we were housed in temporary barracks. It was like being incarcerated in the middle of Waterloo, Gettysburg, or Verdun.

Very soon it became evident that there were no plans underway to "give us work that suited us." In fact, there was no work, no contact with the outside world, and no news except an ever-growing fund of rumors.

Nor was there any mail. I received the first letter from my mother in London on August 31, my twenty-first birthday, two months after I had last heard from her directly. A friend of mine had written ten letters and ten postcards to his parents in London, and by the middle of September he had not yet heard from them. On October 10 Osbert Peake, representing the Home Secretary, was asked in the House of Commons whether he was aware that letters from internees took seven weeks to reach England. He replied that there had been certain difficulties, but that postal arrangements were now working smoothly.

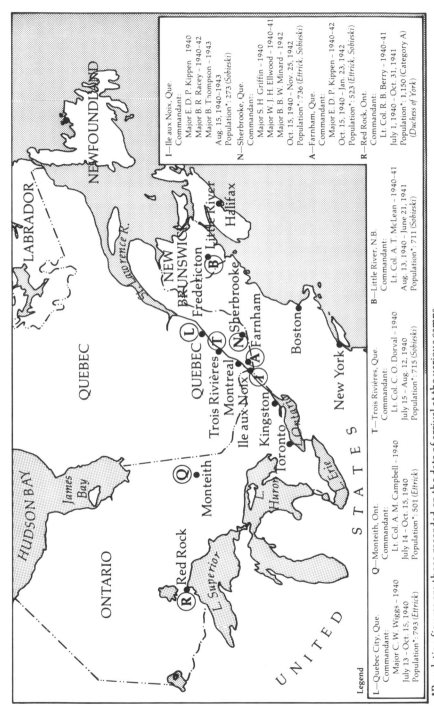

Legend

L—Quebec City, Que.
Commandant:
    Major C. W. Wiggs – 1940
July 13 – Oct. 15, 1940
Population*: 793 (Ettrick)

Q—Monteith, Ont.
Commandant:
    Lt. Col. A. M. Campbell – 1940
July 14 – Oct. 15, 1940
Population*: 501 (Ettrick)

T—Trois Rivières, Que.
Commandant:
    Lt. Col. C. O. Dorval – 1940
July 15 – Aug. 12, 1940
Population*: 715 (Sobieski)

B—Little River, N.B.
Commandant:
    Lt. Col. A. T. McLean – 1940-41
Aug. 13, 1940 – June 21, 1941
Population*: 711 (Sobieski)

I—Ile aux Noix, Que.
Commandant:
    Major E. D. P. Kippen 1940
    Major B. R. Racey – 1940-42
    Major B. Tnompson – 1943
Aug. 15, 1940-1943
Population*: 273 (Sobieski)

N—Sherbrooke, Que.
Commandant:
    Major S. H. Griffin – 1940
    Major W. J. H. Ellwood – 1940-41
    Major B. B. W. Minard – 1942
Oct. 15, 1940 – Nov. 25, 1942
Population*: 736 (Ettrick, Sobieski)

A—Farnham, Que.
Commandant:
    Major E. D. P. Kippen – 1940-42
Oct. 15, 1940 – Jan. 23, 1942
Population*: 523 (Ettrick, Sobieski)

R—Red Rock, Ont.
Commandant:
    Lt. Col. R. B. Berry – 1940-41
July 1, 1940 – Oct. 31, 1941
Population*: 1,150 (Category A)
    (Duchess of York)

*Population figures are those recorded on the date of arrival at the various camps.

Our stay in Camp L was the time for making new friends, building a new community, starting the "Popular University," and engaging in lively political discussions and intellectually stimulating pursuits.

It was also the time for restoring one's health with eating. We had been hungry in the English camps, and after the seasickness and outbreaks of dysentery on the *Ettrick* the food, consisting of Canadian Army rations, was magnificent. We couldn't get enough of the bacon and eggs each morning, and of the real butter and jam we could spread on our bread.

Three political issues were debated endlessly. Actually, they were three aspects of the same question: How best to persuade the Canadian authorities that we were refugees.

1. Should we be prepared to write postcards and letters on prisoner of war stationery, thereby condoning the Canadian viewpoint that we were Prisoners of War, Second Class?

2. Should we agree to wear prisoner of war uniforms—a blue denim jacket with a large red patch on the back, and the blue pants with a red stripe down each side?

3. Should we accept the good offices of the International Red Cross, or the Swiss consul who reported to the German government?

On the first two issues we decided to yield because high-principled resistance to them would have been self-defeating and useless. On the third issue we stood firm, and the inmates of the other camps reacted in the same way.

Yet, however much we tried to explain to the Canadian authorities who we were, they had great difficulty grasping it. The British intelligence officer, Captain Godfrey Barrass, knew precisely who we were and had successfully indoctrinated our corpulent, pleasant and well-meaning commandant, Major L. C. W. Wiggs, a former coal merchant from Quebec City and, I think, the only camp commandant we ever had who was popular enough to be given a nickname; we called him Piggy-Wiggy. (Camp life and school life always had much in common.) In the words of Captain Barrass, "Wiggs was a kind man willing to give the shirt off his back to anybody who needed it."

A more representative view of us was held by Colonel H. de N. Watson, who inspected our camp on August 2 on behalf of the Director of Internment Operations. Colonel Watson was not pleased. He found life in Camp L was "a very casual affair," noting that this may have been due to the influence of the British intelligence officer who "referred to the prisoners as 'Refugees of Nazi Oppression' and said that 'they had nothing in common with the Nazis, and in fact hated them.'" The colonel found this very confusing, especially since Barrass appeared to have "undoubtedly influenced the officers and staff of the camp to think along the same lines." Another thing Watson found difficult to take was that the prisoners had not been instructed to salute the officers and, as he reported to headquarters, little attention was being paid to the commandant while he made his rounds. Not only was this lack of discipline appalling, he thought, but relationships between the prisoners and the officers were so relaxed that "this state of affairs could actually lead to fraternization." This had been brought home to him when a number of officers and staff were invited to a camp concert given by a "number of first-class musicians."

> It was pointed out to the camp commandant that this was
> not very good policy . . . and that, . . . it placed the officers
> and staff attending under a certain obligation to the prison-
> ers, which is not desirable.

Colonel Watson also found it hard to understand why the concert was concluded with the singing of "God Save the King" and "O Canada." Probably much to his relief, he became commandant of a camp for Nazis a year later where life was simpler.

A tragic incident had occurred during our second night in Camp L. It reflects how charged the atmosphere was at the time. Ernst Scheinberg was a young boy who had suffered severe mental impairment as a result of having been brutally beaten in a German concentration camp. The terrible voyage aboard the *Ettrick*, the reception in Quebec, marked by uncertainty and hostility, and the sight of bayonets, barbed wire and watchtowers proved too much for him. He became hysterical, began kicking and screaming and then tried to choke somebody in his hut. A guard was called. He put the poor fellow into the hospital isolation cell near the main gate. The boy tried to force his way out through the window. The guard shot him in the head.

This horror was successfully hushed up in the camp. I did not hear about it until long afterwards, because each one of our seven huts was a separate world.

Prince Friedrich of Prussia, Count Lingen. *Central Press Photos Ltd.,*
London, England

Arrival in Quebec. *Artist unknown.*

Hut in Camp L, Quebec City. *Artist unknown.*

Dismantling Camp Q, October 1940. *Artist, Gerry Waldston.*

Camp B. Work in the Forest. *Courtesy, Edward Weil.*

As internees were forbidden to own or use a camera these photographs were taken secretly with a home-made camera and film "borrowed" from the R.C.M.P. *Photographer, Marcell Seidler.*

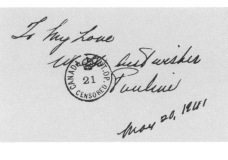

A romance across the barbed wire fence started in Quebec City between Peter Field and Pauline Perrault. They exchanged love letters and Pauline often enclosed photographs of herself, some of them bearing messages such as the one above.

Peter then was transferred to Sherbrooke and in October 1941 was granted permission to leave the camp and spend the weekend with Pauline and her family in Quebec City.

Top. Set for G.B. Shaw's
Androcles and the Lion performed in Camp B on January
23, 1941. *Sketch by John
Newmark.*

Above. Christmas 1940. The
Priests' Hut in Farnham.
Left. Father Anton
Ummenhofer, 1941. *Drawing
by Dr. Walter Ruhmann.*

Stone walls do not a prison make,
Nor iron bars a cage

The Sergeant-Major. *Artist unknown.*

In all respects, other than the lack of comprehension by the high military brass, Canada looked great to us. The location of our camp was magnificent, especially as it provided a glorious view of the mighty St. Lawrence. In fact, everything looked astoundingly *big* to us. The St. Lawrence seemed broader than the Rhine, the Elbe and the Danube combined, and it had the additional advantage, unlike European rivers, that it had never been the scene of bloody wars. Bigness in our eyes was synonymous with innocence, or rather naiveté—which struck us as a very attractive feature; we had had enough of non-naive Europe for a while. Not only was the river broader than any other we had ever seen, but the sunsets were more intensely blood-red and the thunderstorms noisier. All in all we were overawed by the grandeur of North America.

Within the camp the presence of royalty, more specifically that of Fritz Lingen, the old German Kaiser's grandson, added glamour to our lives. Everyone knew who he was, and except for a few arrogant professors, stubborn republicans and glum-looking communists, we all felt better for being in the company of an anointed prince, even if he had no immediate prospects to sit on a throne. It was good enough for us, and we considered it potentially useful that he was related to King George VI of England and of Canada. But had he not been the *good* prince he was—decent, courteous and anti-Nazi—we might well have ignored his illustrious presence.

Noteworthy, of course, was the attraction the Prussian prince had for the Jews in the camp. No doubt it was flattering that when he encountered any of us during our endless promenades through the camp, he would bow slightly and say *Guten Morgen, Guten Tag, Guten Abend, Herr Rosenzweig, Herr Levinsohn, Herr Cohen*, etc. Based on our recent experiences we were no longer accustomed to being treated with such civility by German gentiles. I am tempted to go even further and meditate on the special relationship between Jews and royalty in general—about "Court Jews," and the fact that through the centuries it had been a weakness of many to be prepared to pay a steep price for a smile from royal lips, as some sort of insurance against Cossacks or their equivalents. One might also speculate that during the Kaiser's reign many Jews in Germany did better than ever before, except that they could not become officers in the peacetime army or rise to the rank of full professor at universities. Somehow we projected this sense of belated gratitude on to the prince. We were attracted to him the way Falstaff was attracted to *his* prince, because—who would dare to deny it?—royal blood has magic.

The men who were even more in awe of the royal presence than we were the Canadian officers, especially Piggy-Wiggy. He appointed Lingen as our camp leader, and while making his daily inspection rounds, he never seemed to know exactly whether to stand at attention saluting His Royal Highness or whether it should be the other way round. After all, is there anything that gives more class to a commandant than to have a cousin of the King in his camp? One can imagine the talk in the officers mess, or at the Military Club in downtown Quebec City. . . .

How Lingen's true identity became known to the Canadians was the subject of many legends, one of which was that he had revealed his background on a form he had been asked to fill out. I don't remember filling out any forms and therefore consider it unlikely that *he* would have done so. According to another theory, he summoned a guard on arrival and addressed him in a clipped Prussian parade-ground voice, handing him his card: "Take this to your commanding officer!" This also strikes me as unlikely, since it is out of character. It is much more likely that he assumed, as did everyone else, that the whole world instinctively knew he was anointed.

A third and more plausible supposition was that soon after landing in Canada the prince wrote a letter to his godmother, Aunt Alice, a granddaughter of Queen Victoria and first cousin of Lingen's grandfather, Kaiser Wilhelm. She also was the wife of the Earl of Athlone, the Governor General of Canada, who at the time was in summer residence in the Quebec Citadel, a stonethrow from Camp L. This letter would have been duly intercepted by the intelligence officer, Captain Barrass, and its contents conveyed to the rest of the military personnel.

One thing is certain; it was Captain Barrass who established a connection between Lingen and his Aunt Alice—he told me himself. One day the prince came to him "looking incredibly elegant," to ask whether he would mind going around the corner to the citadel to advise his aunt and uncle of his presence in the camp. Barrass, of course, was delighted to do so. Strangely enough, he had not put two and two together and had never given a thought to Lingen's relationship to the Athlones.

He went over to the Citadel, spoke to an aide de camp, and was promptly invited to tea with their Excellencies. "It was quite a surprise to them that Freddie was in Quebec. They seemed to know him very well, and were very pleasant and very kind to me. How very clever these people always are at making commoners feel at ease."

Subsequently, Barrass was invited to dinner at the Citadel and seated next to Acting Major-General H. D. G. Crerar, then Vice-Chief of the Canadian General Staff.

As for Lingen, I am told, he soon wrote to his aunt and uncle asking that some badly needed sports equipment be sent to the camp. They did so and henceforth we were able to play soccer with a royal football. (They also may have sent cricket equipment, but certainly not a baseball.) It seems that later that summer a meeting was arranged between Lingen and the Athlones, but Barrass told me he had nothing to do with that as he had left Quebec for Ottawa by then.

Inside the camp a kind of court had gathered around Lingen, without any effort on his part to recruit his courtiers. In some strange way those who felt it right and just to be part of the royal entourage flocked towards him. Victor Ross was a member of the entourage. His role, he told me, was that of a court jester.

> There was an Austrian baron and a man called Löwenstein; they took this Kaiser business very seriously. I had a ready Jewish wit, a commodity that was quite scarce in that circle. Löwenstein had a special face which he put on in the presence of the almighty. He believed it to be a set and serious mien. . . . We concocted a story that I was in correspondence with the Queen. Lingen knew very well that it was a joke—but we played it on our baron. A tremendous game was going on, that I was in fact connected with the Royal Family. This the baron liked much better than the thought that I was really a Jew from Vienna. . . . We had tremendous fun with him. We tried to get him to call me by some aristocratic name. . . .
>
> Lingen quite liked me, well enough to invite me to his home after the war . . . but there was no real intimacy; I was a good bridge player. He did not play very well. I "bestowed" the favor of my superior play. I normally played for high

stakes with good players; with them I played for low stakes. That was my contribution to their circle, my condescension toward them as they were condescending towards me.

The other celebrity in Camp L was Hans Kahle, the former commander of the Eleventh International Brigade during the Spanish Civil War, immortalized by his friend Ernest Hemingway as "General Hans" in *For Whom the Bell Tolls*.

He was a commanding figure, tall, impressive-looking—a man of action, not at all an idéologue; a man who was admired by almost everybody. He was straightforward and uncomplicated, and above all, in contrast to almost everybody else, actually had risked his life fighting the fascists. Nobody expected him to justify the Nazi-Soviet pact which was still in force in the summer of 1940. Had he done so, he would undoubtedly have echoed the Moscow party line.

The son of a Prussian officer, Kahle was born in Berlin in 1899, where he attended the *Kadettenanstalt*, the equivalent of Sandhurst or West Point. When war broke out in 1914 he was only fifteen, but by 1918 he was an officer in the German Army. Immediately after the war he drifted toward communism and in 1922 became the military leader of a workers' revolt in a north German port city. As a result he was wanted by the police and had to flee to Mexico, where he called himself a journalist. In 1927–8 an amnesty was declared in Germany and he returned. Between that time and 1933, the year the Nazis came to power and he fled to Paris, he was ostensibly active as a communist journalist.

His experience on the ship to Barcelona was characteristic. He became increasingly annoyed listening to bitter ideological in-fighting among the left-wingers on board. As none of them had any military training, he assembled all those who could speak German—Swiss, Austrians, Germans, Dutch and Danes—and marched them up and down the deck. That, he thought, was a more useful exercise than arguing about the finer points of communist theory. When they got off the boat, the German group was the only one which marched like soldiers; all the others seemed like rabble. Consequently he was made a battalion commander, although he said he had never commanded more than a platoon in his life. He worked his way up from a battalion commander to being the commander of the entire Eleventh International Brigade. He was a superb strategist and enjoyed a formidable reputation as "the defender of Madrid." In camp he gave lectures on the strategy of the Spanish Civil War, and more than one internee, including myself, had the singular privilege of having strategic subtleties explained to him while sitting next to him on the toilet, where he invariably drew explanatory diagrams with a pointer on the cement floor.

Kahle and Hemingway had been genuine friends in Spain. In fact, Hemingway had even considered writing a book about him and then changed his mind, reflecting that, "We have too much together for me ever to risk losing it by trying to write about it." A personally inscribed copy of *For Whom the Bell Tolls* arrived in camp while Kahle was there, and Hemingway's biographer, Carlos Baker, recorded how much it had meant to the great writer to have heard that Kahle had considered it a "true and great book."[20] It seems Hemingway also was helpful in obtaining Kahle's release early in 1941.

In his farewell message to us, Hans Kahle wrote the following in our camp paper:

> Camp L became our new home. . . . Racial and political refugees of different creeds stood together in order to change our most unfortunate prisoner of war status, a change that is the main key to the narrow door which leads to liberty and work. We had to draw the line which separates us from those who pay allegiance to Nazi Germany. The organization of our camp with its manifold activities had to be built up. . . .
>
> This job was well done. . . . There was friction, and often we had too loud and violent discussions. But they only took place in order to solve all important problems of the camp in a spirit which was satisfactory to the vast majority. . . .
>
> We know each other now. We have lived and suffered, laughed and worked together. We have built up a sound and efficient community. This moral asset should by no means be destroyed! Goodbye, Camp L.

To what extent Kahle and Klaus Fuchs were friends is hard to determine. There is some evidence that Fuchs already was a communist agent by the time he was interned. According to one theory, it was Kahle who during the summer and fall of 1940 inducted him into the Soviet intelligence system. A few of us are certain that Fuchs was a member of Kahle's "cell" in the camp.

Unlike Kahle, Fuchs was a quiet and introverted figure. However, he was quite capable of engaging in a plot, such as the one hatched just before the camp broke up in mid-October. One person—we shall call him L.—was to hide in the rafters of the hut while the camp was being dissolved, and then to make his way to the United States where, as their emissary, he was to tell the world the truth of what was happening in Canadian camps to anti-Nazi refugees. This was not a communist plot, but a plot nevertheless. It went wrong. For once the sergeant-major was paying attention during roll call. One man was missing; there was a recount, and everybody was sent back to the huts. Two or three more recounts followed and finally L. was discovered. Some of us knew that Fuchs was a communist, but the question whether or not a man was a communist was not uppermost in our minds at the time.

About four years after the war, Walter Wallich met Asik Radomysler in a London street. Both had been at Camp L and had returned to England together with Fuchs in December 1940. They hadn't seen each other since then, and over a cup of coffee immediately began to reminisce about old times. "You know about Klaus Fuchs, don't you?" Radomysler said. "He's at Harwell!" (Harwell was Britain's main atomic research center, where Fuchs was head of theoretical physics.) "You know what that means?" Radomysler continued. "With his background . . . oughtn't somebody do something about this?" Wallich shook his head. "That's something for M.I.5 to worry about, they know he's a commie. Everybody knows he's a commie," he said. Six months later the world found out that Fuchs had been handing over vital secrets to the Soviets.

The artist René Graetz, an Alsatian who spoke German with a heavy French accent, was another left-winger we had in camp. At the time, he was passing through his "centaur period," painting them by the dozen. His artistic endeavors elicited from Kahle, who prided himself on being a philistine, the following question: "Why do these horses wear underpants?" I remember other colorful camp characters, not necessarily communist, such as a fully-fledged juggler.

More significant were the Nazis. According to somewhat unreliable official records, there were ninety of them in Camp L. Obviously, we knew much better than any British or Canadian intelligence officer who had Nazi sympathies and who did not. In the summer of 1940 they hardly concealed their feelings, although some put on a thin monarchical camouflage or joined nationalistic Christian groups.

Unlike the other two camps which housed internees in the B and C Categories, the number of Jews in Camp L was relatively small—approximately 60 percent. The rather large number of Nazis, on the other hand, and the presence of dedicated communists such as Kahle, made for lively political disputations, not so much *with* the Nazis, as *about* their right to participate in democratically run institutions. This is the theme that runs through a diary written by Peter Heller, then a nineteen-year-old pianist from Vienna with well developed literary and philosophical tastes.

> *July 28:* Conversation with our people about the Nazis who are trying to throw their weight around in the camp university.
>
> *Weiss (blinks, nervous behind his glasses, always missing the point):* Our general line towards the Nazis has already been settled by the senior committee, and that is my view as well. The Popular University should not take things into its own hands. Arndt and Lingen suggest that the Popular University has gone too far by locking out the Nazis. As long as the Nazis don't talk politics. . . . *(Weiss blinks in annoyance)* Each group should be represented proportionally.
>
> *Cohn (sharply but quietly):* Sure. The Jews still want to play at democracy. There is no place in the world where democracy exists in such a pure form as in Camp L. My dear Weiss, how can there be any talk of sharing a community with the Nazis? To be separated from them is not only our personal desire, it's a matter of the gravest importance. Community? We are no community, my dear Weiss, we are a pile of manure. We are "bloody prisoners"—a bunch of people who have been thrown together because no one has any use for them. If we (I mean the 85 percent refugees here) have any goal at all, it is *not* to be confused with the Nazis. And if that should lead to trouble in the Popular University, then perhaps the commandant will be forced to realize officially that there is a difference between us and the real "enemy aliens." If there's a row, all the better. The authorities will finally have to see the light.

August 11: Relay race between the eight huts. In the afternoon distribution of prizes by His Imperial Highness Lingen (cigarettes, diplomas). Commandant gives a little speech. He is pleased that we go in for all kinds of sports and stay fit, so that we'll be in good health when we are released into the world and "make lots of money." I didn't participate. I lay on my bed and read Nietzsche. The others were all very inspired.

At half past nine there was a hut debate: "Cabaret" as our jokers call it. Subject: *Separation from the Nazis*. The Nazis are now all moving into Hut 14. "Is it necessary to allot them ten tickets to our variety evening? And do we really have to accept the representative of the Nazi hut in the senior meetings?" The commandant insists upon it. If this is the decision that is finally reached, we will ban everything important from the hut-leaders' meeting and discuss only technical matters in the presence of the Nazis. The majority is for complete exclusion of the Nazis from our camp life. But the democrats say, "That is not democratic." Brauer and Memelmann, who are still hoping to return to the Weimar Republic and are so absurdly idealistic that one goes mad, speak in defence of Hut 14 and talk of innocent people and neutrals. I suggest a definitive separation. What weak, contradiction-loving hair-splitting Jews we are!

An innocent man actually walked into Hut 14 by mistake. Yesterday he was back in his own hut as a recognized "refugee from Nazi oppression."

Loesch in Hut 14 is a lamp-post of a man. He has a long face and wears thick glasses in front of his bulging eyes. He also has a long, sad nose, an unsteady walk and dangling arms. He is supposed to be an energetic organizer, though— and has allegedly organized the Nazi Party in England. He's now writing a five-volume work on *Tramps in the Salvation Army*. "But you can't get hold of any material here," they say to him. "Adolf Hitler," Loesch replies, "wrote the greatest book of the century without any material."

A fat, white-haired *boche* taps me on the shoulder at a variety evening. "Tell me, young man, why do they play only the English anthem; why not also 'Deutschland, Deutschland über Alles,' or the 'Horst-Wessel Lied'? We are Germans here, after all . . ." He is old.

August 9: After many hours of splashing rain there was a

cool, quiet dusk. Sunlight broke through a hidden crack in the heavy, red cloud banks—but neither the rays nor the sun were visible. The astonishing effect was that in the middle of the grey, muffled landscape only the village on the other shore of the St. Lawrence could be seen shining in a dramatic, supernatural glow. The rays must have been reflected on the wet roofs, and particularly the church and its immediate surroundings were fairly flashing in a blinding, white glare, which was intensified by contrast to the damp, rich, dusky green of the hilly background. Within a few minutes the glow had vanished.

Loewenberg said at once, "Two thousand years or so ago, you would have immediately believed in some damn thing or another—in a good omen or something."

Mr. Penkuhn, the extraordinarily stupid engineer, who has a very thick notebook full of inventions (including a new system of writing music without sharps or flats—but don't tell anyone because it's not patented yet) knew better; he attributed the phenomenon to hidden floodlights. "An extremely effective floodlight illumination, for festivities and so forth. We had it in Berlin, too."

In the meantime there were things happening in the sky. Icy grey masses passed quickly by, herds of heavy, racing tanks—but the grey blanket above was torn open, and one's gaze leapt down from the moist, red cloud banks steering into the golden, absorbing endlessness.

August 19: A special hut meeting: the commandant has especially requested that the scattered woodpiles be carefully stacked—without pay. An important visitor is expected; who it is, we don't know. Taebrich, the hut leader, says the request ought to be granted, as an exception. A bitter, idiotic, half-hour-long discussion about wood-piling follows.

The Radicals: "Protest! A matter of principle!"

Righteous mass stupidity. Any illusions I might have about direct, simple democracy evaporate. Everything unimportant is discussed to death and the important things are forgotten. How about a strictly constitutional aristocracy? But just take a look at our "aristocrats"; the arrogant Cambridge clique! [All work connected with the running of the camp was unpaid. All additional work was paid at the rate of twenty cents a day. What was considered "additional work" was the subject of much discussion.]

September 26: Another disgrace for England: Dakar! Defeatism. The pro-British are confident and assured. They want to be sent back. Among them are people who have lived a long time in England and had good experiences there; Cambridge students who made up their minds with aggressive certainty to be English and nothing but English. Others have young wives or families or money over there.

Then there are the more extreme socialists and communists, who have set their hopes on Russia; also the outspoken skeptics who feel they are free spirits; and the cynics, also outspoken, who are proud of their amorality and definite in their egoism. They think exclusively of themselves, but aren't any the happier for it (many of them are genuine penniless emigrants who have been chased from one country to another, from one camp to another.)

In the discussions about the war, pessimism dictates the tone. It is the prevailing trend. One merely appears ridiculous to the majority when one uses big words (freedom, democracy, equality, etc.). The sad chewing-over of the bad news doesn't help. So I go back home to my Nietzsche.

What happens at roll call? Everyone talks and wrestles and laughs, and it takes a quarter of an hour for the people to line up. "Well, what do you expect from a bunch of civilians?"

New regulation: the beds must be made before roll call, and they are not to be touched until two o'clock in the afternoon.

"Where are we supposed to sit, then?"

"The commandant assumes that you have better things to do until two o'clock than sit on your beds."

"I don't, sir. I don't."

"You! You old bookworm! Don't keep interrupting! No clothes are to lie or hang around. Everything in suitcases."

"What suitcases?"

"There is a possibility that all clothes will be confiscated until the end of the internment."

Let's not get excited. They'll change their minds. After all, we can't stand up all day, and since the beds are the only place to sit . . .

There are apparently several pairs of lovers. M. tells of two people who held each other tight in the first critical night. And how one stroked the other's chin with his dirty hands.

"In a year we'll all be ready for it."

"I tell you, people have already started taking a closer look at muscular thighs. But hardly anyone admits it."

End of September: The camp was of the opinion that we were sure to be spending the winter here. The commandant said . . . and so on. A few well-informed people knew better—and now we're being moved. That annoys not only the conservative spirits, like my friend Cohn; the whole camp is unpleasantly agitated.

Northern Delights

The second group of *Ettrick* passengers was sent to Camp Q near Monteith in northern Ontario. They had to wait to be robbed until they arrived at their destination. The medical examination was held out in the open while the local residents watched from some distance away—the ladies among them using binoculars to get a better view.

The twenty-three-hour-long train ride was exciting and romantic, though none of the internees knew where they were going; that was a military secret. Some of the windows were barred, but our boys had got hold of some screwdrivers to open them and catch a glimpse of the northern vastness unfolding before them. As a precaution, the place-names on the few railway stations they passed had been carefully covered. To find out where they were these "dangerous men" used home-made compasses and made complicated calculations based on the distances between telegraph poles. All this was great fun. Naturally, once they arrived at their destination, they saw a truck with *Monteith, Ontario* painted on it. So much for military secrecy.

The physical set-up of Camp Q could not compare with Camp L, partly because it was a converted prison farm, cut out of the wilderness, which though close to the small community of Monteith, engendered a feeling of complete isolation, and also because the commandant, Colonel A. M. Campbell—unlike Piggy-Wiggy—never understood our situation. When he said goodbye to our camp leaders after our three months' sojourn, he told them that he considered them traitors to their own country and that he would rather have had Nazis who were "at least clear-cut enemies" than refugees who were "neither fish nor fowl, nor good red herring," according to Ernest Borneman. Most Canadian officers, even those who had some understanding for our position, expressed similar preferences at various times. Very few, however, shared Colonel Campbell's opinion that we were "traitors to our country."

The first night in Camp Q was grim; it was pouring with rain. The farm building was not big enough to accommodate everybody, so tents had to be put up for the younger men. As Harold Frye recalls, "I walked towards the camp with a friend, and an officer stopped us. 'Do you speak English?' he asked. 'Yes,' I answered. 'Then come with me,' the officer said. 'You're the camp leader, and bring your friend with you. He's going to be your assistant.'"

Frye does not know why he was chosen as many others also could speak English. He and his friend entered the commandant's office. "You're all soldiers," Campbell said. "You'll know how to behave." "Oh no," said Frye, "we're not soldiers." He tried to explain, but it was to no avail. In fact, the tone of the relationship was firmly set on the first night when one of the officers, before turning out the lights, curtly announced, "If you want trouble you can have it—and plenty of it. I won't wish you a good night, because I don't."

Later the camp elected its own leader and assistant leader; Frye and his friend shared a room with them in the prison building. "My position was difficult," Frye recalls, "because I was the commandant's liaison man and therefore suspect in the eyes of many of my fellowmen."

There were many crises in the camp. On one occasion Campbell ordered the internees to clean the soldiers' latrine. This was not considered work pertaining to the running of the camp; it was *ultra vires*. Our lawyers decided it was a breach of the Geneva Convention, carefully briefed their leader with precise legal arguments, and instructed him to make representations to the colonel. "I am the Geneva Convention," Campbell was quoted as replying. "If I tell you to work, you work." This impasse could only be resolved by the camp leaders doing the work themselves, with the positive result that Campbell never repeated the order.

Other crises were caused by drunken guards who amused themselves by taking potshots at the tents. Luckily, they were never drunk enough to hit anybody.

The internees worked on the prison farm. One day the colonel decided to reduce the rations by the amount of vegetables grown on the farm, the equivalent of one hundred pounds of meat and seventy pounds of potatoes. (It remains a mystery how these amounts were calculated.) There were violent protests, and finally Campbell was forced to yield. But it proved more difficult to dispute his right to impose twelve days' detention and half rations on those who refused to answer a question with a straight yes or no. That was not in our nature.

After the rain-soaked beginning, most of us had a good time in Camp Q. The rigidity of Campbell's regime helped form an *esprit de corps*, and soon we forgot about extraneous disturbances and concentrated on important matters, such as establishing a camp school and lectures. New friendships were formed and discussions were lively. Life in the open air, the *aurora borealis* which none of us had ever seen before, and the northern wilderness had a great impact on us; it was a new thrill to hear the nocturnal howling of the trans-Canada trains on their way to or from strange-sounding towns like Timiskaming.

For the younger crowd tent life was a new experience. In William Heckscher's tent there was a priest who, he told me, "was devastated because there were no women; another man entertained us with marvellous tales that enabled us to escape our situation 'through the magic of words.'" In other tents there was a circus group which had been in a German concentration camp. On the third Sunday afternoon, when everyone was depressed, Willi Amtmann sat on his top bunk and played the fiddle for a couple of hours, which gave us much pleasure.

It was in Camp Q that Fred Wolff discovered a talent for cutting hair. At first he did it for fun, receiving cigarettes or whatever else was legal tender in exchange. Later, in Sherbrooke, he became the official camp barber—getting paid twenty cents a day. Many remember him trimming their locks. H. A. Baer became the canteen bookkeeper. He was amazed that he got paid for his services, especially when his outstanding accounts were transferred to the next camp he went to.

By far the greatest event was the emergence of the smash hit "You'll Get Used To It." Freddy Grant had written the song just before leaving Huyton, and it was first sung at a camp show put together by the composer. There were no instruments other than an old upright piano and some violins, but there was a lot of talent in the camp.

You'll Get Used To It

You'll get used to it.
You'll get used to it.
The first year is the worst year
Then you get used to it.
You can scream and you can shout;
They will never let you out.

It serves you right, you so-and-so;
Why aren't you a naturalized Eskimo?

Refrain: Just tell yourself it's marvellous
You get to like it more and more and more.
You've got to get used to it!
And when you're used to it,
You'll feel just as lousy as you did before.

You'll get used to it!
You'll get used to it!
The first year is the worst year,
Then you get used to it.
You will never see your wife
For they've got you in for life.
It makes no difference who you are,
A soda jerk or movie star.

Freddy Grant recalls that "by October 15 when the camp broke up, everyone was singing it, including the guards, and it remained our camp song throughout internment."

After Grant's release he was invited to a dinner party in Montreal. He played "You'll Get Used To It" on the piano. His hostess suggested he see a friend of hers, "a fellow who's a comedian who could probably use that song. He's got a little show called 'Tin Hat Show.'" The "fellow" was John Pratt who loved the song and decided to include it in his show, after making a few changes in the lyrics. Six months later Pratt auditioned for an American show. "I'll hire you if you sing that song," the producer said. Pratt agreed. "You'll Get Used To It" became an enormous hit. Later it was included in the British film *This Is The Navy*.

The Sports Stadium

The refugees who arrived on the *Sobieski* were split into two groups; one went to Trois Rivières, and the other to Fort Lennox on the Ile aux Noix, an island in the Richelieu River near Montreal.

It was about seven o'clock on a hot summer's night when the Camp T group arrived at Trois Rivières railway station. The town's population had turned out in large numbers to watch the "enemy paratroopers" being marched to the Exhibition Grounds. Heading the procession were talmudic college students—the Yeshiva boys—who instead of a flag bore before them a Torah scroll, the five books of Moses. They were followed by about twenty Catholic lay brothers in ordinary clothing who were outwardly not distinguishable from the other refugees.

The burghers of Trois Rivières were puzzled. These people did not look like ferocious prisoners. But the internees were equally perplexed. Why were all the street signs in French? Why were the sounds they heard floating towards them French sounds?

Spurred by the sergeant's repeated exhortations to hurry up, the procession reached the Exhibition Grounds. Although work was still underway to turn the sports arena adjacent to the baseball diamond into an internment camp, the machine guns were already in place at the gate. Our people swallowed hard and entered the building. It quickly became apparent that the arena was occupied by the Category A Germans who had arrived two weeks earlier on the *Duchess of York*. When they saw the Torah scroll at the head of the procession being carried by a rabbinical student, one of them shouted, "*Das sind ja Juden!*" To translate these words with, "Look, these guys are Jews!" would be missing the blood-curdling ring of the phrase out of the mouths of Nazis; this was followed by the singing of the rousing chorus of the most despicable of all their songs, "*Wenn's Judenblut vom Messer spritzt, dann geht's nochmal so gut!*" (When Jewish blood drips from our knives, things go twice as well).

The new arrivals stopped. Rooted to the spot they refused

to proceed any farther. After a hasty conference it was decided to choose spokesmen who would ask to see the commandant. Colonel C. O. Dorval and his adjutant Major J. A. Marchildon agreed to receive the delegation. Dr. Richard Hübsch was one of them. He explained that there would be violent clashes unless the Germans and the Jews were separated. He pointed out that many in his group had suffered mental anguish and physical abuse as a result of Nazi persecutions. "It is unthinkable, gentlemen, that we can live together, even for a single day," he said. While Dr. Hübsch made his plea, Colonel Dorval was gazing out of the window, to avoid all eye contact with him. Only a few minutes later, he abruptly dismissed the delegation.

Although shattered by the seemingly cold reception the two men had been given, they felt they had made their point, for soon barbed wire was strung down the middle of the camp. The arena became the refugees' reserve; the kitchen, however, remained "in enemy hands," and the enemy was said to withhold half the rations. Besides, some of the people were reluctant to eat whatever food the Nazis prepared, fearful that it might be poisoned. The 123-strong "kosher group" consumed very little at first, but when their dietary demands finally were met, it was done in the same spirit as the wording contained in this report:

> The question of kosher meat is being dealt with by feeding the Orthodox Jews fish, or letting them go without. This type of Jew seems (sic) to be people of very unclean habits, and are difficult to discipline and deal with. They have no idea of cleanliness within their kitchens and quarters, and the Commandant is experiencing difficulty in dealing with them. While the condition of the kitchens was far from satisfactory, the Quartermaster was using forceful methods and was quickly obtaining results.

In this connection it should be pointed out that the arena had not been cleaned before the internees moved in. The floors were filthy and everything was covered with dust.

The first night was the roughest, partly because of the heat. I shall not dwell on the sanitary conditions, except to report that within half an hour of arrival all the toilets were blocked. Ditches had to be dug in the sand-filled corral which had been used for livestock shows not long ago. The internees slept in the bleachers above. One former inmate told me that what struck him most was that some of the older "intellectuals" were among those least able to cope with the appalling conditions. "They went hysterical," he said.

Gradually everyone settled down. Roll calls for the two groups were conducted separately. As tempers cooled, there even was some contact between the two groups. Some time early in August one Category A internee decided to secede and join our group. This was duly permitted and was followed by an announcement suggesting that as a *quid pro quo* any refugee who wished to join the A contingent was free to do so. One sixty-eight-year-old man by the name of Meyerhofer accepted the offer. "I am a German," he stated. "I rather belong to these people than to the Jews." He said he was tired of all the quarrelling about food.

Trois Rivières gave us our first taste of baseball. Night games were being played two or three times a week in the stadium next door, but the windows in the arena were so high up that four or five tables had to be stacked one on top of the other in order to get a glimpse of the action. Watching the games from this precarious vantage point was an enriching experience, especially because it required daring and courage to ascend and maintain one's balance on the teetering structure.

Soccer, on the other hand, we played ourselves, and one of the rabbis turned out to be an excellent goalie. The camp also marked the emergence of Abraham Poljak, the author of *The Cross Is The Star of David*, a novel devoted to the missionary cause of converting the Jews to Christianity. It is unlikely that he made any converts in Camp T, but he was a great success as a violinist, though his repertoire was limited to the works of Sarasate.

Trois Rivières lasted less than one month. When it broke up, its inmates boarded a train which took them on a twenty-four-hour-long journey—via the Gaspé Peninsula—to Camp B in the New Brunswick forest. There, most of them remained for more than a year.

The Fortress

On Monday July 1 Major E. D. P. Kippen visited Fort Lennox on the Ile aux Noix to assess the feasibility of converting the fortress into an internment camp for dangerous men. The passengers from the *Sobieski* were to arrive there on July 15.

Major Kippen, an investment dealer from Montreal, was more sophisticated than most of his colleagues. He knew something about prisoners, having been one himself in Germany during the First World War. The antiquity of Fort Lennox did not faze him, although it had not been inhabited since 1880.

Before the conquest by the English in 1759, the Richelieu River was the chief highway to the cities of Montreal and Quebec. Situated twelve miles below the outlet of Lake Champlain and ten miles from the United States border, it was the perfect spot for a fort. In 1760, the English forced the French to surrender it, only to yield it to the Americans who had invaded Quebec during the War of Independence. Before the War of 1812 a new fortress was built. It is hard to imagine that 138 years later it would house orthodox Jews and an assortment of refugees.

Major Kippen decided it would make an excellent internment camp. With the lightning speed that never ceased to amaze us Europeans, he had water and light installed within two weeks, kitchen utensils imported and watch towers erected, three lines of barbed wire strung, with cat-walks for sentries in between. A sophisticated electric alarm system was devised with—to quote the official document—"emergency pistol grip flashlights." Unfortunately one detail was overlooked—a sufficient number of beds.

On July 15 it was pouring with rain. The prisoners in barge loads of thirty-five were brought across the Richelieu River from St. Paul, accompanied by a fleet of motorboats with heavily armed troops on board. By midnight seventy-six of them were still waiting on the dock in St. Paul. The next day their luggage arrived, and many of the soaked-through cardboard suitcases and boxes had disintegrated.

"The desperation was global," Martin Fischer told me. He had been singled out as the camp leader, not only because he spoke English, but because, as apparently the authorities quickly discovered, he had already performed special duties in the Kitchener Camp in England. On that first night, he told me, people were crying; they were breaking down. It took two or three weeks before enough beds and mattresses had been brought into the fortress and sleeping arrangements had been sorted out.

The man in charge of Camp I was Sergeant-Major J. Breslin, whose voice could shake the very foundations of Fort Lennox. The question soon arose among the internees whether one should walk slowly or run toward the sergeant-major when he yelled from a distance, "Hey-you!" These and other matters were speedily resolved by the camp's diplomatic service. One particularly ticklish issue was that of the horse that pulled the cart carrying the daily rations. The horse had fallen ill. Soon the order came through that, since three internees were the equivalent of one horse, three internees should pull the cart if they and their comrades wished to eat. The official reasoning was challenged. No one I interviewed remembers how the matter was finally resolved.

When I asked Major Kippen what he felt about the requests for kosher food, he replied with a smile, "Oh, that was quite a problem. It wasn't so easily produced, you know, and to persuade the authorities to go along with this was not so simple. 'Can't these people eat ordinary food?' they asked me. 'No, they can't,' I said. 'You see, it's their *religion*.' But in the end they came around!"

Looking back, most of the orthodox alumni of Camp I to whom I have spoken take the view that they were well treated by the authorities. Difficulties usually arose not because of bad will, but because of ignorance, and they remember the various crises with good humor. As to the French-Canadian guards, who were invariably senior citizens, many of them never understood who our people were. Those of us who spoke French to them—usually Berlin or Viennese school French—were, of course, particularly suspect: being educated, the guards decided, they must be Nazi spies. Since they had no fundamental objection to Nazi spies, everybody got along perfectly well.

Arrival in the Forest

Camp B was a former unemployment relief camp, officially called "Little River," situated twenty-two miles from Fredericton and ten from Minto. About two miles from the camp was the chief landmark of the area—a covered bridge across the "Little River."

Today there is no indication where the camp site had been, except that the trees growing there now are not quite as tall as those around them. But on August 5, 1940, a crew was feverishly at work to put the finishing touches on the barbed wire fences to enclose the fifteen-acre compound. Four huts were still under construction; the dining hut and the detention hut were in the frame stage, while the hospital and recreation hut were partly completed. No lights had as yet been installed, and telephone communication with Fredericton consisted of a "bush line" ending in an instrument attached to a tree near the administration building. On August 10 the Director of Internment Operations advised the camp staff that approximately seven hundred prisoners of war would arrive one week later and that, as they were active Nazi servicemen and members of the German Merchant Marine, they were to be considered dangerous. The *Commandant's Journal*, an obligatory logbook, noted that "in view of the almost fragmentary state of the wire and the lack of safeguards in the compound generally, this information was received without enthusiasm by the camp staff, particularly as it had been understood that at least two weeks would elapse before the prisoners were to be taken over." On August 11 the R.C.M.P. was asked to close off traffic on the morning of August 13 at Devon and on the Minto Road, above the railway crossing, at Allbright's Corner. Motorcyclists were posted to keep a liaison between the moving column of prisoners and the camp.

At 8:20 a.m. the group of orthodox internees from Trois Rivières arrived, together with a large contingent of non-observant Jews and miscellaneous gentiles. Camp commandant Colonel A. T. McLean, from Moncton, New Brunswick, met the train. When he saw them descend he shielded his eyes and exclaimed, "Oh, what children have they sent me!" His logbook entry reads as follows:

> Immediately upon their arrival in the Internment Camp it was found that instead of being "Class A" prisoners, these men were entirely "Class B and C" (Civilian Internees) and practically all of them were inimical to the Nazi cause. This situation eased the danger of escapes and rendered unnecessary some of the stringent precautions previously arranged for.

Some of the officers watching the arrival were not as philosophical as Colonel McLean. They openly showed their anger and disappointment that they had not been sent adult Nazis. Out of a 715-man contingent, 280 were between sixteen and eighteen years old.

Here are some first impressions of Camp B as recorded by Kaspar Naegele in his diary:

> There was no station. There was just wood and a stony road crossing the rails. Some picturesque cowboy-like . . . Mounties waited for us with beautiful new cars. The train guards lined up on either side while we stared into the woods. The deserted road . . . the complete isolation of the place! . . .
>
> The procession moved slowly, sweating in the midday sun. We were full of expectations: Barbed wire? A camp? Work? Did they know we were not prisoners of war? A bridge came. We crossed it. The march in between the woods seemed never to end. Then suddenly a bend in the road. Barbed wire!! Guard towers! Grey huts! Boards and beams everywhere, pipe-ditches, workmen rushing around. No doors. Wood all over the place. A workmen-and-soldiers camp opposite. We went in. Guards on the towers with rifles on their shoulders, ready to shoot. They did not know who we are! All that struggle over again! We lined up, having jumped over boards and ditches—outside a long hut. Wires hanging down: no bulbs. Luggage was taken and we were searched. But the Commandant himself brought some water for us. . . . Our group was finished. Ditches, puddles, dirt, rubbish. We climbed up a ladder into one of the huts. There were no blankets. There was no water. Outside there were latrines. . . . In the camp not a bit of green. . . . There was one tap for the whole camp. . . . The latrines for most of the people were terrible. For me they were amusing. The water business was pretty awful. Most of the people despaired . . . L. collapsed completely. The others were bad-tempered.
>
> I saw a lot of opportunity for work in the primeval forest camp. Two months ago the camp had been woods. Not one tree was left inside the camp. The adjutant demanded discipline: "We do not want to do any unnecessary shooting!"

Hot and tired from the twenty-four-hour train ride, the

internees immediately took off their clothes to have a meagre but highly beneficial shower under the one and only water tap.

The pursuit of politics was livelier at Camp B than on the Ile aux Noix, partly because its inmates primarily consisted of a more articulate group of non-observant Jews who had never encountered orthodoxy and had little understanding of it. To these assimilated Jews orthodoxy smacked of ghetto-life; they wanted no part of it, as it had taken more than a century to shake off its memories. These divisions within the Jewish community existed both inside and outside the barbed wire fence. Among the orthodox were various factions ranging from ultra-orthodox Hasidim—mainly from Vienna—to the Frankfurt groups. They each had their own concepts as to which rules should take precedence. Not everyone, for example, insisted on *Eruv*, the symbolic wire or ribbon which encloses a community on the Sabbath. Yet, a wire was strung across the main gate of the camp. To the non-observant this symbolic action appeared ludicrous; after all, were they not already locked up in an enclosed space? Their argument failed to win support among the orthodox. The non-religious simply were unable to grasp that all rituals are symbolic and lose their significance once they are rationalized.

As to members of the Jewish orthodox community on the outside, once they became aware of the presence of their brethren in Canadian camps, they assiduously supported them, supplying religious articles and books. They were more zealous than their counterparts in Great Britain. This may be due to their greater political strength within the Canadian-Jewish community.

If the non-observant Jews had trouble relating to the orthodox, the military personnel were even more bewildered. One day a rabbinical student was called to the commandant's office.

"You are intending to flee," said Major Racey, who had succeeded Colonel McLean. "We may have to punish you. You may have to be sent to another camp."

The student stared at the major. "I?" he stuttered. "Impossible."

"We have proof," the commandant announced sternly. "Don't deny anything." He pointed to a letter lying on his desk, addressed to someone in Brooklyn, New York. He picked it up and started to read, "'Dear friend, do not wait any longer. Send me a chauffeur.' You see? You asked for a chauffeur. Isn't that proof enough?"

The prisoner smiled broadly. "But Major," he said, "you read it wrong. We have the High Holidays in a few weeks and I asked for a *shofar*." (A *shofar* is a wind instrument made of a ram's horn, used in the synagogue on the High Holidays.)

It took the intervention of the orthodox camp leaders *and* the highest rabbinical authorities in Montreal to convince Major Racey that the student had no intention of escaping in a chauffeur-driven limousine.

On the other hand, the internal organization of Camp B was carried on with Prussian efficiency. Every internee was on unpaid duty for three hours a week. There were liberal mess-orderlies and kosher mess-orderlies; liberal pot cleaners and kosher pot cleaners; liberal scullery duties and orthodox scullery duties. "Killing flies," according to available records, was "non-denominational." A group of rabbinical students had to spend three hours every week on *Klaubdienst* (screening vegetables to make sure they were kosher). Julius Pfeifer reports: "One day, when I accidentally entered the kitchen, I found out the truth: the boys were sitting around, each with a little hill of beans in front of them on the table, and on their knees, hidden under the table, a Gemora (a section of the Talmud). Those swindlers!"

On arrival, everyone had been given the prisoner of war uniform. One orthodox young man objected to wearing it on the Sabbath. "How can you chant 'Livshi Bigdey Sifarech Ami' with *kavonah* (devotion) while dressed as a prisoner?" he argued. The next Sabbath morning he appeared in his crumpled civilian suit at roll call. The sergeant-major ordered him back to the hut. "Change your clothes or go to jail!" he screamed. The boy decided to go to jail, well-equipped with talmudic literature. His friends brought him lunch and supper, though deep down they showed little sympathy for his predicament. He finally relented on his principles and was released.

Yet, the orthodox group's insistence on ritual observances served one useful political purpose; it helped identify us in the official minds as refugees. In fact, it may well have been that the group from time to time played up its orthodoxy with just that purpose in mind.

The Rabbi With the Axe
A short story by Carl Weiselberger[21]

In the hut of the orthodox Jews, the rabbi was sitting reading the Talmud. His thin head with the black hat went up and down above the big book. The rabbi was still young, twenty-five at the most, but he looked like a man in his forties with his pale face, small reddish beard, and his eyes reddened not by infection, but by excessive reading and studying. He had the emaciated face of an ascetic—which wasn't surprising! Since his internment he hadn't eaten a single bit of meat, not even when it had supposedly been kosher; he didn't trust the butcher in the small Canadian town—how could one be sure? He also refused to partake of butter, cheese and milk—could one be sure? He was actually pleased that there was so much to abstain from—the more, the better, one might say. It was a way of doing penance . . .

On this occasion he was puzzling over the question of whether Jews should do base labor. His head, especially the small reddish beard, swayed back and forth over the big book. It says in the Proverbs that he who cultivates the earth shall have food in plenty. But the Talmud adds, "If you become a slave to the earth, you shall have food in plenty. If you *do not* become a slave to the earth, you shall not have food in plenty." The head with its beard swayed, turned, searched for an explanation: what ought one to do? What does that mean, that one should become slave?

At this moment four soldiers armed with rifles and mounted bayonets burst into the hut and roared hoarsely, "Get out! Immediately! All men out of here immediately! Get to the gate! Get to work!"

"Get to work!" There it was: forced labor. Until now the orthodox, the rabbis and the Hasidim, had been spared. The others, who were less pious, the "liberal" Jews of the camp and the interned Christians, had already assembled at the gate, been counted like a herd of sheep, picked up axes, hoes, shovels and saws, and had gone out to dig ditches, fell trees, chop wood, and God knows what else—forced labor! Apparently there hadn't been enough volunteers, so they burst into the orthodox hut to come and get them. Take them away from the holy books. With rifles flashing. The small, weak, pale boys with their nodding heads and curls at the temples, and the pale, thin rabbi. They snatched them away from the holy books in the midst of their studies—Almighty God!

There was no resistance. With their rifles threateningly lowered, they were standing there—it's the same all over the world.

The rabbi and his flock were driven to the gate, set up in rows of two—oh, it took so long for them to be ready! Then they had to pick up heavy axes with very sharp, blue blades, axes in the very hands that had just been turning the ancient, holy pages . . .

"Silence! Attention!" shouted the corporal, or whatever he was. The next command was "Quick march! Forward march." Totally military.

One two, one two, they went past the barbed wire of the camp (strange to see it from the outside, for a change!), down the road, into the forest, straight into the Canadian wilderness. Cut down trees! Jews cut down trees! With these axes! They, of all people   one two, one two—the ground was all wet. And terribly uneven. Whoops! Every minute one stumbled over a root or a rock. Up and down. The soldier with the rifle was running ahead so that one could hardly keep up with him, and in the middle the other escorts were driving them on; "Go on, boys, go on!"

The pale rabbi marched at the head. His thin head rose and fell with each step, as a matter of habit. His long legs stalked along over the obstacles, bent clumsily; the right shoulder, connected to the arm carrying the axe, hung down crookedly. It didn't occur to him to carry the axe over his shoulder. The question of whether Jews should do base labor was still haunting him, smouldering in his mind. If you do not become a slave . . . but the train of thought was broken by the steps and stumbles, and the axe destroyed the rest, chopped it to pieces—it was terrible. The day was lost. He would have made it to the thirty-third chapter if they hadn't bothered him! Chopping wood—doesn't Rabbi Nehoroi say, I abandon all professions of this world and teach my son nothing but the Torah? It is man's pleasure in this world and foundation of the world to come. This is not true of any other profession. Chopping wood—the ground was sopping wet. With every step he stumbled into a puddle—once he almost fell, but managed to grab onto a low-hanging branch at the last minute, thank God!

Why does it go on to say, he continued brooding, why does it go on to say the reverse, that he who cultivates the earth shall have food in plenty, and in the Talmud even, "If you do not become slave to the earth, you shall not have food in plenty"? "Halt!" commanded the corporal, or whatever he was. "Here!" So this was the place. A small clearing in the forest. With an extremely vague wave of the arm, he designated the area where they were to chop. "And only birches, no pines; you understand?" he added, and then explained rather more kindly, "The birches burn better in the bad months; when it rains torrents, you won't be able to go out, so as much as possible has to be chopped now." An explanation for the forced labor . . . Two boys were the first to start. A small redhead with curls over his ears, and a thin, pale boy. They began hacking randomly at the trees. One of the escorting soldiers took the axe away from one of them and showed him how to do it properly, sideways and downwards! What a guy. He could knock down a thick tree with just a couple of strokes! Typically Canadian. He grasped the axe with both hands, swung it in the air over his head and slammed it down onto the trunk. Good God, if it hits you on the foot . . .

So that was the way to do it. Timorous and cautious, they attempted to do it the same way. And lo and behold, it worked better than they thought. Even the thin rabbi with the small reddish beard raised his axe and hammered at a birch with all his might. He hadn't even looked for the thinnest; no, on the contrary! I am older and stronger than the small boys, he thought to himself, and working well and bravely is also a *mitzvah* and a service to all of them, to Judaism. The blows he made dashed the rest of what he had been studying to pieces, of course. What will be the prayer tonight, he wondered worriedly.

"The hour of prayer is the centre and the blossoming time of your life," (these words from the *Kusari* occurred to him) "and the other hours are but paths that lead to that hour." Is chopping wood a path? Whoops! He almost cut his foot . . . God preserve me! One must step back a little; now, that's better! He was breathing heavily. He heard himself panting like an animal. His breath was as white and thick as a horse's in the cold autumn air. He never would have thought that a man could pant that way.

But it doesn't matter. It must be; it must be. And they should see that Jews also—wham! wham! the axe hit the trunk, penetrated to the white, to the tree's marrow. What had the tree done to deserve this? "There are fourteen situations which make an animal unfit to be slaughtered," was going through his head; why, he didn't know. But the axe blows destroyed the thought. They were going deeper and deeper into the life of the tree, and the tree was groaning and swaying. The rabbi was glad he could do it, too; after all, I'm only twenty-five, he thought, and for the first time he felt that twenty-five was actually still young. "Watch out! Watch out! My tree's about to fall!" shouted the small red-headed boy; "Move aside! My tree's about to fall!" How proudly he said "*my* tree" and how he looked about for admiration! The small boy with the red tufts over his ears stood there pressing against the trunk with both hands, with all his might, until it slid onto the forest floor, all its branches rustling and cracking. "Well! That one's done!" "Bravo, bravo, Mottel!" shouted the other boys and applauded. The first tree to be felled!

But now it had to be stripped. With the axe. "You have to be especially careful there," the rabbi warned him like an old expert stripper of Canadian birches. Oh, if only *he* were that far! But he needed a while yet. He had sought out a much thicker tree, after all. In the next few minutes a second and a third tree fell and then another and yet another. Rustling and crackling they swept down, the felled trees. You had to jump to the side. They kept on falling, rustling and crackling between the other trunks. God knows, wondered the rabbi, amazed and confused for a moment, have we really cut them down? If God wants, trees will fall even when they haven't been cut down, they will fall here, there and everywhere, they will lean over and fall . . . all by themselves. The whole forest goes down on its knees when He wants, He just breathes on it from above. Maybe a miracle occurs when righteous Jews are in a forest . . . and the trees fall down by themselves.

But that was just the thought of a strange moment. The trees, as he knew by the exhaustion of his hands, were not falling down by themselves, by God.

Yossel, the delicate, pale youth with the big, dark eyes (the most eager to learn of them all), also had an odd idea. While he was leaning the axe against a tree, in order to catch his breath a bit, he had a pious vision. Perhaps the rabbi's thought had leapt over to him like a spark, and had inflamed his imagination. He looked into the green twilight of the forest and a joyful fright came over him: he thought he saw the Messiah suddenly appear out of the deep forest, riding a white horse through the pines with a golden trumpet in his hand, and all the Jews of the world were suddenly free—free all at once! "Hey! Go on, boy; don't daydream! What's been cut down must be carried away at once!" admonished the soldier.

Carry away! The heavy trunks! Mottel and Shloime set about carrying off a stripped trunk. It took a long time for them to agree about who should take the front and who should take the back. Then they were finally ready, there was a slight misunderstanding: Mottel and Shloime went off in different directions, one to the left, the other to the right, so that it looked as though they were going to stretch the tree trunk. "Hey, watch out! You're going to rip the tree apart!" joked the others. Cutting down trees in the woods . . . Actually it was a fine thing, an exciting change . . .

After two hours of work there was a break. "Just sit down," said the soldiers. They sat down. On rotten tree trunks. Something quite new, quite different, thought the rabbi. In the middle of the forest instead of behind barbed wire in the camp. The sun was shining golden-green through the needles of the trees. It was wonderful. A forest is wonderful! felt the rabbi. He had never experienced a forest in this way. So totally deep within it with all one's senses, with one's soul. The forest is wonderful. It yields more than just wood to heat with in the winter. And shelter for animals. It is so good, good in itself. And beautiful. The earth with all the stems and grasses and roots. It all smelled full of strength and life. The dead tree, however, on which he was sitting, was covered with moss. He laid his hand carefully upon it and stroked it. It was as soft as an animal's fur. The moss was made up of extremely fine, soft, little plants. Many, many tiny little plants. All together they were "moss"; how strange—God is capable of so much! Many dead trees were lying there on the forest floor and moss and fungus was growing on them. And the other trees were alive and full of thick, green needles and leaves on which the sun was playing . . . And the air was so strong, so wonderfully different. Usually one didn't notice it at all, but here . . . The same way he felt that his heart was beating heavily from the hard work. From the work and perhaps also a little from amazement and joy over the new experience . . . The forest was endless. Tree after tree. Tree after tree, as far as one could see. Green, dusky depths. Inside there were certainly deer and stags and elks, maybe even bears, Almighty God. A world unto itself of God's. And up above between the treetops there was the sky with its gliding clouds. It was all very big and terrifying.

The small, pale boy with the big, dark eyes (the most eager to learn of them all) was sitting on the trunk next to him under a green fir. He was sitting with his knees drawn up, and he felt them to be strangely empty, since there was no book on them. He was daydreaming. He dreamt he went into the forest, into the endless, green forest and then came out on the other side in the big, free world. Over there was America. Big cities with millions of Jews, with synagogues, schools, books. America . . . Oh, he will get an affidavit for his father as soon as he's there, for his father was in Germany. "Go on, boy!" the soldiers called. The break was over. They picked up their axes, which were leaning against the trees, and began hacking at the trees again. Funny, now it went much better and faster. Surprisingly many tilted over and crashed down. And they were carefully stripped, with short, quick axe blows, so that the branches and little twigs fairly flew off. And then they were carried away to the clearing, almost without any arguments or debates.

At half past eleven the soldier shouted, "Stop! Stop work!" In order to demonstrate their industriousness, some ignored his command and kept on swinging at their trunks, so that they could fell them at the last moment. "Come on!" urged the soldiers, who wanted to get home. "Line up in twos!" They were to be counted. Counting was a mere formality. Okay, okay. No one had run away. Where could he have run to, anyway? Then the command was "Quick march!" and the line of treecutters marched off. Over roots, rotting logs, stones. Over rivulets and ditches. Up and down. But it was now much easier than on the way there. When one of them fell down, they burst out laughing. The young rabbi was now carrying his axe over his shoulder, just like a Canadian lumberjack, and he jumped nimbly over the puddles and holes.

Finally they came out onto the road. "One two, one two," ordered Mottel. And the Hasidim, the Yeshiva boys with their rabbi at their head, marched almost stiffly, like soldiers. Each one had his axe over his shoulder, the shaft held tightly in his right hand. Workmen, proper forest workers . . .

The rabbi was marching at the front. A foreman, a leader. They began to sing songs, Hebrew songs about Palestine, and about work. A car rushed by them. Then there was a hum in the sky. An airplane. Oh, the world was so big, so bright, so free. Clump, clump, clump, they marched on until they came to the barbed wire of their prison camp. At the gate they handed over their axes. And after being counted once again, they marched through the gate to their hut.

It was strangely muggy inside. Muggy and more cramped than usual. But as soon as they were properly home again, they reached for their books, got them out from behind the beds and cushions, and sat down to read and study. The rabbi with the small reddish beard sat bent over the Talmud like a man of forty, rocking his head and his whole body, engrossed in the question that had been interrupted before: "Should a Jew do base labor?" In the Fathers' Proverbs it says, "He who cultivates the earth shall have food in plenty." But the Talmud says, "If you do not become slave to the earth, you shall not have food in plenty." Rabbi Nehoroi, though, says, "I abandon all professions of this world and teach my son nothing but the Torah . . . This is not true of any other profession." The rabbi's thin head bobbed up and down, swayed back and forth. Somewhere in the distance, in a dusky, dark corner of his soul, trees were crashing, rustling and crackling, to the ground.

The Little Third Reich on Lake Superior
On July 26, less than two weeks after our arrival in Canada, M. J. Coldwell, leader of the C.C.F. in the House of Commons in Ottawa, addressed a question to T. A. Crerar, Minister of Mines and Resources, also responsible for immigration. He wanted to know what had been done to separate anti-Nazi Austrian and German civil internees from those who were pro-Nazi. Coldwell had received a letter from the "Council of Austrians in Great Britain," an organization that listed among its patrons such

distinguished personages as the Archbishop of York, the Bishop of Chichester, the Right Honorable A. Duff Cooper and others. They were anxious to know the fate of former Austrians, hoping that "the welfare that has been carried out for them by refugee organizations" in Great Britain could be continued in Canada. The letter "implored" Coldwell to press the Canadian government to discriminate between Nazis and anti-Nazis.

On the next day the Secretary of State P. F. Casgrain advised Coldwell as follows:

> Among the people who came here from England recently there would appear to be some people in the category of which my honorable friend has spoken. These people are in separate camps. I am given to understand that some liaison officer of the British government will be coming soon to Canada and the matter will be submitted to him upon arrival by the department.

Casgrain had not been well briefed. It was true that civilian internees and prisoners of war were in separate camps, but it was not true that Nazis had been separated from anti-Nazis. Camp R in Red Rock, Ontario, on the shores of Lake Superior was a typical example of the authorities' failure to separate people with diametrically opposite ideologies. It accommodated 1,145 Category A internees who had come over on the *Duchess of York*. Of these, 178 were anti-Nazis, including seventy-eight Jews. The rest was made up of communist merchant seamen and political and religious refugees. It was impossible for any opponent of Hitler to live in peace within a compound dominated by a pro-Nazi majority.

Camp R was different from all the other camps. The huts had not been hastily constructed, but had been erected some time ago to house the workers of the Lake Sulphite Pulp Company, a former pulp and paper factory which had closed down and sold the property to the government. The sloping ground was surrounded by red rock on three sides; on the fourth were railway tracks and beyond that Lake Superior. With eight rows of six huts, each accommodating twenty-eight beds, the camp was crowded, but not overcrowded. Excellent food was served by ship's stewards dressed in white. The commandant was Colonel R. B. Berry, a straightforward soldier more concerned with security than with the administration of justice.

The camp leader was Commodore Oskar Scharf, the former captain of the *Europa*. He and Hanfstaengl had become acquainted in June 1934 when "Putzi" had sailed to New York on the *Europa*, just before the Roehm purge.

News that he was aboard had leaked out, and there were demonstrations at the dockside when the *Europa* arrived in New York. Thousands of people were carrying placards reading "Oust Nazi Hanfstaengl!" and "Ship the Hitler agent back!" Much concerned with the safety of his ship, Scharf had handed Hanfstaengl his binoculars and told him that there was no question of his leaving the ship by the main gangway. To avoid trouble, plainclothes men from the New York Police Department had shepherded Hanfstaengl ashore incognito.

Scharf was a decent man. He had quarrelled with the Nazis before the war, was subsequently deprived of his command, and sent on the small transport boat *Alster* to Norway where he was captured by the British. He knew most of the leading Nazi personalities back home and talked about them in a most interesting way, according to the British intelligence officer, Captain K. Kirkness.

A man of fifty-five, he was universally respected by all in the camp, making both militant Nazis and those opposed to Hitler's regime feel he was on their side. Joseph Senoner had an illuminating encounter with him. He was a sixteen-year-old Catholic merchant seaman from Austria who had chosen to live among the Jews. One day, as he was walking back to his hut, two men took him by the arm and told him Commodore Scharf wanted to see him. He was surprised to find the Commodore in the company of prominent Nazis. When they asked him why he was "living with the Jews," Senoner just stared and said nothing. But when they tried to intimidate him, he turned to Scharf and said, "If you want to ask me something, I'll talk to you privately." Scharf requested the others to leave, and Senoner explained why he had chosen to live where he did. "They are my friends," he said. Scharf thanked him and dismissed him without further ado.

Scharf's second-in-command as camp leader was Baron Constant von Pilar von Pilchau, the suave Baltic shipping executive who had plotted to seize the *Duchess* and take her back to

Hamburg. Strangely enough, he did not seem to be an out-and-out Nazi, but a man of great discretion whom nobody could quite make out. Less mysterious was Edwin Gulcher, with whom Hanfstaengl had nothing in common at all. He was either a Gestapo man or an agent of Dr. Goebbels—"the little demon," as Hanfstaengl called him. Gulcher was in charge of sports and recreation. His main claim to fame was that he seemed to have been involved in the murder of the communist leader Rosa Luxemburg in 1919. He was a small wiry man, with a grim expression on his face—not one to laugh at Hanfstaengl's jokes.

Another influential inhabitant of Camp R was Count Montgelas, a strong anti-Nazi who had been foreign correspondent of the *Vossische Zeitung* during the Weimar Republic. He had lived in the United States and was a friend of Dorothy Thompson and Sinclair Lewis. There was also Dr. Gustav Lachmann, the well-known aeronautical engineer of whom intelligence officer Captain Kirkness wrote that he had "probably been turned into a Nazi by internment." Another "celebrity" was Wilhelm von Richthofen, a cousin of the famous Manfred, the air ace of the First World War. Wilhelm was an insignificant man, an anti-Nazi who was not especially liked by anyone. More unusual, perhaps, was Otto Slabke, a seventy-one-year-old man who had been interned throughout the First World War, although he had lived in the United Kingdom since his boyhood. He had married a Scotswoman, but spoke neither English nor German properly.

According to British Intelligence Officer Kirkness, probably the most interesting internee in the camp was Ernest Hanfstaengl—historian; composer of music and brilliant pianist; literateur; amateur politician.

> His appearance is almost as strange as his history. About six feet three tall, he is built in proportion, and has a large, curiously shaped head set deep into square angular shoulders. Lank wisps of hair hang over his eyes; a prominent forehead juts out over the rest of his features. He speaks very rapidly, switching from German to English and back to German so abruptly that considerable concentration is necessary to follow his conversation. An interesting item is that he appears to be very popular in the camp, and seems to

have no difficulty in establishing a *modus vivendi* with both Nazis and refugees. He is very fond of discussing politics and the course of the war, which, in his opinion, is to be a long one.

Hanfstaengl's views must have clashed with those who throughout August 1940 prepared themselves for an early reunion with their families and friends in victorious Germany. Outside the Nazi huts hastily painted billboards appeared with the inscription, "To be let by September First." Their families had written to them that September 18 had been declared "Day of the Internees and Prisoners of War."

Whenever a "fracas" occurred in the camp, Commandant Berry would punish everyone involved. Walter Ruckersberg told me how he was beaten up by the Nazis because he was a Jew and suffered an eye injury with considerable internal bleeding; he was put in a cell as punishment for fighting. "Had it not been for the intervention by the medical officer, Captain A. A. Klass, who liberated me after a few hours, I might have suffered permanent damage to my eyes."

Jewish religious services were held in a corner of the Jewish hut, deliberately interrupted by the Nazis who practiced boxing with maximum noise in the adjoining hut. After weeks of urgings, space was made available outside the compound about half a mile away. The worshippers were escorted there by military guards, and the doors were locked during the services so that nobody could escape.

The most spectacular outburst of anti-Semitism occurred on October 1, when Dr. Hans Novotny and Dr. L. Seewald, two Jewish internee doctors working in the hospital, were beaten up by the Nazis.

Karl Kruger reports:

> We went to the perimeter to shout to the guards to intervene. Nobody came. Very much later the sergeant came on his own. Nobody else had wanted to come into the camp. . . . The sergeant took the two doctors out. After that they worked in the hospital outside the compound . . . as doctors.

As a result of this incident the anti-Nazis went on a hunger-strike for two days. Only then did Commandant Berry promise to separate the refugees from the Nazis. Yet, his promise was not fulfilled until nearly four months later.

Nothing about this ever leaked out to the Canadian public, but British M.P. Colonel J. Wedgwood somehow found out about it. On January 24, 1941 he asked in the House of Commons whether it was true that "seventy refugees, mainly Jews, are dominated by several hundred Nazi sailors in Camp R."

About two years after the "doctors' incident" Commodore Scharf was repatriated to Germany, where several complaints were made against him and he was investigated by the Gestapo. Presumably, these were complaints from Nazis in Camp R who had accused him of being disloyal to Hitler. How serious his position was is shown by the self-serving report he made on August 1, 1944, to the *Oberreichsleiter* of the Party in which, probably to save his life, he turned the truth upside down when describing the attack on the two Jewish doctors:

> A major incident occurred on October 2 when our merchant seamen were brutally beaten up in hospital by two Jewish doctors and two male nurses. Everybody was punished, including the two doctors. They got seven days' arrest and only in the spring of 1941 were we finally relieved of the Jews and all these other elements. Immediately after they left, there was a much better atmosphere in our camp.
>
> We were not allowed to hang up pictures of Hitler, nor show any German flags, although I protested about this several times. Otherwise life was quite pleasant. We went swimming, had regular cinema performances, could play football. Several of us tried to escape. One got as far as the U.S. and was recaptured and returned.[22]

Commandant Berry had good reason to worry about escapes as several rather daring attempts were made. The most flamboyant escapee was Don Manuelo Fischer, the veteran of the Spanish Civil War. According to Karl Kruger, he was "a very comical man . . . always in the fresh air, doing exercises, keeping fit." Joseph Senoner recalls, "He was quite a guy, with a magnetic personality." Eugen Spier remembers him as a man who "demonstrated radiant cheerfulness."

Fischer was extremely popular in the camp. On August 19, Spier had breakfast with him. Having observed on previous occasions that Spier preferred strawberry jam to bacon, Fischer grandly offered him his jam rations for the coming week. Spier didn't give the matter much thought until that evening when at roll call it was discovered that Fischer was missing. He had not been seen since breakfast, after which he had taken a shower in the bath hut outside the compound. Fischer had managed to smuggle into the hut extra clothing and everything else he needed, including his Spanish passport. He hid in a box-like shelf and had his friends turn it against the wall. There he stayed, unobserved, until everybody had returned to the camp. During the noon-hour he came out of the box, opened the window and escaped. He made his way by train across the border to the United States, which was still neutral at the time, confident the Americans would never send him back to Canada, to his native Germany or to Spain, especially since he had fought against Franco. But the American police picked him up, turned him over to the Mounties, and on November 3 he was returned to Camp R, cheerful as ever. After completing twenty-eight days of solitary confinement, he was resolved to try again soon. The case received wide publicity in both Canadian and American newspapers, many of which expressed the view that the Americans should have given him his freedom.

On September 24 Herbert Cohn, a Jewish seaman anxious to go to Palestine, was less successful. His main purpose was to go to Ottawa to tell the world what was going on in Canadian internment camps. "He built a tunnel," Hein Doerr told me. "It was a beautiful job, all boarded up nicely, a few feet away from the road. But somebody squealed." When Cohn was asked why he wanted to escape he gave his reasons and added that he wanted to join the Canadian Army to fight the Nazis.

Eugen Spier in his account of the escape did not mention that Cohn was betrayed by someone. He described how the ground gave way, and the guard who had stood on it suddenly disappeared. "It looked as though the earth had opened its mouth to swallow the man alive."

Cohn only received seven days' detention, but according to the *Commandant's Journal* of November 4, six weeks later, he was given twenty-nine days for saying that the commandant's word could not be trusted.

The third escape took a tragic turn. On October 4 Ernst Mueller and Rudolf Rauschenbach disappeared from a fatigue party. According to the *Commandant's Journal*, they were discovered that evening on Mount How. A Canadian soldier called out to them. "Mueller rushed at him, Private Moar, J. R., shot Mueller twice and killed him, and then Rauschenbach was brought to the Guard Room for custody." But Hein Doerr told me that Mueller, who wasn't a Nazi, "raised his hands and said, 'Don't shoot; I have a family.' The soldier shot him twice through the stomach."

Captain J. A. Milne, the British intelligence officer who had reported Baron Pilar von Pilchau's plot to seize the *Duchess of York*, criticized the behavior of the camp guards. His information came from internee Schmitt. "Almost without exception, the soldiers in Camp R could be bought for twenty or thirty dollars. They were also known to borrow money from the internees in order to meet their gambling debts. The internees had made money selling to the soldiers model ships in bottles, woodwork, and other hand-made articles. Two internees who recently escaped were able to buy their railway tickets to Port Arthur."

As to Hanfstaengl, if he had found satisfaction in wielding political power or exercising diplomacy, the camp would have been a perfect arena for him. But he was basically a bohemian and a dilettante, and he had no other ambition but to get out. In spite of his friendship with President Roosevelt, dating back to the Harvard Club of 1908, for the moment his chances were nil. He had excellent connections in England and the United States, but none in Canada. There was nothing he could do, for the time being, but to lie low and play Wagner on the piano in the recreation hut.

He could not have felt comfortable with either Nazis or anti-Nazis. In his memoirs he wrote that he and his group was "roughly handled," but he did not specify how. Instead, he complained about the Canadian winter:

> The few stoves gave practically no protection against the bitter winter cold, even though we kept a day and night watch to keep them alight. A spilled cup of coffee froze on the ground where it fell.... By October 1941 it was clear we would not survive another winter there, and we were moved into the casemates of Fort Henry, near Kingston.

SEVEN

Military Government

In the fall of 1940 Colonel H. Stethem succeeded General Panet as Canadian Director of Internment Operations. A man of fifty-two, he had enlisted in the Royal Canadian Dragoons in 1911, had distinguished himself during the First World War, and served in Siberia after the war.

So conscientious was he in his new job that on one occasion, while on an inspection tour to a northern prisoner-of-war camp, he personally participated in the pursuit of two escaped prisoners of war. Inadequately dressed for an outdoor chase in the Canadian winter, clad only in light shoes and slacks and a raincoat, he did not give up. Although he fell several times in the deep snow, he persevered until the prisoners were caught. Back in his office in Ottawa, he was on the verge of pneumonia, but he had done his duty.

He found it more difficult to do his duty toward the interned refugees than toward the Nazi prisoners, because he had to overcome a deep dislike of them. Similarly, he had a profound distrust of the voluntary organizations, both gentile and Jewish, which from the very beginning of his administration were a considerable nuisance to him. But just as he tried to overcome his dislike of the refugees, he made a determined effort to cooperate with the officials of the welfare organizations. All these activities seemed to him to be a deflection from his main challenge, which was the discharge of his responsibilities towards Nazi internees and prisoners of war.

Being cooperative and courteous towards those who came to see him to ask for recognition of the special needs of the refugees did not come easily to him. One of these was Godfrey Barrass, the British intelligence officer in Quebec. This is Barrass' account of the meeting:

> He played the old trick: he kept me waiting and then, when I was in his office, he didn't offer me a seat. "Do you know," he said, "what we think of you?" It was news to me that I had been given any thought at all. "Well," he said, "we think you are a fifth columnist." I quietly sat down without waiting for permission. "There are two things you can do," I said, fully realizing that he would do neither. "You can either put me under arrest, or you can apologize. But I don't think you have the guts to do either. I don't really care what you do because I'm going on leave."

Stethem kept many others waiting in his outer office and was overheard raving through the closed door and "indulging in tirades against refugees and Jews and voluntary organizations." The only times when a smile was seen flickering across his face were when he promised to "twist their tails all right," or when he shouted into the telephone to advise a district commandant that "we can hit these fellows harder than they can hit us," and telling him that his men were not making sufficient use of their rifles. He was so disliked by his own staff officers, and all the clerks and typists who worked for him, that his headquarters office in Ottawa was not a very cheerful place.

As Director of Internment Operations, Stethem had to act through the general officer commanding the district; this led to endless delays. During his first year in office he never visited any of the camps, though Colonel H. de Watson, one of his officers, made at least one personal inspection tour of Camp L and Camp T. The result was that each commandant was very much left alone to make his own rules. In no respect was this as evident as in those concerning compulsory work.

During the sixteen months of my own internment in Canada I was never personally forced to do any kind of work other than unpaid chores related to the maintenance of the camp. Such activities, though under the jurisdiction of the resident sergeant-major, were administered by our own "minister of works." This meant that if anyone preferred talking to working, as I usually did, it was possible—through subtle diplomacy—to extricate oneself from unwelcome or distracting chores. Other camps, however, instituted compulsory labor schemes, mainly because some commandants firmly believed that there was a direct connection between idle hands and the devil.

The British Home Office, in its initial instructions to the Canadian government, had made clear that "there shall be no compulsory conscription of labor," but that there was no objection in principle to arrangements providing employment for those internees who were willing to work. "Such arrangements would be of the greatest value in helping to maintain the morale and in preventing the physical and mental deterioration of the internees."

Colonel Stethem had either never read these instructions or did not consider it necessary to pay attention to them. Apparently Colonel A. T. McLean, the well-meaning commandant of Camp B in New Brunswick, also decided it was a good idea to compel his inmates to engage in forestry work, for twenty cents a day, just as the unemployed had labored during the Depression on the same site in a similar camp for slightly better wages.

Although the 123 orthodox Jews in Camp B had no objection in principle to be compelled to work, unless it interfered with their talmudic studies, they categorically refused to do so on the Sabbath. It is not clear to what extent Colonel McLean was personally involved in the dispute that ensued; he may have left the matter in the hands of his adjutant.

It is difficult to imagine him as a callous slave-driver, for on one occasion he asked those people who had been chefs at first-class European hotels before their internment to prepare a dinner for a group of New Brunswick "potentates" he planned to entertain. They went all out. Some inmates acted as waiters and happily served the important guests. At the end of the party McLean made a speech praising all of them, and then coined the following much-quoted phrase: "Not only do we have great cooks and great waiters in Camp B, but we also have more brains than in the whole country put together!"

On one occasion the sixteen-year-old Gustav Bauer was caught with bread in his hut—a grave offense. He was arrested and placed in the clink. It so happened that it was the day before

Yom Kippur, the Day of Atonement, October 11, 1940. The wheels were put into motion to get him out. This is the letter the rabbi wrote to Colonel McLean:

Sir:

There is one day in the year when God is atoning the sins of men (Third Book of Moses, Chapter sixteen, XIII). It is then that all the Jews are praying for forgiveness of their sins and that, so we are sure, God receives their Prayers. This day will start tonight.

Regarding the extraordinarity of this day, may I ask you, Sir, to be merciful and to grant the internee Gustav Bauer, who was sent to the jail today, to be present at the Prayers. I am sure, God will reward you for this.

I am, Sir yours,
Most obedient
Rabbi

McLean yielded to this eloquent appeal and Bauer was released and took part in the prayers.

Yet, on November 9, a Sabbath day, soldiers with bayonets came to the camp to pull people out for compulsory work, according to John Newmark's diary. Following an emergency meeting, a formal complaint was sent to the commandant who forwarded a request for guidance to Colonel Stethem in Ottawa. On November 22 the following reply was received:

It is becoming increasingly evident that the group of ortho- dox Jews do not propose to adapt themselves to the circum- stances in which they are placed, and that there is a distinct lack of cooperation on their part. . . . Strictly speaking, it would be quite in order to state that the internees will carry out compulsory labor six days a week, and the only day which shall be observed as a day of rest will be the Lord's Day, as recognized by Canadian legislation.

The memo went on to order that a nominal roll be compiled of those who declined to work on the Jewish Sabbath, "in order that same may be noted in connection with any question that may arise in the future, regarding permission to reside in Canada or to immigrate to countries other than Palestine."

It was further decreed that, because of the lack of coopera- tion of a large proportion of internees, no light manufacturing plant would be established in Camp B, and that internees would be placed on "compulsory labor on forestry work." Regarding the question of pay, preference was to be given to "those of the Jewish race who have shown a spirit of cooperation and adaptability." The recalcitrants "will be used on work connected with camp maintenance and unpaid labor." The memo concluded:

> Internment Camp B . . . has been granted certain privileges in regard to mail, newspapers, magazines, radios, etc. and, if any large proportion of the camp population show that they are antagonistic to authority or show a lack of cooperation with those who are trying to assist them . . . it may be necessary to take away some of these privileges, in consequence of which all the camp will suffer as a result of the attitude adopted by their comrades.

In due course, forms were distributed to all inmates, requesting them to sign one of two declarations: "I am unwilling to work on Saturdays under any circumstances, as it is against my religious convictions as a member of the Orthodox Jewish Faith" or "I am willing to work on Saturdays if required to do so."

The news soon leaked out, reaching the World Agudas Israel Society in London which passed it on to the Home Office and to Member of Parliament Josuah Wedgwood, who raised the matter in the House of Commons. On January 26 and 29, 1941, the following despatch was circulated by the Jewish Telegraphic Agency:

> The Jewish internees of orthodox belief were compelled to do labor six days weekly with Sunday the only rest day, and punishments were proposed for violators to the effect that their names were to be noted and that they would be barred from emigration.
>
> They were compelled to do all camp work on Sunday including that work normally done by the guards and they would receive other punishments.

A Jewish representative from Montreal visited Stethem, and Rabbi Kraus of Fredericton called on McLean. The offensive memorandum was erased from the record.

The "Official" Lists

As fall approached, it became evident to us in Camp L in Quebec City that big changes were in the wind. Here are excerpts from Peter Heller's diary:

September 17: At last it is public with a semi-official announcement: the "Aryans" are being separated from us, to a Camp S where there already are other "Aryans." We are going to a Camp N that has just been finished.

Following this news, every camp institution is immediately writing a letter of protest to the commandant's office, etc. The political refugees, the rabbis, the camp university, the hut leaders, etc.—all emphasize that for us "there has always been and always will be only one criterion, namely Nazi or anti-Nazi, and there has always been complete collaboration among all anti-Nazis here in the camp," etc.

The political, "Aryan," refugees are afraid that they will be carted off to a Nazi camp. Then the very people who left Germany for reasons of principle and not because as Jews they had no choice, would be locked up with their mortal enemies. We all find that not only sad and upsetting, but also tragic, in the most real sense of the word. Unfortunately the most awful squabbles are starting. A few Jews, of course, think that's not really the way it is with political refugees. You can never trust the Aryans, they say. They need only change their views and then everything would be fine for them. Other Jews say they would rather go to a Nazi camp with the political refugees than go on living with such unprincipled, nationalistic, even fascist, Jews. R. is extremely worried about who our future camp leader will be if through the separation we lose the Hohenzollern Lingen. "Will there still be paid labor?" "Will my things be searched?" "Is my diary in danger?" . . .

People are refusing to send back the lists. Ottawa wants a list of professions, Gentiles, Jews. The huts only fill out "profession." The majority are against separation by these criteria. The list that is improperly filled out comes back. Excited hut meetings. "Aryan" volunteers register. (Among them are Jews, in order to thwart the racist separation.) Ohmann, the seal, brings up the tasteless comparison with two men in a boat; (i.e. when things get critical, the Jewish refugee should throw the non-Jewish political refugee overboard.) Someone gets hit.—First pamphlet: statutes of the National Party. Heymann, "the Jewish Nazi," starts a list. Popper, the anti-National Jew, eavesdrops on the National Jews. An anti-pamphlet appears, written by Brauer-Markowitz. Great excitement. Apologies. Rumors about those who want to seize power after they're rid of the present camp leaders (Lingen, etc.) through the separation. Intrigues, lies and obscene propaganda from the National Jews. Commandant discontinues all lists. Appeals to "law and order" (signed by Abrahamson and Lingen, as representatives of the two "races"). Rumor: the commandant is setting up the lists as he sees fit, with the help of his secretary, Hoffmann. Two piles of suitcases ("ominous") right and left.

Rumors: the commandant will have to defend himself before a court-martial, because he allowed one of the Catholic priests to visit a monastery in Quebec. He supposedly has to retire from the military. He got our refugee committee to give him lists so he could make a stink in the Home Office as a private citizen. He is completely on our side. "Piggy," they say, "is incompetent but decent." New election of a "tour leader." (We elect a man who promises not to run for camp leadership in the next camp, Dr. Franck).

Here is a letter dealing with the same subject.

> Camp L
> Internment Operations
> Canada
> September 27, 1940

The Commandant
Camp L

Sir:

You informed Count Lingen this morning of a telegram from the Director of Internment Operations, Ottawa, ordering the dissolution of this camp into groups based on the racial descent of the individual internees and the transfer of these groups into other camps.

This camp consists of 89 percent refugees from Nazi Oppression. We, as the representatives of these refugees, have urged again and again since our arrival here for a separation from the minority in this camp who support or tolerate the Nazi regime. We should like to take this opportunity of repeating this request. But at the same time we would like to express our most earnest wish that the majority of refugees should not be torn apart. They have now lived together in internment for several months and would consider a separation from their friends a severe hardship.

Above all, however, we should like to protest with all emphasis against a separation based on racial grounds. It is true that the majority among the refugees are Jews. But by no means all. Many of the others are persons who, though no longer of Jewish faith, are Jewish or partially Jewish by descent and had to leave Germany because of racial persecution. What is still more important, many others are refugees from Nazi Germany on political grounds. They are men who had to leave Nazi Germany ... because of their belief in the principles for which this war is being fought. ... It would be intolerable if these political refugees were now transferred to camps containing Nazi prisoners and were forced to live with their Nazi opponents. Both racial and political refugees have in common the enmity against Nazism and loyalty to the British cause.

> Yours truly,
> F. Lingen
>   Camp Supervisor
> Abrahamson
>   for the Refugee Committee

Though Ottawa tried to stick to its guns, the authorities did not have the means to separate Jews from gentiles without the cooperation of the internees. In any case, there were no acceptable definitions or criteria.

One hundred and forty-one men were to be sent to Farnham, Quebec—that was to be the "gentile" camp. Only eighty-nine signed up, and the rest was made up of various shades of non-gentiles. Similarly, the "Jewish" group that was to be sent to Sherbrooke, Quebec, contained a sizeable number of people who were non-Jewish friends of Jews. They maintained they had joined the group to protest against the introduction of the Nuremberg Laws in the administration of Canadian internment camps. No doubt, another reason for the non-Jewish political refugees to join the Jews was their fear that if the Nazis won the war, they would be sent back to Germany together with the triumphant victors.

EIGHT

Sherbrooke

We arrived in Newington, near Sherbrooke, on October 15 during a heavy rainstorm, just ten days before the federal government had acquired the property consisting of two repair sheds, one for locomotives and the other for railroad cars, from Quebec Central Railway. The railway tracks and oiling pits that ran through the sheds were filled with black water. Soot was everywhere. The place had six old-fashioned lavatories without ventilation, two urinals and seven low-pressure water taps which also had to serve the kitchen. The windows were broken and the roofs were leaky; so were the noisily hissing heating pipes.

The floor space allotted to each of the 736 internees amounted to twenty-nine square feet; that was contrary to British Ministry of Health regulations which required a minimum of thirty-five square feet for each person incarcerated in a British prison. The beds had been sent by mistake to Montreal; however, the mattresses intended for the Farnham camp had been delivered to Sherbrooke.

The appalling conditions of the camp were not the fault of its commandant, Major S. N. Griffin, who faced an impossible task. He was a conscientious and brave soldier who had won the Military Cross in the First World War. The ensuing battle with us was to be his last; in December 1940 he suffered a coronary thrombosis and died on April 15, 1941, four months later.

Immediately after our arrival we decided to go on a hunger strike unless we received assurances that we would be sent to a habitable camp. Major Griffin was unable to give us such assurances.

Here is an excerpt from his journal.

October 15: 618 prisoners arrived from Camp L. [One hundred and eighteen men from Camp Q were to arrive the next day.] Owing to the appalling condition of the camp, a considerable amount of severe trouble is being encountered in the form of a passive resistance strike. The internees refuse to prepare their supper and unload their bedding, fixtures, etc. The causes for this behavior outlined by their spokesman are chiefly:

(a) That it had been indicated to the internees that they were moving to a camp better equipped than Camp L;

(b) The faulty routing of the bedding equipment . . .;

(c) The deep-rooted belief that they had been ousted from their comfortable quarters at Camp L to make way for Nazi prisoners;

(d) The conviction that passive resistance would result in immediate removal to a new camp.

On the morning of October 16 a meeting between our chosen representatives and Major Griffin took place. We still refused to prepare meals or do work of any nature. Rumors persisted that we had been threatened with removal to Nazi camps, and would be locked into the sheds until we had changed our minds.

What *did* change our minds—at least the minds of our elected leaders—was the appearance of a type of Canadian officer we had not encountered before.

Assistant Adjutant, Second Lieutenant J. A. Edmison had come to address us on the morning of October 16 in Shed A. He was a thirty-seven-year-old lawyer and alderman from Montreal who had taken arts at Queen's and law at McGill University. Together with his close friend Carl Goldenberg, who later became one of Canada's most distinguished labor arbitrators and a senator, he had taken a strong anti-appeasement position before the war. As a lawyer he had acted on behalf of the Black Watch regiment. He was an honorary member of the B'nai Brith, and active in the Society for Christians and Jews. Having attended several Jewish functions in Montreal, he was thoroughly familiar with the Jewish situation in Canada. Apart from his law practice, he was head of the Legal Aid Bureau in Montreal, interested in prison reform and active in the John Howard Society.

Edmison had received his commission in the summer of 1940, but not until he was asked to assume the duties of staff officer at Camp N in Sherbrooke did he report for active duty.

On that critical October morning, he went to see Griffin to ask for permission to speak to the internees. Griffin hesitated at first, but then agreed, provided Edmison understood that "he was on his own"; he even asked him to sign a paper to that effect.

I shall never forget the impression Edmison made on me. Here was a man in Canadian uniform who knew who we were, who realized that there were men among us who had been in German concentration camps. Using a table top as his platform, he appealed to us, trying to persuade us to cooperate with the authorities who would do their best to help. His main point was that, if we were more flexible, we could make the camp more livable. He said, even the officers had to put up with sub-standard accommodation. "But if you remain recalcitrant," he went on, "do not harbor any illusions about the support you may receive from the Jewish community in Canada. I am well acquainted with them."

According to the *Commandant's Journal*:

> He pointed out that their present course of conduct was highly damaging to their own cause, that it would arouse resentment rather than sympathy, and would aid the spread of anti-Semitism in Canada and severely handicap the efforts of Canadian Jewry in working out plans for post-war Jewish immigration. He appealed to the more educated and reasonable men among them to get down to work at once and make the quarters as comfortable as possible under the existing conditions. A reply was demanded by 1300 hours today.

Today, arguments designed to break the resistance of men who had every right to feel betrayed appear iniquitous. But the fact that a singularly decent individual whose sympathies and motives were beyond reproach was able to use them is a reflection not on him but on the general situation of Jews in Canada in 1940. The Jewish community had a low standing in the eyes of the political establishment. Throughout the Hitler years its attempts to have Canada's doors opened just a little wider to admit desperate refugees were frustrated again and again. Edmison knew this and correctly assessed that the leaders of the Jewish community were unlikely to antagonize Ottawa by going to bat for people who, after all, were safe in Canada, had enough to eat and a roof over their heads (even if it leaked), while Jews in Europe were in constant danger of their lives.

At 12:30 p.m. our leaders agreed to cooperate for a period of three days. We abandoned our hunger strike for lunch. Support for our leaders' decision was far from unanimous, but the divisions within our ranks at least were manageable.

In the afternoon, 118 men from Camp Q arrived at Sherbrooke. In the view of the camp commandant they were "better disciplined and more cooperative than the prisoners from Camp L." They agreed with our position and it was resolved that, while we were prepared to perform necessary tasks during the trial period, we would not help with other work such as building new latrines. We still were anxious to press for a transfer to a habitable camp.

On October 18, the day before the trial period was due to expire, Commandant Griffin spoke to us. He was the first to admit, he said, that there was much to be done to improve conditions in the camp. "I suggest to you strongly that if we cooperate with one another with efficiency, we can work wonders in this place." He then informed us: "Sherbrooke is not going to be a temporary camp. Both you and I are going to be here for a long time!" He told us that for everything done to improve the camp, we would be paid twenty cents a day. The only unpaid work would be ordinary fatigues, which if performed daily and in rotation would not require more than 25 percent of the camp's enrollment. He went on to say: "There are among you many clever and qualified men; to them, I throw out the challenge to assist in the planning and erection of this new camp. You will tell me what materials you want and I will supply them without delay. . . . The winter is fast approaching and every day's delay is serious."

Finally, Griffin announced that Saul Hayes of the United Jewish Relief and War Relief Agencies in Montreal would visit the camp to discuss "various immigration and diplomatic tech-nicalities." He concluded by calling on everyone to "stop talking and arguing. . . . I speak to you now not only as Commandant but as man to man, and I hope that a lot of things will be different from now on."

To show how much importance Major Griffin attached to this matter, he had carefully written out his speech before it was delivered, and he presented a copy of it to our spokesman in the presence of the assembled camp.

Unfortunately, the commandant's valiant efforts failed to make an immediate impression. The committee that was formed to draw up plans came to the conclusion that these plans could not be carried out unless we were moved out of the camp during the renovation. The internees from Camp Q signed a formal letter to the commandant stating that, after listening to his speech, they felt that he was not fully aware of the gravity of their situation.

Another officer appeared on the scene. Major D. J. O'Donahoe was a tall, red-faced Colonel-Blimp-like entrepreneur who had found his way into the army. It was he who had taken the initiative to organize our voluntary paid work projects— wood-working shops and light manufacturing facilities for making tables and benches, ammunition boxes, palliasses, kit-bags and socks. When "Major Balls," as O'Donahoe came to be known, addressed us outside Shed B, he blithely endangered the fragile harmony Major Griffin had established earlier.

I was standing at the back of the crowd, not far from Peter Heller, who later wrote that he thought this "monumental blond sea elephant" was drunk.

"Do you all understand English?" he started off, a question greeted with a mixed chorus of yes's and no's.

"I'm not going to threaten you," he continued, "but I've had bad reports about this camp. If you're asking for trouble, you can have it; plenty of it. And don't you try any monkey business."

The concept "monkey business" was new to us. We had many learned scholars among us, but none of them had ever heard of monkey business. Since O'Donahoe was mumbling, anyway, those in the back rows were sure he had called us *monkeys*. He may have noticed a certain lack of responsiveness in his audience and decided on a change of key. Pointing to one of us he brightly observed, "This fellow needs a haircut." Somebody said, "Hear, hear." He narrowed his blue eyes and looked us over. There was no doubt about it, we were a scruffy-looking lot. As hot water was almost impossible to come by, our general appearance and the unwashed prisoner-of-war uniforms we wore did not make us look particularly appetizing.

"I understand you are all Jews," he continued in the manner of a British colonial officer amiably tickling the chin of a gurgling Zulu baby. Again there was a chorus of yes's and no's. "That's all right," he went on happily, as though to say "that's not your fault." "But you've got to wash. Otherwise you get lice."

The best was yet to come.

"If you play ball," he announced, "I will play ball. If you won't play ball, I won't play ball."

This idiom was even less familiar to us than the "monkey business." "What's he trying to say?" those of us who heard him were wondering. "Why *should* he want to play ball with us? What kind of ball game?" (Hence the nickname.)

"Major Balls" then decided to talk turkey. "You want us to win this war, don't you?" (Yes, yes, yes.) "We're going to start right here. Will you help?" (Yes, yes, yes.) "I understand some of you have been in business. That's great. You're going to be asked—no, you're going to be *ordered*—to work." He then outlined his plans for the camp workshops. "We will teach you something useful, so that when you get out of here at the end of the war you won't have wasted your time. This"—he pointed to the railway sheds—"is going to be your home." (Laughter.) "Some of you have a certain grade of reasonable intelligence. You won't misunderstand kindness for weakness. By the way, can you all hear me?" (No!) "Well, the other fellows are going to tell you," he laughed. "I don't want to scream. As I was saying, we'll get you machines. Have you any people who know about making furniture? Joiners? Woodcutters? Tailors? I want to have a word with them."

And so the meeting broke up. The major went into a huddle with our furniture makers, joiners, woodcutters and tailors. Within an hour of O'Donahoe's address, Griffin made a smart move: he appointed the Defender of Madrid, Hans Kahle, camp speaker.

A Love Story

In September 1940, when the leaves had begun to turn in Quebec and the valley of the St. Lawrence was golden-yellow, several of our poets were polishing their sonnets in praise of the Canadian autumn. Thanks to the personal initiative of Major Wiggs (Piggy-Wiggy), a proud citizen of Quebec who wanted us to appreciate the beauty of his city, we had been allowed to go for occasional walks in small groups, heavily guarded.

It was around that time that Peter Field's love affair began. Peter Heller in his diary mentions a boy in Camp L,

> who fell in love with one of the girls who go by the barbed wire every day. A small blonde girl, fifteen years old. (God only knows how he found out her age!) But he seemed to know everything in great detail. What time she goes by, . . . today she had on a new blue hat, . . . the boy runs along beside her—twenty metres away—next to the barbed wire, and waves. . . . Today she looked over at him. No, she didn't wave, she just looked. The poor boy is quite beside himself. He wants to write a letter to the commandant to be let out—just for a few hours—on his word of honor, and be allowed to visit the girl. He says he will go mad if he is refused.

Well, the boy did not go mad. Peter Field was twenty-six then and he looked like a junior tenor ready to sing Siegfried at the Wagner Festival in Bayreuth. Before the war he had been selling books in Germany, Poland and Holland. On arrival in England, after a hair-breadth's escape from Holland, he was interned in a Liverpool barracks—"a real hell-hole." But he didn't mind; he was so amazed that he was still alive.

The girl's name was Pauline Perrault. Field describes her as "fifteen going on twenty-one." She was a granddaughter of Charles Alphonse Fournier, former M.P. for Bellechasse, a man with excellent connections in Ottawa, noted for his resemblance to Sir Wilfrid Laurier. Pauline, whose parents were separated, was an only child living with her grandfather, her mother and her aunt in an apartment on the Grand Allée, the most fashionable residential street in Quebec City. Everyone in the family adored her, especially her grandfather.

Her home was a few minutes' walk from the camp, and by

making a slight detour on her way to and from school, Pauline was able to pass the camp and wave to the prisoners. They appeared to her as glamorously enchained captives. One of them, in particular, was the most handsome of them all.

"Around the barbed wire," Peter Field told me, "there was a walkway, and then there was another barbed wire, and watchtowers in intervals of a few hundred feet. Beyond that was another walkway where Quebeckers would stroll by. I think she came by every day.

"At first I didn't pay much attention to her, especially since I wasn't sure that she was waving at me. But then, later, I noticed that she was. Once, I called 'hello' to her, when we were within shouting distance. I got into trouble; a guard stopped me: he may even have got ready to shoot. I was arrested and put into the clink for a few hours. But our camp spokesman got me out.

"Outside the compound there were high hills of dirt and we internees were given shovels and wheelbarrows to straighten them out. We were digging away, moving and taking away the soil.

"We had a good time playing games with the guards. They were older men. One of them stood on top of one of those dirt hills, holding his gun. We undermined him, by digging and digging until he fell. . . . Pauline saw us, while we were working there.

"One day the guard said to me, 'You like Blondie? She asked me about you.' I was doubtful about that; I thought he was telling me a story. I didn't believe him, frankly. But when he asked me if I would like to have her name and address, I said yes. If he'd get it for me I would give him my pocket knife.

"A couple of days later he told me he had her address, and he threw a piece of paper at me. We were working with the wheelbarrows and he didn't want the others to see him give me anything. I promptly dropped my pocket knife and he picked it up, as we had agreed. That was that. All this happened within a few days before we were moved to Sherbrooke."

Sherbrooke was only about three hours away by train, but from the lovers' viewpoint it might have been as far as Singapore. Torrid love letters began to be exchanged, which must have been most entertaining to the censors. Pauline regularly sent parcels with all sorts of goodies to Peter, and he duly distributed them among all his friends. In several of the letters she enclosed photographs of herself, including one in which she reconstructed the moment of their distant yet close first encounters along the barbed wire fence. She posed on the monuments to generals Wolfe and Montcalm, the fallen heroes of the Battle of Quebec.

The lively correspondence continued for many months until in late summer of 1941 it finally was possible to make arrangements to visit the internees. Peter Field told me:

"There had not been a girl in the camp until then. We some-times saw girls outside, but never in the outer compound; never.

"When Pauline arrived with her mother and aunt about eight hundred guys pressed their noses against the barbed wire to watch the scene. She did all the right things; she ran toward me, fell into my arms and kissed me. She loved every minute of it and played it up to the hilt. The men just howled.

"We must have been together for an hour or so; they had brought me so many gifts and packages that someone had to get permission to come with a wheelbarrow to cart all the stuff into the camp. It was absolutely incredible what these people lavished on me."

He must have made such a good impression on Pauline's mother and aunt that they decided to ask her grandfather to pull some strings in Ottawa so that Peter could visit them in Quebec over a weekend. Of course, parole was unheard of. According to unconfirmed reports, Charles Alphonse Fournier, either directly or indirectly, appealed to Prime Minister Mackenzie King. Permission was granted and the date was set; Peter could go to Quebec City from Friday, October 3 to Sunday, October 5, 1941. (Sadly, Pauline's grandfather died a week later.) Almost a year had passed since Peter and Pauline had first "met." Peter Field continued:

"I was asked to sign that I would be back by Sunday, mid-night. At the time, the place was full of rumors that we would be released soon. I was very much aware that I was sort of a test case, and that if there was trouble, if I was late coming back for example, everyone would suffer.

"As far as money was concerned, I had a one hundred-dollar bill which I had saved from Holland; I kept it hidden in my little bag. Wearing my one and only suit, and I suppose I must have had a coat, I was driven to the railway station in Sherbrooke. Never having lived as a free man in an English-speaking country before, and since I spoke more German than English in the camp, the mere experience of asking for a ticket in English was entirely new to me; it was all very strange."

On the train to Quebec City Field met another girl and they began to talk. She was working for a mining company in Thetford Mines and she promised to visit him. "She did, too, some weeks later. But when she got into her taxi to go home, she fell and broke her leg. This was a most unpleasant experience for her, and we never saw each other again."

Pauline was at the station with her mother and aunt to meet Peter and there was great jubilation.

"They took me to their apartment and soon dinner was served. They were very hospitable to me; everybody was happy. After dinner Pauline and I walked to a drugstore. I had a sundae, my first black and white sundae. Then we went up to the roof of her apartment house where we sat around and necked. I was surprised that her mother allowed us to be alone together. I must say I was amazed by the whole set-up, that they gave her so much freedom.

"On Saturday morning Pauline came into my room wearing her negligée. She did not make it easy for me, but I behaved like a gentleman. She was a very precocious city child. . . .

"We went out and explored the city. I bought a dark blue suit, very much like a Bar Mitzvah suit, using thirty of my hundred dollars. For my return to camp the family gave me an elegant leather suitcase. They insisted I go back to Sherbrooke first class, and that I eat in the dining car. It was a marvellous weekend."

On the way back to Sherbrooke, there was an awkward moment in the train. When Field sat down in the dining car and ordered dinner in his heavy German accent, "there was a man sitting opposite me; he looked at me in a strange way and said, 'You know, there are spies hiding everywhere.' I was terrified; I was sure I would be arrested. But the waiter assured me the man was drunk."

On arrival in Sherbrooke, Field hailed a taxi. "To the camp, please," he said to the driver, very much aware of the incongruity of his situation. He arrived early, just after ten o'clock, but the lights already had been put out. Someone spotted him walking across the camp to his hut, wearing his brand new suit and carrying his brand new suitcase.

Suddenly, all the lights came on. "It was incredible. Everybody came rushing out of their bunks. They shoved me onto a top bunk and shouted 'Story! Story!' And I told them everything— more or less."

Peter Field was released a few months later, but not until he had been interviewed by an immigration officer who showed him his dossier containing reference to an illegal visit to Quebec City. When Field explained the circumstances, the officer said to him, "The Prime Minister's Office never informed us."

Peter visited Quebec City a few more times, but gradually the romance petered out. Pauline grew up; they just drifted apart. But there may have been another reason for the breakup; when he told the family "that I was a refugee, they were kind of disappointed. They probably would have preferred a real prisoner of war."

The Sergeant-Major

In civilian life Sergeant-Major Macintosh had been a used-car dealer in Sherbrooke. He was tall and stocky, with puffy bags under his pale blue eyes and a mustache which was wrongly conceived. A normal mustache is like the upper half of a circle; his was like the lower half. The widest distance between its two sides was immediately under his nose. This made him look like a stage caricature of a sergeant-major.

He was the *compleat* sergeant-major. No doubt he treated the troops under his command the same way he treated us. The difference between them and us, however, was that they were soldiers and we were not. Anybody who answered him with a mere yes or no would get back a bellowing: "Yes, *what?*"

A friend of mine, a timid fellow, had protruding teeth. During roll call, Macintosh would pounce on him: "You, there! Wipe that grin off your face!" When an elderly frail professor of art from London University had not folded his blanket properly, Macintosh would scream at him, "You goddamned son-of-a-bitch! Will you never learn?"

There was a story about him which was not necessarily

invented. One day he had a conversation with a boy he favored. (Outrageous favoritism was an important ingredient of his administration.) The boy was not Jewish, but he spent much of his time in a predominantly Jewish group.

"Why are you hanging around with all those dirty Jews?" Macintosh would ask. "Jews are very fine people," the boy explained, "After all, Einstein is a Jew."

Macintosh looked around. "Einstein? Einstein? In what group is he?"

Emil Fackenheim sums it up this way:

> In the concentration camp I found some very ordinary people with whom I formed very close ties. For example, they were able to adopt the view that the Nazis were just bastards. Never mind trying to explain what social conditions produced them, whether they were left-wing fascists or right-wing fascists, they're sons of bitches and that's the end of it. That was all you had to know.
>
> Now I could never have said a thing like that in our Canadian internment camps. Some of the officers were stupid fools, but they weren't vicious. If you take somebody like the sergeant-major in Sherbrooke who always screamed at us—such a figure would be unthinkable in any concentration camp. I cannot imagine how anybody who really was there could say, except in moments of extreme bitterness, that the two things were the same.

As I mentioned before, the sergeant-major had his favorites. The camp musicians were occasionally permitted to entertain him and his friends on Saturday nights. This provided an agreeable change of scene—because the sergeants' mess was *outside* the compound. If you were a *particular* favorite of his, you were sometimes allowed to go along on the garbage truck to the city dump and back again. This was considered a *great* favor; after all, it was a treat to see downtown Sherbrooke. The truck driver was a nice man, and on at least one occasion he took the favorite to the entrance of the local whorehouse, put three dollars in his hand and said, "Go in, have a good time. I'll pick you up in half an hour." I understand the offer was refused.

Sergeant-Major Macintosh had another human quality: he was a Canadian patriot. This took the traditional form of being anti-English, a trait possibly due to his Scottish origins. Once he asked a man—not a particular favorite of his—who had expressed the desire to join the British Army and fight the Nazis, "Why in hell would you want to do a thing like that?"

"To teach men like you the meaning of democracy," was the answer.

When we got to know the sergeant-major better, we would occasionally take the liberty of answering his questions with a clipped "Yes, mein Fuehrer," instead of the obligatory "Yessir." He seemed to enjoy that. At Christmastime the Camp Committee even went as far as to ask one of our camp artists to draw a nude for him. That softened him up, at least during the holidays.

His régime had another important characteristic. If one was a law-abiding citizen in Sherbrooke and quietly played poker, studied Plato, played football, performed the few easy camp chores or made kitbags in the workshops, one would be left alone.

However, some of us had to learn the hard way that it was bad policy to argue with the sergeant-major or with any of his sergeants, corporals or guards. One night Helmut Blume and some of his friends decided to clean the dining hall, after everybody had gone to bed. It was a congenial chore; they could be by themselves and occasionally scrounge a few tidbits from the kitchen. Just below the ceiling of the hall a loudspeaker had been installed on top of a partition. Blume decided it required cleaning and, equipped with a rag, he climbed up on a ladder.

Suddenly, one of the guards, his gun at the ready, shouted, "Get off that fucking ladder!" "I'm cleaning," Blume called down. The guard took aim, repeating, "I said, get off the fucking ladder!" At this point, Blume thought it prudent to descend. Once standing on the floor he quietly tried to convey to the guard that he was not "used to being spoken to in that tone of voice." The guard was not impressed: "Tomorrow, you will be paraded before the commandant for not complying with an order." Blume remonstrated, "But I did come down the fucking ladder!" It made no difference. The next day he was marched into the commandant's office. When asked what had happened Blume told him that the soldier had used language to which he was not accustomed. The commandant looked at him with amazement, "Not accustomed, eh? Fourteen days' fatigue!"

Fourteen days' fatigue meant cleaning the soldiers' latrines which, though unpleasant, was very different from solitary confinement. That was no joke. George Brandt received four days in the cell for provocatively whistling repeatedly the theme from Laurel and Hardy films in order to get the goat of a sergeant.

George Brandt sums it up this way:

> The sergeant was an unbelievably low type, a dreadfully effeminate, disgusting, slug-like individual. He set a trap for me and I fell into it. He had soldiers lying in wait for me. . . . I was pounced on and marched off. There was a summary enquiry. . . . The solitary confinement was extremely unpleasant. There was no light and no toilet facilities, just a bucket with some disinfectant that caused maximum difficulty to your breathing. That was done deliberately. I was actually struck by the sergeant. I had to lie on a wooden plank. It was an interesting study in claustrophobia. I put my eyesight at risk reading by very sparse light a book about the war in China.

Ernest Borneman kept a careful record of the various acts of harassment committed by the sergeant-major's troops.

> *Incidents:*
> Refusal to let internees use the lavatory after 10:15 p.m. under the pretext that "all have to be in bed by then." Diarrhea patient gets half crazed.
> Pulling away blankets to see "if internees are undressed." Homosexuality running high among soldiers. On New Year's Eve drunk guards coming into dormitory to rape internees.
> Soldiers' mess and guard room are so dirty that soldiers refuse to clean them. So internees have to be found to do the job as penal labor . . .
> Sergeants invent defaults: for not being shaved, for leaving milk bottles in dormitory, for hanging up towels to dry over heating system. Attempts to tell the truth are considered "insolence" and held as cause for additional punishment.
> Fourteen days' fatigue for refusing to clean guard room. Sergeant slaps B. calls him a "dirty German swine."
> C.O. complains halls are dirty. Football banned for a week.
> Sergeant-major hits T. because he doesn't take his cap

off quickly enough. Medical officer hits internee with gloves across cheek because he did not stand at attention; says "You just go on protesting and we'll put some M.G.'s on you."

The Case of the Illicit Correspondence

On Friday January 2, 1941, at 11:30 at night Sergeant-Major Macintosh handed to the acting new camp commandant a nickel together with an envelope addressed to a Miss W. Henson, 417 St. Peter Street, Montreal, hereafter called Winkie. The sergeant-major stated that the nickel and the letter had been given to Private D. J. Home, one of the guards, who told him that he had received both from internee No. 222.

On January 25 Fred Lycett (No. 222) together with two of his friends—Ernest Guter and Gerard Arnhold—were arrested and placed in separate detention cells.

During the previous summer in Quebec, Lycett, Guter and Arnhold, who called themselves the Three Musketeers, had operated the steam-boilers in the camp. They had used their privileged positions to turn the boiler-room into a kind of club where coffee that had been cunningly "abstracted" from the kitchen was served to friends. The three also had provided laundry facilities to a privileged few.

Two older members of the club—a crippled veteran of World War I and a middle-aged lawyer—had hatched the "plot" there, namely to resurrect the imperial monarchy of Germany when the war was over and to put our man Lingen on the throne. The Three Musketeers were around eighteen years old at the time and enjoyed the sensation of witnessing so historic an occasion.

Fred Lycett, the son of an English father and a German mother, had been brought up in England. He could not speak German—nor did he have any connection with Germany—when he was interned in Wimbledon. Nor was there anything Jewish about him. However, since he had spent the first few years of his life in Germany, his German quickly came back once he was associating with people who spoke the language. Gerhard Arnhold, the son of a well-known banker, had been with me in Cambridge; Ernest Guter was a student from Berlin.

The trio had made friends with one of the guards, Corporal Bernard Henson, nicknamed Barney, who at one time must have mentioned to them that he had a daughter called Winnifred, nicknamed Winkie. The mention of Winkie must have excited the boys. Would Corporal Barney take a letter to her? Barney, who was a nice guy but not too bright said, "Why not!"

The following is taken from the legal dossier that was subsequently compiled:

The first letter was written on September 28, 1940 (Exhibit A). The Musketeers declared that "they had taken the opportunity of looking after your Dad."

Exhibit B was a letter from Winkie to "Fred, Jerry and Ernie," dated October 1, telling them that she is sending cigarettes with the letter, and adding, "Make sure you get them. I don't trust my Dad as much as I ought to." She went on to say, "So you are looking after my father. Well, from my experience I can tell you he needs looking after."

Exhibit C is an undated letter to the effect that her father had asked her not to write letters "officially" because they might all get into trouble if she did. She also told them that "Dad was unable to contact those people you wrote to me about."

Exhibit D is a letter from Lycett to Winkie dated October 25, by which time he was in Sherbrooke. Lycett wrote he had received her letter and went on to ask whether her Dad had found a way of getting in touch with Prince Frederick. "It is very important to us." (Lingen was in Camp A in Farnham, but no correspondence was allowed between camps.)

Exhibit E is a letter from Winkie to Lycett and Exhibit F is a long-hand, undated draft letter to "Dear Barney:... I don't suppose for one moment that the good old days in the Boiler House will ever come again, but one never knows... I miss His Royal Highness..."

So it went until Exhibit Z. What these exhibits did not show was the number of letters to persons other than Winkie which Barney had posted for the Three Musketeers.

Guter recalls: "It was a lot of fun. But we also had a serious purpose. We got letters out from many of our friends to M.P.s and to other influential people in England and the United States who could raise questions in public about why we were sitting in Canada."

Once caught, the Three Musketeers spent twenty-eight days in solitary confinement. The laces were taken out of their shoes to prevent suicide. There was no communication between them. They had to sleep on planks; no pillows or mattresses were provided. There was a heating unit in the cell which couldn't be shut off; being constantly on full steam, it created sweltering heat. The daily dessert was usually an apple which they put on the radiators—within a couple of minutes they had baked apples. No watches were permitted. Once a day, at about four o'clock in the afternoon, they were allowed to take their buckets outside and bury the contents.

Corporal Henson (Barney) was court-martialed. There is no record what his punishment was.

The man who contributed to keeping up Gerard Arnhold and Ernest Guter's morale was Lt. Alex Edmison. He lent each of them copies of the then current bestseller *Anthony Adverse*, a book with 1,224 pages. (This was one of the reasons why Arnhold later named his first son Anthony.)

Guter recalls: "I read it at least half a dozen times. Edmison was one of the nicest men I've ever met. I saw him again after the war in Montreal when Thomas Mann was invited to speak at McGill. I went up to him to introduce myself and I mentioned *Anthony Adverse*. He remembered me very well. He was one of the first Canadians to visit Bergen-Belsen. He showed us slides. I did not know then that my parents had died there."

Some time in late winter of 1940–41 Lt. Edmison received this undated and unsigned report:

> Particular exception must be taken to the attitude of the Camp Sergeant Major Macintosh ever since arrival. At the beginning the treatment was very strict and exacting but Major Griffin whose sense of justice was beyond reproach prevented occurrences which have become more and more frequent ever since. The C.S.M. endeavoured to live up to the standards set by Major Griffin without, however, commanding his sense of justice. Probably well-meant but inappropriate efforts to turn internees into Guards-men are bound to fail. Strictness arbitrarily applied, officers' orders continually countermanded the very moment they were given, rude and appalling language and indulgence in anti-Semitic remarks are particularly objectionable. The C.S.M. in fact openly tries to bully the internees by stress-

ing that he and he alone runs the camp, taking or threatening disciplinary action, such as barring internees from doing paid work for ninety days and the like, actions which are, it is believed, entirely outside his province. It is needless to say that the other members of the Provost Corps try to copy the C.S.M. whenever an opportunity arises. Such behavior and the ill-conceived idea to run this camp on strictly military lines only without giving any consideration to the status of the internees and the problems of the work programme give rise to unnecessary friction and tension; it is prejudicial to the morale of the camp and detrimental to the progress of its work.

There is no doubt that the sergeant-major's government, even if one tried to ignore it, had a depressing effect on all of us. The lack of privacy, the overcrowding, the sight of the two ugly railway sheds, the feeling of confinement, the constant rumors, and above all, the absence of any real hope for release, had taken their toll. We pursued our various activities, but suffered increasingly from a new disease we called *internitis*, the symptoms of which were a combination of despondency, touchiness, and worst of all, self-absorption and self-pity. From the point of view of the Canadian officers we were a sorry lot—bitching and proclaiming *ad nauseam*, "There has been some mistake, we are refugees, we are loyal to Britain and—we want to get out!"

Granted, these officers had to justify their existence, but they were free and we were not. As they could not accept our constant harping, they somehow had convinced themselves that in some way we must have deserved our confinement; consequently, we could not be as loyal to Britain as we constantly proclaimed we were.

On December 27, 1940, Captain J. A. Milne, the British intelligence officer, addressed an open letter to us written in German, probably translated for him by one of the internees.

I want to help you. I don't think you understand at all the situation you are in, and I'm perfectly prepared to sit down with some of you individually to tell you what is on my mind. I don't appreciate your attitude towards England. You don't seem to realize that England has saved you from a tortured existence and certain death by giving you shelter. Nor do you seem to realize that it is customary to intern enemy aliens at the outbreak of a war. Did you not know that in England three men have recently been executed who had posed as refugees? They had been Hitler's spies. And I myself have come across two cases here in Canada of men who were 25 percent Jewish and were exposed as Nazi agents.

You are complaining because life is not comfortable for you. It's still far more comfortable than for hundreds of thousands of Englishmen. Why are you so bitter? Because you were deported? Would you prefer to live in England, being bombed every day, having to observe the blackout, and live on rations? You are full of egoism and self-pity. You don't hesitate to write letters of lamentation to bombed Britain and neutral America, in order to throw a false light on British measures regarding you. If women receive these letters, they will have to reply that you should be more manly!

You must realize that there is only one thing that counts, and that is the war—a war Britain is fighting not least to preserve Jewish equality and to gain respect for Jews.

Those of you who agree with me should do their best to enlighten those who don't. If there are some in your group who won't see the errors of their ways, tell your leaders. If that won't help, let me know. This is not a matter of betraying your comrades. It is simply a sensible thing to do. No one who has good will and is prepared to listen has anything to fear.

I have only one guideline: anyone who is against England is for Hitler. Anybody who is against England is against Humanity.

No doubt Milne's references to the three executions in England and the apprehension of Nazi agents in Canada were made in good faith. But he had been misinformed. No such events had taken place.

However simplistic his open letter may have been, it was motivated by honest conviction and genuine impatience and irritation caused by our sanctimonious and righteous attitudes. We may have deeply resented it, but we could not deny that the lecture was at least partially deserved. After all, like us, he was a European. Some of our Canadian officers were a little less sophisticated. An officer in Camp T in Trois Rivières comes to mind; a day or two after our arrival he declared, "I'm told some of you think you would like to stay in Canada. All I can say about

William Heckscher, 1941.

Gregory Baum, 1941.

Four pictures reproduced from the Montreal Standard of February 7, 1942. *Above left.* Creative leisure on the Ile aux Noix. *Above right.* A demonstration of loyalty. *Left.* We make camouflage nets. *Opposite.* Hut meeting in Camp I. *Courtesy, Montreal Standard.*

Constance Hayward.
*Courtesy, Hyndman
Photography, Ottawa.*

Senator Cairine R. Wilson.
*National Photography
Collection, Public Archives,
Canada.*

Saul Hayes.

Lieutenant-Colonel R.S.W.
Fordham. *Public Archives,
Canada*.

Alexander Paterson. *Bassano and Vandyke Studios, London, England.*

Hanfstaengl Senior and Junior in Bush Hill, Virginia, 1942.

Hans Kahle Memorial Stamp issued in 1946
by the East German Democratic Republic.

Our toolmakers at Machinery Service Limited, Ville LaSalle, Quebec, 1943.

that is that the only way you can stay in Canada is six feet underground."

After our arrival in Sherbrooke, one of the officers summoned our two rabbis, Emil Fackenheim and Heinz Fischel. "You fellows are men of the cloth. You must have some sense. Tell me what this fuss is all about." Fackenheim told him that we were not worried about minor inconveniences which were due to wartime conditions—these we were quite prepared to accept. "However," he continued, "we are concerned with our dignity, to be recognized as refugees. Many of us have been in German concentration camps."

"Oh," said the officer, "you've been in a camp before? In that case you must know how to behave in the presence of an officer. Kindly stand at attention."

The New Commandant

After Major Griffin suffered his coronary thrombosis on December 7, 1940, he was succeeded, at first as acting commandant, by Major W. J. A. Ellwood, a much younger man from Montreal. His blue eyes and little mustache made him look like a British officer from the First World War. He left the running of the camp to the sergeant-major, but to judge from his *Journal* of February 22, 1941, he had his own views of the internees:

> In spite of the fact that a certain percentage may be heartily anti-Nazi, it cannot be forgotten that they are German-born Jews. Jews still retain the same instincts they had nineteen hundred and forty years ago and these in particular are very apt to try and take advantage of privileges which if once given result in demands for more.
>
> The combination of this insidious instinct and the well-known characteristics of the German habit of breaking every pledge ever made, is not a particularly easy way to handle except by maintaining strict discipline and rigid enforcement of Camp rules and regulations.

NINE

The Camp Experience

Learning Behind Barbed Wire

There were many inspiring educators in the camps who had a lasting influence on the lives of our young people, of whom more than 30 percent were under twenty. The schooling of most of them had been interrupted.

After the ordeal of Nazism and the difficulties of refugee life in England, the camps provided a perfect learning opportunity, especially since we had a plethora of teaching talent—a talent not only available for formal teaching once the schools had been established but, just as important, also for informal discussions and lectures. For example, few of us who participated in a seminar on the Italian Renaissance by the art historian Dr. Otto Demus will ever forget it, and similarly, the lectures given by Wolfgang von Einsiedel on the French Revolution made an indelible impression on us. Von Einsiedel had been a well-known journalist at the *Vossische Zeitung* in Berlin and was a charismatic lecturer. To this day Gregory Baum remembers his definition of revolution: "The violent revelation of circumstances which are already in a state of transition." In a later stage of internment, even Major Kippen, who had been an investment broker in private life, gave some lectures. His subject: stocks and bonds.

The academic talent assembled in Kippen's camp—Farnham—exceeded that of many Canadian universities. Among them was the embryologist Johannes Holtfreter, whose teaching career before the war had included positions at the Kaiser Wilhelm Institut in Berlin and an associate professorship at the University of Munich. In 1939 he had become a researcher at the Zoological Institute at Cambridge. Kurt Swinton, a man of considerable organizational abilities and seemingly unlimited energy, was another leading figure in the administration of the Farnham school. A qualified radio engineer, he gave highly entertaining lectures on popular science, including atomic theory.

Two outstanding teachers were Alfons Rosenberg in Camp B and William Heckscher in Camp A. Rosenberg had been a teacher in Germany, and later in England. He arrived in 1937 at Cranbrook School in Kent; I had left shortly before, having spent two years at that school. Again, in internment, we failed to meet; we were never in the same camp. But repeatedly I heard enthusiastic accounts of his initiative in establishing the camp school and his devotion to it. The same is true of William Heckscher. (We were on the *Ettrick* and in Camp L together, but we did not meet until after our release.)

Although several outside committees were instrumental in setting up the camp schools, one of the chief animators was Dale Brown of the Y.M.C.A., the Canadian representative of the European Student Relief Fund (E.S.R.F.). He worked closely with Dr. Jerome Davis of the Y.M.C.A.'s War Prisoners Aid. Both men regularly visited the camps.

Dale Brown's encouragement and assistance were exemplary. He became a personal friend of many internees after they had been released, and kindly sent me an illuminating essay by his special friend, William Heckscher. Here are some excerpts:

> The fight for a tolerable atmosphere in which a *vita contemplativa* can prosper requires about 50 percent of your alertness. Rooms set aside for silence are an exception. There is usually a canteen, or a kitchen, or a piano which intrudes into your *Lebensraum*. "Private" study, in the sense a student outside would understand it, simply does not exist. I have, in eighteen months of internment, not had a single minute which I might have called my own, without outside disturbance. Vast areas of thought I had to shelve until the day of my liberation. Boethius could not have written his *Consolation* in a modern internment camp. Dante at best might have made copious notes.

How is it that students pass their exams all the same? How is it that they exchange views, imbibe their lectures, study their texts?

Whenever people said to me: well, there was nothing to distract their minds; no women, no outings, no financial worries, I felt insulted—simply because one doesn't like one's tribulations pettified *ex post*. Experience has taught me that the very fact that everything seems to be adverse to learning makes people study. Their road leads "uphill." But they feel proudly that the aims they achieve are the result of their own fight, their own will power. Each single student who studies in an internment camp is his own master in the first place; his coaches and teachers are the walls against which the pupil flings his mental "squash" balls.

On a hot summer afternoon I remember I had fallen asleep, when suddenly I awoke, sensing that there must be "something on." I turned round and saw ten boys assembled at the foot of my bunk, staring at me with sad eyes: I should have given them a lesson on *Twelfth Night*, and I had over-slept my time. It is the dynamic push on the part of the young students which carried along their teachers, and made them the happiest men in internment, because they were made to feel that they had a task to fulfil.

This is the one, internal, side of the picture. The two essential factors from without are the European Relief Fund and the Commandant of the Camp. The Commandant is the virtual ruler over the hundreds of souls under his jurisdiction. Our Commandant was silent, military, human and gentlemanly. What he did to assist the students was not laid down in any of the regulations, which only provide for discipline and the physical wellbeing of prisoners. It was he who set aside a special schoolroom within the compound, who worried about young men who were falling behind, who arranged for a regular "p.t." hour, who delegated a teacher to do the final invigilating, and who did all this at a time when the refugees under his care were still technically prisoners of war.

The European Student Relief Fund, in conjunction with the War Prisoners' Aid organization of the Y.M.C.A., provided books, and all the material on which studies depend, such as blackboards, chalk, pencils, exercise books, table lamps. Examination fees were paid and every single wish was followed up with meticulous care. To those helpers as well as the ones who made their help possible by contributing to their funds, a constant feeling of gratitude radiated, as it were, from within the barbed wire. Only a few had a chance of voicing their gratitude individually. I am sure that every single man who profited by those gifts was somehow aware of the thrill that lies in help given by unknown people to unknown people. Surely, these material gifts and facilities are the *conditio sine qua non* of spiritual life in the camps.

There was something else, which only a few were privileged to enjoy: the imponderable gift of human contact with a civilian who was not part of the ubiquitous conformity. The fact that one could sit down over a cup of coffee and discuss almost at leisure one's problems and cares, was a source of strength. The fact, moreover, that one was allowed to write letters to the representative of the E.S.R.F. was an unfathomable boon.

William Heckscher was a remarkable figure. He was the ideal headmaster. The adjective with which several Old Boys of the Farnham Camp School described him was "elegant." He had grace, style, and patience.

One of Heckscher's early childhood memories was that of his grandfather, a mathematician and astronomer who taught French prisoners of war during the First World War. The family lived near Potsdam in Germany, and his grandfather ran some sort of gardening estate on which one hundred French *poilus* were employed. "They used to come dressed in their French uniforms, and in the evening my grandfather would lecture to them in French; they took feverish notes," Heckscher remembers. "I was a young boy at the time. Like everything in life that's good, my work in Farnham was just imitation. Being progressive is always resuming an old tradition. Nothing is renewed which hasn't existed before."

The story of the Farnham Camp School began with a visit to the commandant by one of Canada's most distinguished educators, Dr. H. M. Tory. He arrived as an emissary of Toronto's Canadian National Committee on Refugees. At seventy-six, and supposedly retired, he had been president of the Khaki University at the end of the First World War, president of the University of Alberta and then of the National Research Council. He was still to mastermind the conversion of

Ottawa's Carleton College into Carleton University. In fact, he was *the* grand old man of Canadian education. Having been on the faculty of McGill University as a mathematician, he had excellent contacts there, especially with the registrar, T. H. Matthews. At Matthews' instigation and that of the Jewish committee in Montreal, the students from all the camps were able to take the McGill matriculation exams with the full support of their commandants.

William Heckscher recalls Dr. Tory's visit. "One night I was fast asleep. To my horror one of the guards came into my hut, tapped me on the shoulder, and said the commandant wanted to see me. When I came out of the hut the fog was so thick I could hardly see the guard walking ahead of me. In the commandant's office sat an old man. He asked Major Kippen whether the prisoner spoke English. 'Yes,' replied Kippen. As I was very sleepy I asked him whether he would mind terribly if I sat down. Kippen didn't think this was such a good idea, but the old man said, 'Yes, please sit down,' so it was very difficult for Kippen to say no. I sat down, and he turned to me to ask whether I knew why he was there. I said no. It was because of the fog, he explained. 'I am Dr. Tory,' he said, 'and I have a taxi full of books waiting outside. I am on my way to the military camp.' Major Kippen interrupted Dr. Tory, 'Oh, no, don't mention that.' Then he turned to me: 'You're not supposed to know that there is a military camp nearby.'

"I didn't know and frankly I didn't care. Dr. Tory went on to ask me about our school, whether we had pencils and writing gear. I said, 'Well, we make do, but it could be better. The real trouble is that we don't know what to prepare for. We need to know about university admissions, examinations, and so on.' Well, Dr. Tory was marvellous. The fog had turned out to be a highly profitable fog. He had been sent by Heaven."

Spectacular results were achieved at the Farnham school. In June 1941, forty-two of our students, some of whom had learned English only recently, passed their junior matriculation; one of them, we were told, received the highest marks in the province of Quebec.

"My life was changed in Farnham," Gregory Baum told me. Never having done well at school in Germany and having had no schooling whatsoever while he was in England, he attended a few classes at the camp school but couldn't keep up, especially in mathematics and physics.

Baum went to see Bill Heckscher. "I don't think I can do it," he told him. Heckscher smiled. "I don't believe that. Find yourself somebody to help you," he said. "So I found somebody and that's how I got into the school system. Several of us turned to the sciences, not because we thought we were necessarily gifted in that area, but in camp we found out that scientists were part of an international world. The scientists who had been kicked out of Germany were able to carry on their work in another country more easily than the humanists. The lawyers were particularly helpless; but science is international. The whole thing was a great experience. We discovered the manifold meaning of things. Later on I graduated in mathematics and physics."

The other camp schools also flourished. In September 1941 the Sherbrooke Camp School Board listed the following classes:

A) Junior Matriculation Class (enrolled: 27)
   (26 periods per week of 40 minutes each)

B) Senior Matriculation Class (enrolled: 14)
   (6 periods per week of 45 minutes each: not yet fully organized)

C) Engineering Class (enrolled: 19)
   (24 periods per week of 50 minutes each)

D) Education Plan (usual attendance of 50 and more)
   (6 periods per week of 50 minutes each)
   (providing serial lectures on selected topics for those juniors not participating in either A, B or C)

E) Evening Lectures (total attendance per week 140 approximately)
   (35 periods per week of 50 minutes each)

F) Vocational Training Classes (wood and metal work) (enrolled: 22)
   (4 periods per week of one hour each for theoretical instruction)

G) Musical Circle (to be started in October) (enrolled: approximately 50)
   (1 period per fortnight of one hour each)

The Sherbrooke Engineering School had a teaching staff of eight: university professors and graduate students. The syllabus included classes in advanced mathematics, mechanics, thermodynamics, strength of materials, theory of machines, property of materials, machine drawing, descriptive geometry, physics and chemistry.

Twenty-five students were also enrolled in agricultural studies, for which Macdonald College of McGill University provided valuable assistance and guidance.

To write their matriculation exams our students had to travel to Camp S on St. Helen's Island in Montreal, and Heckscher usually went along. Once Dale Brown even arranged a dance for the boys at a Jewish club, on the evening following the exams. Heckscher and the boys were driven to the club in trucks, accompanied by the guards with their bayonets fixed, ready for any emergency. Josef Eisinger was one of the boys who attended the party. Here are excerpts from his diary:

Sunday, September 21, 1941
Since my last entry many important things have happened. It all started on September 7. We went to Camp S where we were heartily welcomed by the Italians. There we met 23 candidates from Camp I, some of whom we already knew from Camp B. During the exams I acted as assistant invigilator and secretary to Dr. Heckscher. The Italians were very nice indeed, though most of them were fascists.

But the real thing started on Wednesday at three thirty. At that time we went by bus to an exquisite club in Montreal. After an interesting ride through the city we arrived at the Montefiore Club and all our expectations were surpassed when we met—*girls* there. We had a gorgeous evening, excellent supper on *table-cloths*, and *china-plates* and *cups*. We were served by *waiters, butlers* and *maids* and the whole thing seemed like a dream to us. Some ladies from the Committee were also there, and a few lucky ones of our boys found sponsors . . . It was the most interesting evening I have ever spent. But it is better to keep the impressions in one's mind than to write them down.

After the supper at the Montefiore Club two guards took Heckscher aside and whispered to him, "It's time to go to the whores." So he walked with them to the red light district and left them there, after arranging to meet again later at a certain corner on St. Catherine Street.

Heckscher meanwhile went to a little café, had a cup of tea, wrote a letter and mailed it to his brother who was serving in the United States Army at the time. (Later he found out that his letter was subsequently retrieved from the mailbox by Mounties in plain clothes; obviously they had been following him.)

He then bought a copy of *Life* magazine and waited for the two guards to reappear. They were late; when they did show up they were both drunk. "Somehow we found our way back to the camp on St. Helen's Island," Heckscher recalls. "The commandant was furious with all of us, and threatened me with a court-martial for trying to escape."

Back in Farnham, Heckscher was summoned to Major Kippen's office. "Trying to protect the guards, I took the blame. When Kippen declared in a not altogether convincing voice that I would be court-martialled, I asked him, 'What does that mean? I am not familiar with these strange English words.' Kippen chided me for not taking the matter seriously; 'This isn't a joke,' he said. But by that time we were on such good terms that I was even allowed to sit down in his presence. At the end of our interview Kippen said to me, 'You know, Heckscher, I wish I could send my two sons to your school.'"

The Flowering of the Arts

Camp B in New Brunswick was the first to put on a major theatrical production. On January 23, 1941, they performed George Bernard Shaw's *Androcles and the Lion*. Before then they had staged various reviews and cabarets, and while we were at Camp L (Quebec) we even had a D.E.O. (Director of Entertainment Operations) to organize similar artistic endeavors.

But a three-act play, with sets, costumes, and original music, required much more. It could only be undertaken if there was some measure of stability; it required that neither the director nor any of the actors and designers would expect to be released to go to the United States or return to England during rehearsals. (Remaining in Canada was not yet a real possibility.) In short, such a venture presumed abandoning the hopes of attaining imminent freedom as well as a ready response to Freddy Grant's imperative "You'll Get Used to It!"

The man who had chosen *Androcles and the Lion* was John Newmark; it was a brilliant choice. Not only did the play contain numerous parallels between the absurdity of our internment and Shaw's satirical depiction of Christian virtues, but it also had the advantage of requiring no more than two female parts— Lavinia, the wife of the gentle, animal-loving tailor Androcles who manages to tame the lion, and Megaera, the "pampered slattern." There was no shortage of talents to play Magaera, the lion, the gladiators, Christian martyrs, and a Roman centurion, for which the sergeant-major was the perfect model, but it was difficult to find the right Lavinia.

Fortunately it wasn't a large part. Eventually, Hans Schindler, a very young boy, played her, wearing a bedsheet as a kind of Roman toga. The performance was a great success.

Another Shaw production, *Man of Destiny*, a play about Napoleon, gave the young professional actor Anton Diffring a chance to play the unnamed lady. It was deliberately performed in German, so that the officers would not be offended by Shaw's diatribes against the English; according to one witness, this was the reason why the play was chosen.

Then there was the production of *Faust* in the Camp B Recreation Hut. The absence of a suitable boy to play Gretchen caused a trickier problem. It was decided to present her voice only. When Faust first meets her in church, and later in her home, she was simply heard, through an open door. It was not hard to cast a suitable falsetto voice to speak her lines. Nor was it hard to depict God in the *Prologue in Heaven*. A piece of board was removed from the false ceiling in the recreation hut and an actor was installed above it under the roof; the Divine Voice came booming through the gap.

Two plays with all-male casts were *Journey's End* by Robert C. Sherriff and *The First Legion* by the American playwright Emmet Lavery; the latter takes place in a monastery, and the leading role of Reverend Paul Duquesne, S.J., again was played by Anton Diffring.

Other productions were: *Oliver Cromwell* in Camp I and *The Green Cockatoo* by Arthur Schnitzler in Camp B. John Newmark had to be stabbed at the end of the play and had to topple down a flight of iron stairs. In Camp A, *The Proposal* by Anton Chekhov was performed. The director was Gerhard Hintze, another professional actor. Anton Diffring played the lead.

According to Franz Kraemer's review, the fact that Fuerstenheim, the author of a parody on Hoffmannsthal's *Tor und Tod*, had been a pig-breeder in England "made his play still better." It was performed in Camp A.

If theatrical productions called for monumental efforts on the part of designers, carpenters, tailors, directors, actors and prompters, making music required nothing but talent, a few instruments and some rehearsal space. There was no shortage of talent. Camp B alone had nineteen pianists, including John Newmark, Wolfgang Gerson, Harry Coleman and Len Bergé. Willi Amtmann played the violin, and Carl Amberg the cello. There were flautists and accordion players. The Canadian Red Cross and the Y.M.C.A. generously donated a good supply of instruments and sheet music.

In Sherbrooke we had Gerhard Kander, a promising young violin virtuoso with an amazing technique, who all day could be found practicing in the boiler room. Since all the musicians were excused from routine duties, he spent the time when he was not practicing reading detective stories and studying law books. Another violinist of remarkable talent was Hans Kaufman, an admirable exponent of Mozart and Beethoven. He could also play lilting Viennese airs, which delighted even the most dour Prussians. A genius by the name of Paul Huber had such a remarkable musical memory that he scored the orchestral parts for the D-Minor piano concerto by Mozart from the piano solo part alone. He wrote it for two violins, two flutes, a viola and cello as no other instruments were available in the camp. John Newmark, whose memory in contrast to Huber's was so bad that he had to sight-read "God Save the King," then performed the concerto, with Huber conducting. Another outstanding contributor to the musical life was Walter Stiasny. He had been conductor and coach at the Vienna State Opera, and professor at the Music Academy.

Many of us had a richer musical life behind barbed wire than we had before or after internment. I cannot ever hear the *Wandererfantasie* by Schubert or the F-Minor *Ballade* by Chopin without thinking of Helmut Blume practicing these pieces in the little lean-to in Shed A in Sherbrooke. We had, in Camp L, heard him play the D-Minor *Toccata and Fugue* by Bach-Tausig on an upright with two keys missing.

Once John Newmark had arrived in Sherbrooke there were two great pianists under one roof—Blume, the romantic virtuoso, and Newmark, the elegant, polished chamber-musician. We, the audience, endlessly discussed their respective styles. Whenever the two played together the event was comparable to a Stanley Cup play-off game.

Our officers often attended our concerts and were so impressed by the variety and quality of music they heard that they frequently commandeered the musicians to play during Sunday dinner at the mess. These performances were in addition to the sergeant-major's requests to provide music for his Saturday night entertainments. Shortly after Newmark was released, he gave a concert in Sherbrooke together with Adolf Busch and Rudolf Serkin; Sergeant-Major Macintosh appeared backstage afterwards, slapped Newmark on the back, beaming with pride that one of his "prisoners" had risen so high! I am afraid Newmark acknowledged the salute with minimal grace.

On December 7, 1941, Newmark and his friends were listening to a broadcast of Artur Rubinstein playing the *Emperor Concerto* in Carnegie Hall. Someone burst into the hut, shouting, "The Japanese have bombed Pearl Harbor! Now the Americans will be in the war!" Newmark hushed him and whispered, "Quiet please. The war will go on for a long time, but Rubinstein is an old man. Who knows how long we'll still be able to listen to him!"

In the visual arts the dominating figure was Oscar Cahen, a skilled and humorous illustrator and commercial artist who during the later stages of his internment managed to sell some of his work to the *Montreal Standard.* No one could have predicted then that he would later become one of Canada's leading abstract expressionists and co-founder of Painters Eleven. Had anyone told him then that his works would one day be part of the National Gallery's collection in Ottawa, he would have uttered his unforgettable, high-pitched laugh. Some detected his talent early. Reviewing an art exhibition in Camp L, Dr. Otto Demus observed that it was difficult to categorize Cahen's

"Allerweltstalent" ("universal talent"). "Decorative improvisation," he wrote, "seems to be the centre of his bubbly-spirited gift. The 'real' Cahen appears more in his 'Jazz band' drawings than in the somewhat facile portraits." Cahen also was a superb raconteur and all-round wit, who as an artist inspirited disciples such as Jerry Waldstein and Egon Reich. Robert Langstadt was already established as a serious painter and, though essentially a solitary figure, exercised considerable influence on many of his camp admirers.

The Gay Life
The absence of women had a very predictable influence on the lives of many inmates. The only way in which we could have heterosexual love affairs was in our fantasies. But no fantasy at all was required to have affairs with men: we were surrounded by potential male love-objects who were all too real. Father Anton Ummenhofer in Farnham wrote in his diary—no doubt with a shudder—that as many as 50 percent of the camp had succumbed to homosexual love. Whatever the figure, it became higher in direct proportion to the duration of our imprisonment.

By far the greatest number of love affairs were between men who before and after internment were perfectly straight. If you had played a policeman in a play, as one of my friends had done, and you celebrated your triumph at a party in Hut 4 after opening night, you probably could not take your hands off the boy who had played and looked exactly like Mitzi, the luscious chambermaid.

As to the urgency of our libido, to keep it within bounds we were convinced that bromide was added to our soup, or possibly our coffee. It was perhaps this widespread assumption of the use of chemicals that served as an explanation why many of us found our libido surprisingly docile and relatively easy to sublimate.

Of course, there was a small number of men who had been gay before their internment, and some of them may have had to leave Germany or Austria for that very reason.

Harold Frye told me that when he was camp leader he found the homosexuals to be "by far the best behaved and most charming people." Martin Fischer, leader in Camp I, had to deal with one of the cooks who had been discovered having some sort of homosexual relationship. "I was surprised by the vehemence of the response," he told me, "because somehow people began to associate homosexual practices in the kitchen with food. It became an explosive issue, and the demand was made for the cook to be removed from the kitchen. This was one of those situations where it was difficult to restore reason through objectively orientated discussion."

Astute observers of the camps' political scene told me that communists objected to homosexuals for ideological reasons. On one occasion they held a much publicized trial that ended in the condemnation of two boys. As punishment they were ordered to fight each other "until there was a bloody mess." Others felt that the homosexuals were accepted both by the extreme left and by the extreme right with equal equanimity.

In one or two camps, special areas were "reserved" for gay activities, divided from the rest by blankets, particularly so in the later stages of internment when the practice was widespread and more generally accepted. Couples lived together. Older men found it prestigious to be seen with young boys. There were some violently jealous fights, and some young boys who sold themselves.

For some these goings-on were deeply repugnant and they made every effort to protect the young from being exploited. One man who felt particularly strongly about this was our *Muskelzwerg* (muscle dwarf), a man of singular physical strength and compact size who had survived a German concentration camp by keeping physically and spiritually fit through efforts of intense concentration. He became a one-man morality squad, making the rounds at night and shining a flashlight into the faces of men and boys whom he found in bed together. He wouldn't leave until the couple had separated. The *Muskelzwerg* was a jiu jitsu expert. (After the war he taught jiu jitsu to the Montreal police force.)

Once he stopped an older man just as he was about to climb into bed with a young boy. The older man, who had acquired the nickname *Fassadenkletterer* (climber of facades, or cat burglar) because he had been a professional at this game in Germany, had not met the *Muskelzwerg* before. In two moves our dwarf laid him out flat and, for the moment at least, the boy's honor was saved.

Climbing in and out of other people's beds also preoccupied a humorless Freudian analyst in Farnham, a handsome man with just the right beard. His efforts to protect the young proved to be largely useless because instead of listening to them—which one would have thought was his trade—he gave them sex lectures full of psychoanalytical jargon, triggering much merriment behind his back and achieving no positive results whatsoever.

In the end there was only one therapy which worked—girls.

Ordination

In the Priests' Hut in Farnham a curtain divided the sleeping area from the chapel where thirty Roman Catholic priests and lay brothers had put up altars; the lay brothers had decorated the chapel with beautiful carvings and colorful embroideries. On some days early Mass was celebrated at five o'clock in the morning. The only non-Catholic among them was Abraham Poljak, a Christian writer with a Jewish background, who later called the hut "the most original monastery in the possession of the Catholic Church." He described his stay with the priests as "one of the most blessed in my life. . . . They came from all sections of Germany, from the working, peasant and middle classes. Not once did we quarrel. The harmony between us demonstrated that even under the strain of forced imprisonment and taut nerves one can live together productively if there is mutual tolerance and human decency."

One of the priests in the hut was Anton Ummenhofer, a twenty-seven-year-old theology student. Born in Bavaria, he had joined the Order of the Salvatorians at twenty-one. He intended to become a missionary in China. In 1937 he was sent to England to continue his studies and to keep him out of reach of the Nazis. From then until 1940 he studied at Christleton Hall in Chester. He was interned on May 16, one week before he was to have been ordained. Here are some extracts from his diary:

> *Thursday, April 17, 1941*: I had just come from the factory and was sitting at tea, when P. Philibert came over and said,

"Annuntio tibi gaudium magnum!" (I proclaim to thee great joy!) I was jolted; I knew what the joyful message was and yet I could hardly believe it. But it was true: on May 18 I am to be ordained priest. Oh, at last, I believe the most difficult part of my life has been endured. Everything faded like shadows and the sun was inside me, sun was in the camp, sun was in the factory. I kept singing the *Magnificat* and the *Te Deum* at work, both at the same time, over and over. Everything is new, happy and strong inside me. I am going to become a priest of Christ, in fetters, prisoner of Christ.

Thursday, May 8: Today Major Chaplain Chartier came. He confirmed that I "must wear a sign," i.e., of being a prisoner, at the ordination. So now I will walk to the altar at the holy ordination in fetters, in the shameful attire of imprisonment: the trousers with the red stripe! Behold them with the eyes of faith . . . !

May 21, 1941: The night before last was a very restless one for me. I couldn't sleep, I was more excited than I was willing to admit. The spring morning was splendid after the rain; nature was fairly glowing in finery of the most splendid colors; it was like the Garden of Eden after the Almighty had just created it. At around seven the guard came to fetch us; we went through the gates, gave over our "dog tags" and waited in front of the last gate for our "first-class carriage." Then they came with the delivery trucks on which they carry out the camp garbage. But they had laid mattresses on the metal benches. . . . The truck was full of water and filth. We climbed into it and the guards came in after us. . . . Yet, there was jubilation in my soul: we were on our way to the altar, to the longed-for goal of my life.

My blue and red trousers, the truck, our guards—everything was more than merely incidental, everything had deep significance. I experienced here what is so seldom experienced: the thought that is expressed in the ordination itself: *"Agnoscite, quod agitis; imitamini, quod tractatis!"* (Acknowledge what you are doing; imitate what you do!) We who daily commemorate the death of the Lord, we should come to resemble Him both in our internal and external lives. Didn't it look a little like this on the way to the execution? . . .

There was inexpressible jubilation in my heart, and ardent prayers of thanks rose from my soul, out of the delivery truck. Eventually we arrived at the convent. It was a girls' high school, connected to a convent of the nuns of Notre Dame de Namur. We climbed out of the truck and were greeted by the local priest. I glanced up at the facade of the building; in spite of all the solemnity of the occasion I had to laugh. The girls had been locked in and we were now being stared at by a hundred curious girls looking through the blinds. Is the whole world a prison? The reason was that the public had to be kept away; that was also why the chapel was deserted, not even the nuns were allowed to attend.

Major Green led us through the main entrance where two soldiers presented arms. We went up to the second floor and into the chapel. Exuberance overcame me, my heart was about to burst, I felt tears coming. We were going into the House of the Lord and approaching the moment for which I had been yearning with all my soul. *"Laetatus sum in his quae dicta sunt mihi, in Domum Domini ibimus"* (I am rejoiced in these things which have been said unto me; we shall enter into the House of the Lord). Everything was ready; the bishop was already waiting for us at the altar. First the confirmation sacrament was administered to some camp internees. Then I walked to the altar with the chasuble over my arm, and received the holy ordination as if in another world. Afterwards I administered my first blessing to some nuns and the escort in the sacristy. Major Green congratulated me. In the chapel the bishop conveyed the greetings of the Papal Nuncio in Ottawa, Msgr. Ildebrando Antoniutti, . . . and then presented me with a chalice as an oblation. After that we went back to the delivery truck and were returned to camp, where we were greeted with the hymn "This is the Day of the Lord." It was all very beautiful.

Abraham Poljak delivered an address on the occasion of Father Ummenhofer's ordination. Here are some excerpts from it:

> You will remember our last night on the Isle of Man. . . . We were in a big hall, a theatre. We were miserable. From the stage every one of us was called to come up . . . to receive our papers. Most of us were exhausted and hungry: we were sitting or lying on the floor. I was in a corner and watched the goings-on. Suddenly a curious thought occurred to me, like the thought of a man who in a dream or in a vision sees a

scene of the future, and then—after a certain time—finds himself in the situation which he had foreseen. I asked myself what could have been in my mind in happier times some years earlier when I envisioned the scene in that hall on the Isle of Man? Very quickly I answered my own question; I would have thought I was watching an English military comedy. The idea that the officers who gave us our papers were not actors but real officers and we were not theatre-goers . . . but prisoners about to be sent across the ocean—this idea would never have occurred to me. . . . Life writes comedies and tragedies, and tragi-comedies, which even the most imaginative playwright could never invent.

And here we are, ten months later. When I see the peaceful picture in front of me, the beautiful altars, the magnificent vestments, the golden chalices, the richly-laden tables, and around the tables twenty-five men of the cloth, I ask myself the same question: what would have been in my mind when I envisioned this scene? . . . How could I possibly have imagined I would be in a corner of a prisoners' hall in Canada? Only God can think up such enterprises. Only God can convert a prison into a temple— not only in the days of St. Paul but in our own days, in a Canadian internment camp. The military comedy has become a *Divina Commedia*, a display of divine power and wisdom, love and mercy.

We look back now to our misery on the Isle of Man, and we say *May God be thanked!* As in Noah's ark He has carried us through the Great Flood of our days, and through mortal dangers, and He has chosen one of His elect to become His priest. I ask myself: was it not worthwhile to have had to endure one year's imprisonment to become His instrument in the exercise of His power in the world, and to serve Him in a unique demonstration of faith?

The Party Line

In ideological terms the hut furthest away from the priests' was the one housing the communist leadership. In none of the camps did they amount to more than a handful, though in the minds of the military authorities—and of some right-wing internees— there were large numbers of them. Clear distinctions must be made between the leaders, the more sizeable numbers of left-wing intellectuals, and the rank and file of relatively uneducated and often militant merchant seamen.

Throughout the thirties it was hard not to admire the communists' courage and tenacity in their fight against the Nazis. Jews had no option but to be against the Nazis, but non-Jews had a choice. Communists, for example, who went to Spain to fight the fascists had risked their lives for their beliefs, while most of us had endured Nazi persecution without being able to put up much of a fight. In any case, Jews, as individuals, hardly ever belonged to organizations such as political parties or trade unions that could have backed them up. Our dilemma was not between passivity and resistance; it was whether to stay, hoping to survive the dark days, or to leave.

The willingness to act rather than to endure, even if it meant risking one's life, gave communists a certain heroic quality at the time. Their difficulty, however, was that they had to come to terms with the party line which dictated a degree of cooperation with the Nazis, thanks to the Molotov-Ribbentrop Pact. How to overcome this difficulty was the subject of endless soul-searching and much talk. In the end, it all resolved itself when Germany invaded Russia on June 22, 1941, and the communists became our allies.

From the Canadian authorities' point of view, this latest turn of events was of minor concern because from the very beginning they had been far more worried about the communists than about Nazis in the camps. Invariably, the communists were in the forefront of those making demands, *for* recognition of the refugee status, *against* the use of prisoner of war stationery, *against* sites "unfit for human habitation," *against* mail delays, *for* receiving radios and newspapers, and so on. Communists were activists and trouble-makers; the few Nazis in our camps behaved like lambs.

A much stronger reason for the official dislike and actual fear of the communist element was the fact that throughout the twenties and thirties the Canadian political and military establishments had violently opposed "the Red Menace." On more than one occasion the camp intelligence officers had been instructed by our commandants to gather information about the communists, so as to be ready to deal with them, if necessary.

On May 27, 1941 Captain F. W. Staff had reported to Major

Kippen that the communists had "an excellent organization in Camp A . . . issuing exact directions on how to act and react and their orders must be followed. Few in this group are willing to admit or agree that they are communists: they declare that they are 'social-thinking people,' but their social thinking is similar to the attitude the Nazis take regarding their new 'Social Order in Europe.'"

In Camp B in New Brunswick a nucleus of disciplined party organizers, some of whom had worked together in a communist youth club in the London suburb of Hampstead before the war, made considerable efforts to woo and win young minds for their cause. Among them were Dr. Georg Honigmann, who had been one of the foremost theoreticians of the Austrian Communist Party, and Jeno Kostmann, who acted as a kind of Marxist guru. Young people would gather around him and question him on ideology or history; he would sit down with them for many hours to give them his careful answers. Strangely enough, he always seemed to have money without actually working for it and somehow managed to extricate himself from all compulsory work schemes. Rightly or wrongly, it was generally believed that he was being financed by the Party, although, who knows, he may have had a rich aunt in New York.

You had to be invited to attend the formal debates. Invariably, the organizers managed to "abstract" coffee (with whipped cream) and cakes from the kitchen. These debates were modeled along the lines of medieval disputations: the antagonists of communism were usually the social democrats, not the capitalists. In other words, they were *within* the left. The most skilled debater on the side of the social democrats was Dr. Bruno Weinberg, a brilliant international lawyer, who in the later stages of internment fell into disfavor with Ottawa because the officials there were unable to answer the numerous legal briefs he addressed to them. But many remember him more vividly during the early days of camp life when cigarettes were hard to come by; he was ever ready "to give a kingdom for a stub."

When Hans Kahle passed through Camp B in mid-December on his way back to England, he was welcomed in a manner comparable to the reception given General Montgomery in Trafalgar Square following the battle of El Alamein. There were several veterans of the Spanish Civil War in the camp, among others Alfred Hrejsemnou, whose occupation was listed on the official record as "professional officer, Republican Spanish Army." It is not surprising that many boys in their late teens who had been too young for political experience before internment were deeply impressed by the display of anti-fascist courage, idealism, intellectual vigor, discipline and determination. They were converted to the cause during their internment, and remained overtly or covertly loyal for many years after their release.

The chief rivals for the conquest of young minds were the men who were running the camp schools. If these also were men of religion, or at least men who had a feeling for religion, then they became obvious targets for the communists.

On Christmas Eve, 1940, Alfons Rosenberg went to a service. He was not a Christian, but had often attended midnight Mass in Germany and found it a moving experience. Coming back to his hut in a solemn mood in the early hours of the morning, he found the Christmas tree decorated with carrots and empty condensed milk cans. "I immediately knew the communists had done it," he said. He furiously tore these things off the tree, deliberately making a lot of noise.

The next day he was hauled before the leaders in the communist hut. He was asked to defend his action. Rosenberg welcomed the opportunity. A great ideological trial followed. One of the communist lawyers told him that it was men like him who were responsible for the Nazis. Rosenberg was magnificent in his defense of liberal values. He told me that he had been a communist for a short time in his youth, and had taught in Berlin at the Karl Marx Schule. He was familiar with the arguments. . . . It was a great occasion.

In Camp L in Quebec, Rabbi Emil Fackenheim also had an unpleasant encounter with communists. It happened shortly before we were moved to Sherbrooke. Somebody informed him that two suspected Nazis had gone to the commandant and told him that since the communists were about to take over the camp university, *they* should be allowed to do so instead. The suspected Nazis happened to be Protestant ministers. "You're a rabbi," Fackenheim's friend said. "Surely the commandant will trust you as much as two suspect Protestant clergymen. *You* should undertake to run the university."

Fackenheim agreed. "So I went to the commandant," he told me. "He seemed to find me kosher. That was the only time in my life I was a university president.... A week or so later a boy came to see me, 'I take this course in math and they teach me Marx,' he said. I really got scared. I realized the communists had pulled a fast one. They had used me. But I couldn't report them to the commandant. I didn't know what to do. Fortunately fate came to my assistance. Within a week or so we moved to Sherbrooke. They came to see me to ask whether I wanted to be president of the university again. I said, 'No thanks. Once is enough.'"

Heckscher also had an ugly experience with communists. About three months after the camp school in Farnham had been established, the communists, consisting of about eighty tough merchant seamen, declared war on it. The camp school had ninety students, "but compared to the communists, they were," as he put it, "the sissies and the intellectuals." One day he heard that the communists "would get him" unless he stopped "that teaching business." A number of "strong men" in Heckscher's hut offered to protect him, but somehow a physical clash was avoided. On a previous occasion when they beat up someone, the victim had lost an eye. To see this in the right perspective, it must be emphasized that there were other teachers in the camp school who taught with Heckscher who were totally unaware of this and similar incidents, and who never had any trouble with communists.

To Heckscher this was particularly painful because the leader of the communists was a man he liked; Wilhelm Koenen, like Heckscher's father, had been a member of the Reichstag. "He was a Khomeini-like figure," he told me, "a mature, impressive man, dedicated and eloquent. We were both fishermen for men's souls."

Random Impressions
We who were interned may not be the best qualified to judge objectively in what way the years spent behind barbed wire affected us. But when asked, many confessed to having derived immeasurable benefit from the experience. However, there were those who felt it was "a dead period—a period cut out of our lives," which left behind a residue of utter blankness. A

number of older men told me they suffered so deeply during that time that they did not wish to be reminded of it. The causes for the suffering varied; some found the open-endedness intolerable: "It was worse than a prison term; the prisoner, unless he is in for life, knows the day when he will be free. We did not know. . . ." Some said that the absence of women was the most difficult thing to bear; others mentioned the lack of privacy, of never being by yourself—not even on the toilet.

Many found strength in their religious or political convictions. This was certainly true of the Catholic community and among the traditionally-minded Jews. Albert Pappenheim said, "If you're a religious Jew, you always have to overcome obstacles. So what's one or two more? Internment wasn't much of an obstacle to our development, because we continued doing the things we were doing anyway. I look upon the experience as a fascinating interlude in my life."

Emil Fackenheim had been in a German concentration camp. Speaking of the Canadian camps, he said:

> I must say I got depressed at times. In the concentration camp you had no time to get depressed. You had to survive. That was a full-time job. I always played games with myself. I would say, "I give the Nazis a week." Okay, you can stand it for a week. After that you say, "I give them two more weeks." Only once did I get really depressed. I noticed that out of 6,500 people only 250 were left. The next day I was one out of three to be released, a very small number. . . .
>
> Now, who played such games in our internment camps? Nobody. It wasn't necessary. One *could* live with the idea that one might have to stay there until after the end of the war.

We often tried to remind ourselves that in many ways our lives were the same as being in the army. We knew that much of army life was equally absurd and dehumanizing. But this argument never cut much ice. After all, a soldier is a free citizen, however constrained his life may be. Because we were so self-absorbed, we felt that the world had rejected us and we did not know where we belonged.

Yet, the conviction that we had every right to feel sorry for ourselves gave us much satisfaction, though of course we wouldn't admit it. At times, we may have considered ourselves morally superior to those who kept us behind barbed wire, and easily convinced ourselves that they were much worse than they really were. We were we, and they were they, the "Canadians." A chasm was between us, even if there were a number of officers whom we particularly liked and admired. There were also some guards with whom we made friends. Henry Kreisel remembers writing love letters for an illiterate but amiable guard in the wilds of New Brunswick.

Most of us feel that the years spent in this compression chamber between Europe and North America, between Hitler and the post-war world, taught us a great deal about ourselves and about the way a community works.

Each camp had a different flavor, but there were a few things they all had in common. Groups were formed in consonence with common interests and common backgrounds. Left-wing people stuck together; right-wing people stuck together. The Cambridge clique, to which I belonged, stuck together and was much disliked by many for their haughtiness and snobbish insistence on speaking English, in order to set themselves apart from the "mob" who spoke German. The orthodox, of course, stuck together. On one occasion a vain attempt was made to segregate the Austrians from the Germans in the hope of convincing the authorities that Austria had been overrun by the Nazis, and therefore they belonged to a different political group. "We should be released earlier than the Germans," the Austrians maintained. But the authorities did not notice any difference between the two species. They thought the important distinction was between the various religious groups. But, with the exception of the orthodox, religion was of little consequence to the way friendships and groups were formed.

For all of us camp provided an opportunity to meet men we probably would not have met outside. Where else could we have met a *Klettermaxe*—Max the Climber? His real name was Max Telling. He was a "Berlin Original" and had been a stunt-man for UFA films before the war. A whole chapter is devoted to his exploits in a book published in Berlin after the war;[23] one of these was his successful escape from a Canadian internment camp (his first attempt had failed) across the U.S. border, then back across into Alberta, and from there, through the Canadian and American Rockies to Hollywood, where old friends quickly found work for him. After the war he returned to his beloved Berlin where he continued his work in the movies.

Each camp had its "underworld"—its wheeler-dealers who gambled and engaged in shady practices, who bought and sold things, often in collusion with the guards. Some of these men openly admitted that they had been in trouble with the law in Germany and Austria. Victor Ross, the son of a Viennese lawyer, told me about one such man, a former client of his father's. In camp, Ross became his defense attorney, just as his father had been in Vienna. "He called me 'Herr Doktor,'" Ross recalls. "He was a crook, just as he had been a crook before. I was his spokesman, his 'mouth,' to use a slang word."

Many of us had never encountered such types before. Though each group stuck very much to itself, it was impossible to remain altogether immune. This had its special charm. It was like living in a small town, where everybody knew everybody else. If one had the right attitude, this could be a rewarding experience—for a little while.

For some of our younger people camp life provided an illuminating introduction into class awareness. Here is what Gregory Baum has to say on the subject:

> People were very conscious of where they came from. Class differences in Europe were not as much disguised as they are in North America. I mean working class people in Germany did not disguise the fact that they were working class. I remember very well the workers and the sailors in camp, how distant and fascinating their world was for me. As a child in Germany working class people had always been mysterious and attractive to me—and more powerful than the others—and they formed a whole other world to which I had no access. The same kind of mysteriousness I experienced with the sailors and the workers in camp. But my friends were middle-class, bourgeois people. . . . When we elected Count Friedrich von Lingen camp speaker, I remember how aghast the socialists were at the blindness of the middle-class that elected the Kaiser's grandson as their leader.

For all these reasons camp life provided new social insights for us, the children of the middle class. Franz Kraemer told me, "When I was interned I was an eccentric young artist who never had paid much attention to the social and political aspects of life. It was in camp that I learned how to get along with very different kinds of people." He concluded, "Everything I've done in Canada has only been possible because of the things I learned in camp."

Gregory Baum was a Jewish boy from Berlin with a nominally Christian upbringing. Later, after his release, he became a Catholic and went to Germany to live for a time in a monastery. In this connection, he states, "Internment has become an archetype for me, an archetype for intense community, of being dispensed from everything except friendship and intellectual activity.... In the monastery later I didn't find exactly the same thing. It wasn't as intense.... There was a kind of universality about life in camp."

For others, such as Robert Langstadt, the benefit of internment was not so much the communal aspect:

> Sometimes today I have a sort of longing for it. All worries, all responsibilities, were taken off your shoulders. As long as you were able to live with yourself, that was all you had to worry about. I could sit in a corner and dream and I knew that I could eat at night. You didn't need to hustle.

Edmund Klein reacted in a similar way. His adolescence in Vienna had been a period of intense intellectual activity living under great stress, and he had found his year in England unusually difficult.

> The British did me a tremendous favor by interning me, because they made it possible for me not having to worry about matters I could do nothing about.
>
> Besides, it was the only time in my entire life when I had a rest. I could turn off my mind completely. I read prolifically.... It was a wonderful experience.

This feeling of being suspended in mid-air, of being in a vacuum, came as a great relief to many others who had passed through unprecedented turmoil before. So much the better if you had a natural aptitude for being an internee like Max Abush.

> I took to it very well. I would say camp life itself suited me. In Vienna my father had taken care of me and protected me. He had been assistant to the Austrian Army commander holding Russian prisoners of war in the First World War; and half a dozen uncles of mine had been army officers.

Now I was again taken care of. . . . I set myself a routine. I got myself quite active; I was always one of the first to get up in the morning, the first to take a shower. Time passed very quickly. I became self-reliant; I was a born soldier. I had always wanted to be in the army, and this was the next best thing.

For Martin Fischer, who intended to become a psychiatrist, internment provided an excellent opportunity to "study people in crisis." Intuitively and objectively he could provide support to others, some relief, and some perspective. "Perhaps it was a little easier for me than for the others," he thinks.

Unlike Martin Fischer, most of us did not have any clear idea what we wanted to do with our future lives and were pleased to be relieved, at least for the moment, of having to make definite career decisions. But we enjoyed discovering aptitudes and talents in ourselves and others for which we had had little time nor training before. George Brandt was very much aware of having lived a sheltered life so far.

To be on the raw edge of experience was exciting. It enabled me to find out a great deal about my own German and Jewish backgrounds; I hadn't been very aware of them before. It meant meeting an enormous number of people from a variety of social and intellectual backgrounds. . . . We were a group of people who could not quickly be reduced to a common denominator.

A roll call with a group of trained Nazis was extremely easy—a roll call with a group of hopelessly anarchistic Jewish civilians took about half an hour, and usually was an unsatisfactory affair even *after* half an hour. It was, of course, a fact that a great many officers on the other side of the fence had a clear preference for authoritarian structures, and consequently preferred "safe" Nazis to anarchistically inclined liberals and Jews.

To some of us, the fact that we preferred anarchy to discipline was a source of constant anguish, especially if this preference was combined with self-pity, self-indulgence, laziness and cynicism. The idea to "make the best of internment" was anathema to many; it meant giving up the fight to get out and join the struggle against the Nazis. It was considered a cardinal sin to attempt turning the camps into holiday places, to yield to the soft life, without giving a thought to what was going on in the world outside.

There was one man in particular who was deadly opposed to "making the best of it." Having had to flee Rotterdam under circumstances that made it necessary for him to leave his wife and child behind, he tried to reach England in a small boat together with eight men and one woman. They spent four days and four nights in the English Channel without food or water before being picked up by a British submarine. "More dead than alive, I was interned in Pentonville Jail on arrival in Britain," he told me.

Even before he had received the news that his wife and child had committed suicide in Holland rather than facing deportation to a German concentration camp, he was obsessed with the urgency to get out and fight. Once he knew the worst, he nearly went mad with grief and rage. "To be confined behind barbed wire, and prevented from taking revenge, was utterly unbearable," he said. No wonder he was among those opposed to all attempts to make camp life more comfortable. "When I could buy a cup of coffee topped with whipped cream in our canteen, together with a piece of Viennese *Apfelstrudel*, I felt that the battle had been lost."

Part Three

TEN

The Curtain Rises

It was as early as two weeks after our arrival in Quebec that the British government had published a White Paper listing eighteen categories of Class C internees eligible for release. These were mainly people who could find useful employment in the United Kingdom. No mention was made of those who had been shipped to the Dominions.

On August 16, 1940, the *Times* of London had printed a letter signed by nine well-known correspondents castigating the British government for not dealing with the internees according to their merit, specifically mentioning "the fate of the Class C aliens." Release appeals were being turned down, they wrote; the Secretary of State was not prepared to give any reasons for his decisions. On August 22, three days after Hermann Goering had declared that Germany had now reached the decisive period of the air war against England, and two days after Churchill's famous statement that "never in the field of human conflict has so much been owed by so many to so few," a debate began in the House of Commons. It was conducted on a high intellectual and moral level, and the government came under heavy fire for its internment policies. One cannot help but admire British parliamentarians for taking so much time and giving so much careful thought to discussing a problem which was only indirectly concerned with the immediate dangers facing Britain. The reason why they did so was based on their conviction that the problem was closely connected with the nature of the war, touching upon the very essence of Britain's moral position.

In the course of the debate the Home Secretary, Sir John Anderson, made this significant admission:

> I am not here to deny that most regrettable and deplorable things have happened in connection with the internment camps. I regret them deeply. They have been due partly to the inevitable haste with which the policy of internment had to be carried out. They were due, however, in some cases to mistakes of individuals, stupidity, muddling. These things all relate to the past. So far as we can remedy mistakes we shall remedy them.

The question what remedies were available to undo the damage arose several times, especially regarding the "deportations" to Canada. Major Victor Cazalet said he was sure the Dominions would allow Category C internees the same freedom they would have enjoyed if they were released in England. But he saw one practical obstacle: how would they know who was Category C and who was not?

Colonel Josuah F. Wedgwood, the great champion of our cause, specifically mentioned that quite a number of young men from the University of Cambridge had been sent away without being allowed to communicate with their parents. They were not told where they were going. "Their parents do not know where they are, or under what conditions they are living."

He asked the Home Secretary whether the internees who had been sent to the Dominions would be treated in the same way as those who had been allowed to stay in England. Sir John Anderson replied in the affirmative, pointing out, however, that only those covered by the White Paper would be eligible for release, both at home and in the Dominions. This did not satisfy Colonel Wedgwood, who insisted that the White Paper was not relevant to the situation of the "deportees" to Canada.

> The Right Hon. Gentleman seems to base the whole of his internment policy on the danger of invasion here. There is no danger of invasion in Canada comparable with the danger here. Therefore, why not set them free, at least in Canada? . . . These people may just as well go to the Canadian universities and finish their education. You cannot have it both ways. If this general internment is necessary

because of the fear of invasion, then the Government should, at any rate, allow all those B and C internees—not only the boys from Cambridge, but also all the others—to regain their freedom.

It is touching to see that as late as 1940 British politicians assumed that London had authority to decide who was and who was not to be set free in Canada. By then, the British government had already asked Ottawa, in a tentative and tactful way, whether it might be prepared to consider releasing some of the "deportees."

Viscount Caldecote, in his letter to Vincent Massey dated July 22, 1940, tried to explain, if not to justify, why "innocent refugees" had been sent to Canada. He stated that arrangements would be made to return to the United Kingdom any person whose release was authorized, unless the Canadian government was prepared to "allow them liberty in Canada, and they themselves wished to be there." In the same letter Viscount Caldecote assured Vincent Massey that the British government was prepared to consider, in consultation with Washington, whether arrangements could be made for the emigration to the United States of internees with valid visas.

The first official Canadian reference to the possibility of release in Canada I could find was contained in the minutes of a meeting that took place on September 12 of a special committee set up by the prime minister to consider internment matters. It was attended by the Director of Internment Operations General E. de B. Panet (Colonel Stethem's predecessor), Commissioner S. T. Wood (R.C.M.P.), Colonel G. S. Currie (National Defence), F. C. Blair (Immigration) and O. D. Skelton (External Affairs).

General Panet pointed out that two thousand-odd civilian internees being held in Canadian camps were in no sense pro-Nazi, and that the Canadian authorities now recognized that they had been sent over by mistake. It was agreed that, although it was the duty of the British government to take them back to the United Kingdom, under existing circumstances it was not practical to expect that this be done. "The United Kingdom have agreed to take back some sixty people," Panet said, "but indicate they could not take any more."

The next question that arose was whether some of the internees could be allowed to settle in Canada. Reference was made to a few specific cases of men who had first degree relatives living in Canada; they might be favorably considered. But it was also realized that there would be opposition to admitting to Canada a large proportion of Jews. In any case, many wanted to go to the United States. There was no reason, it was said, why those who claimed to have visas—if this could be verified—could not be taken to the United States Consulate and passed across the border. Whatever happened, it was now apparent that the Canadian government was going to have the large majority of refugees on their hands for some time.

Canadian newspapers had paid no attention to us until early September 1940, after reports of the British House of Commons debate and editorials about it had appeared in the British press. The first important story was carried on September 7 by the *Financial Post*, but it did not mention the possibility of release in Canada. Its Ottawa correspondent summarized the facts, noting that "one of the most vexing problems of the war, and one with which Canada is virtually helpless to deal, has been thrust on the government." He pointed out that many of the documents dealing with the internees had been lost at sea. Moreover, it was known that impersonations had been practiced in Britain, and many internees had come to Canada under false names. Referring to the anti-Nazis among them, the correspondent observed that "their reaction under this treatment is reported to be splendid. In some of these camps educational facilities rivaling, it is said, our own universities, have been organized. And all are taking the rigors of internment philosophically."

Under the heading "Would Release Refugees" an important letter appeared in the *Toronto Globe and Mail* of September 11. It mentioned publicly for the first time the possibility of release. Written by Mrs. Sara B. Skilling, the wife of Professor Gordon Skilling (my first boss at the C.B.C.), it stated that "I would like to see an arrangement made with the British authorities whereby these men could be released here in the safety of Canada, and be allowed to settle as immigrants here, or to proceed to another part of the Empire."

Regarding the refugees now in Canada receiving United States visas, Mrs. Skilling conveyed the hope that they would be allowed to proceed to the United States as free men.

The Skillings had visited Czechoslovakia before the war and were thoroughly familiar with the situation of anti-Nazi refugees in Europe. In fact, they had worked with British refugee organizations both in Prague and in London. When it became known in London towards the end of July 1940 that Mrs. Skilling was about to return to Canada these organizations contacted her, begging her to find out where the refugees for whom they were responsible could be located in Canada, whether it would be possible to secure their release and further emigration, and what could be done for their welfare in Canadian camps.

On October 9, a reporter from the *Ottawa Citizen* interviewed an unnamed "internment official" asking him whether prisoners of war and civilian internees were being kept in separate camps. The question of release did not come up. The interview followed a dispatch from London containing a report by Labor M.P. Glanvil Hall, who had stated in the House that no such distinctions were being made. Herbert Morrison, who had succeeded Sir John Anderson as Home Secretary, assured Mr. Hall that he would try to "draw attention to the matter by conversations and see if it can be put right."

The internment official countered—correctly—that prisoners of war and civilians were receiving "absolutely separate and distinct attention," but stated—incorrectly—that the "Nazi-type of internee was kept in separate camps from the refugee-type." Since Canadian officials claimed not to be able to distinguish the one from the other, it is surprising that this statement was made. While it was true that internees in the B and C Categories were kept separate from those in A Category, *some* "Nazi-types" were in all the camps, and 178 "refugee-types" in Category A were in Camp R. The official made one other significant observation:

> Naturally all have to be subject to disciplinary regulations. . . . In camps in England, some of the civilians were allowed considerable liberty under certain conditions. In Canada, we haven't found that to be practical. These civilian internees are looked upon as enemy aliens who must be kept in custody, but they are being given every consideration consistent with safety.

It is unfortunate that the *Ottawa Citizen* reporter was not well enough informed to ask what had made such treatment impractical. He also might have enquired why the "refugee-types" in Camp B near Fredericton might not have been given the same treatment as the unemployed who had lived and worked there when the place was used for that purpose in the hungry thirties. Also, why was it essential, he might have asked, to impose military discipline on civilian refugees, most of whom had never been in any organization more military than the boy scouts.

The first journalist who took the trouble to research the story properly was Grant Dexter of the *Winnipeg Free Press*, who published his results on October 16 in a story entitled "Internment Scandal." Since Ottawa had said virtually nothing about it, he wrote, few in Canada knew of the injustices and hardships which had been inflicted on hundreds of refugees. Basing his article mainly on the debate of August 22 at Westminster, he concluded that the refugees' "outlook was hard and their prospects bleak." Not a word about the possibility of release in Canada.

A little more than two weeks later the *Globe and Mail* carried an editorial on "Internment Injustices." Referring to the case of Cambridge graduate F. G. Friedlaender, a brilliant young mathematician about whom a letter had appeared in the *Times* pointing out the absurdity of keeping distinguished scholars behind barbed wire, the *Globe* had this to say:

It is well understood that the Canadian government has no power to release any internees who have been entrusted to its charge by the British government, but, if the latter does not within a reasonable time take action to remedy what seems an indefensible injustice, it might make representations to Downing Street that it strongly dislikes the idea as being used as an agent for the perpetuation of it.

There was still no direct plea for the release in Canada of men of Friedlaender's calibre—or of any other men who were not suspect, but might be useful to the war effort. The assumption was that this was a matter to be dealt with by the British, and not the Canadians. It was left to the voluntary agencies to take the matter one stage further and inform the Canadian public of a fact Ottawa knew already, namely that the British would be delighted if their mistake could be rectified by the release in Canada of the men who should not have been sent there, or by their emigration to the United States.

However, there was one senior official in Ottawa who recognized that no substantial improvement in our position was likely to occur, unless our prisoner of war status was changed. On October 21, 1940, Norman Robertson, Associate Under-secretary of State for External Affairs, circulated a confidential memo among other senior civil servants raising the question whether perhaps the responsibility for policy and for the internal administration of the refugee camps should be left in the same hands as those who looked after prisoners of war. "There is a real risk," he wrote, "that if nothing substantial is done to mend matters quickly, the situation may deteriorate. . . . The moment may have come to review the adequacy of existing arrangements, and perhaps inaugurate some changes."

The Emergence of Friends

It would have been surprising if there had been a groundswell of voices demanding our release in Canada. Essentially, the country was still opposed to immigration, particularly the immigration of Jews. Even though the war had put an end to appeasement, the prevalent mood was still that of the Great Depression. Out of eight thousand immigrants admitted to Canada during the first nine months of 1938, only 326 were Jews.

Testifying before a Senate Committee hearing in 1946, the research director of the Canadian Jewish Congress provided documented proof that the government had actually imposed restraints on Jewish immigration not applicable to other groups. This policy was a fair reflection of public opinion, by no means only in French Canada. Apart from a few concerned citizens, the main spokesmen for a more liberal approach to the plight of refugees from Hitler were a number of prominent figures in the Protestant churches, the C.C.F.—above all, its leader M. J. Coldwell—and the Jewish community. In the government the person described by a *Globe and Mail* reporter as "the man behind the scenes on all international affairs, including immigration of refugees," was Under-secretary for External Affairs O. D. Skelton. He was one of the most consistent opponents of the relaxation of existing regulations. So, on the whole, was labor.

The most important personalities who emerged in the summer of 1940 to become, in a sense, our lobbyists were Constance Hayward, Senator Cairine R. Wilson, her quite exceptional secretary Sybil Wright and Saul Hayes. Later, Charles Raphael came from London to help iron out immigration problems with the United States, in close cooperation with Stanley Goldner. Another important figure, operating out of Toronto, was Ann Cowan.

Constance Hayward had returned to Canada in 1934 after studying international law and international relations at the London School of Economics. Within a year she was organizing study groups for the League of Nations Society and making speeches on the worsening situation in Europe.

In 1938 she happened to be in Geneva during the Evian Conference, called by President Roosevelt to consider the plight of refugees from Hitler. The hypocrisy on the part of all the speakers who officially pretended to be concerned, yet were reluctant to open their countries' doors to the victims, did not fully sink in until Miss Hayward had returned to Canada. To her, the refugee problem seemed the most burning issue of all, an issue on which the Canadian government could act if the public were informed. She went on a lecture tour for the League of Nations Society, which by then she had joined as a staff member. On October 15, at a regular meeting of its Executive Committee in Montreal, a new committee was formed—the Canadian National Committee on Refugees and Victims of Political Persecution. Constance Hayward became its executive secretary, under the chairmanship of Senator Cairine R. Wilson; honorary chairman was Sir Robert Falconer, past president of the University of Toronto. The founding meeting took place on December 6, 1938, in the Château Laurier in Ottawa.

Constance Hayward and Senator Wilson were friends, though the senator was considerably older than she. (In 1938 she was fifty-three years old, and had been a senator since 1930.) She was chairman of the League of Nations Society and the National Federation of Liberal Women and had been involved in many humanitarian causes. Not only did she know Mackenzie King well, but also everybody who was important in Ottawa.

Constance Hayward remembers coming to Ottawa just before the Committee was formed.

> I stayed with Mrs. Wilson. I arrived early in the morning and she met me at the door. I don't think she had slept that night. We did not really know what we could do. Later Norman Robertson visited me. He knew then in a way I didn't know what we were up against. He knew what the policy was, and he knew what the attitudes were. Early in 1939 a large meeting was organized. Mackenzie King received a delegation and gave us assurances—I think in good faith—that there would be a change in policy in the refugees' favor. But governments move slowly.

In September war broke out. As soon as Constance Hayward had heard that refugees were among the internees sent from England in July 1940, she went to see T. A. Crerar, the Minister of Mines and Resources, who was also responsible for immigration. "I discovered afterwards," she recalls, "that he was more sympathetic than he expressed at the time. I was young and just learning what cabinet solidarity meant. I remember telling him about the refugees, and he said, 'That can't be: they're all dangerous Nazis.' I don't think Mr. Crerar ever deliberately lied to me. I think the word hadn't got through to him."

On August 27, 1940, the Committee asked the retired "Grand Old Man" of Canadian education, Dr. H. M. Tory, to see whether educational assistance could be given to the interned refugees. (The results of his visit have been described earlier.) From then on, the Committee performed one useful service after another. On November 6 its Executive responded positively to suggestions for coordination with the United Jewish Refugee and War Relief Agencies in Montreal. This was the genesis of the Central Committee on Interned Refugees, henceforth to be known as the Committee, under whose auspices invaluable assistance was given to us all while we were in the camps. It ultimately became the chief architect of our release.

The main driving force on behalf of the Jewish internees was Saul Hayes, a devoted and energetic young Montreal lawyer. He had been chosen by Samuel Bronfman, at the time chairman of the Jewish Refugee Committee and later president of the Canadian Jewish Congress.

Sam Bronfman was convinced that a lawyer's skills were

required to deal with the federal government in a new way. Until then the Jewish community had had few successes in its relations with Ottawa. The record of endless petitions, visits from delegations and requests for help during the thirties is a lamentable story of failure. Bronfman, the singularly successful and ambitious businessman, believed that the refugee problem was too desperate to permit a continuation of this policy. The Jewish community was resolved to deal with the government in the same way businessmen deal with large corporations, i.e., in a cool, professional manner. Sam Bronfman could not have chosen a better man than Saul Hayes. He was so effective that on September 20, 1941, F. C. Blair, the Director of Immigration, wrote in a letter, "To prevent the more generous scale of assistance to Jewish cases ... I think the best way to do this would be to get rid of Sol [sic] Hayes."

Hayes told me that it was the *St. Louis* incident in the summer of 1939 that had made him decide to work full-time with the Canadian Jewish Congress as a professional advocate representing refugees from Hitler. The more deeply he became involved in this work, the more convinced he became that, even if there had not been such strong anti-Semitism in Canada, the country would have been opposed to immigration. He attributed this mainly to Quebec's influence on the Mackenzie King government, and to the powerful role played by King's Quebec lieutenant, Ernest Lapointe, who delivered the French-Canadian vote.

A catalogue listing Hayes' activities on our behalf would be a formidable document. From the moment he heard about our existence in Canada in August 1940, he was indefatigable, going to Ottawa again and again to plead for the refugees' separation from the Nazis, for recognition of our refugee status, for the rights of observant Jews to have kosher food and a work-free Sabbath, for concessions relating to letter-writing (two letters a week, instead of one), for radios, newspapers, and magazines to be sent to the camps, and for permission to let movies be shown. Often, together with other members of the committees, he visited the camps and arranged for rabbis to pay similar visits and render assistance.

Throughout this period a great deal of time was spent on the seemingly intractable problem of facilitating emigration to the United States. Moreover, Saul Hayes established close relations with Constance Hayward and the non-sectarian Toronto committee, so that, within the framework of the Central Committee for Interned Refugees, a common front was established vis-à-vis the authorities.

All these efforts required the kind of skills which Samuel Bronfman had considered to be indispensable. Not only did Hayes have to be diplomatic in dealing with men such as Colonel Stethem, but also with those in the government whose hostility toward us is now on public record. In addition, he had to placate critics within the Jewish community. Criticism came from those who said he wasn't doing enough, while others claimed he was doing too much. In the first group were mainly those who had personal connections with internees, or received letters from relatives in England or the United States. They were pressing for action. Those who contended that the Committee was spending too much time and money on the interned refugees took the view that we were, after all, safe and had enough to eat, while thousands in Europe could be saved and needed the assistance from Canada more urgently. It required the highest measure of political savoir-faire to conciliate the critics on both sides.

Early in 1941, at Hayes' request for help, Bloomsbury House in London sent a young Jewish scholar to Canada to help specifically with American emigration problems. Charles Raphael had gained experience helping internees in the Lingfield internment camp in England to obtain American visas. This turned out to have been a far simpler matter than that facing him in Canada. While visiting New York for the first time, he met some of the Lingfield men who, at least partly through him, were now living in the United States. They invited him to an evening at their club.

> I went to the address and as I approached the street on Upper Broadway—not knowing where I was because I was quite strange to America—I heard a familiar sound; it was "God Save the King." This seemed an extraordinary tribute to what we had managed to do for them.

Raphael was invited to give evidence to a U.S. Congressional committee on the way England had handled the refugee problem.

This was before Pearl Harbor, when the Americans were wondering how to approach the matter in case they would come into the war.

When Raphael recently was asked what he thought of the way the Canadians had dealt with the problem of the refugees sent to Canada, he said, "At first they had been highly suspicious. They had agreed to receive some dangerous enemy aliens. . . . Then they were told 'they're really rather nice people. Would you mind releasing them.' They resented this. They felt they'd constructed camps and these camps ought to be filled with dangerous people, and if they weren't, well, they'd better stay there until they *were* dangerous."[24] Another thing he remembered as extraordinary was the absence of public discussion of the subject. On the attitudes of Jews generally, he had this to say:

> We felt it was pure accident that all over Europe every Jew was now at the mercy of Hitler and we knew even then that their conditions were terrible. We had no idea of the extent of the murders that would follow. Every Jew who was not directly subject to Hitler must have felt—there but for the grace of God. . . ."

Raphael did not visit the Canadian camps frequently; that was left to an assistant of Saul Hayes, Stanley Goldner, who had taken his bar exams at McGill in 1940. Apart from his legal studies, he also engaged in newspaper work. Like Raphael, he spent much of his time on a voluminous correspondence. "For a long time," he told me, "there was a lot of anguish and despair and sorrow. Eventually the ultimate results were satisfying."

In Toronto similar work was done by the enterprising Ann Cowan, who later became a highly competent co-optor of sponsors and employers.

On her first visit to Camp I on the Ile aux Noix on September 7, 1941, she accompanied Charles Raphael and was looking forward to interviewing dozens of men and collecting their curricula vitae. Up to that moment, however, no woman had been allowed to enter the compound, let alone one that was young and pretty. This constituted a grave problem for the military authorities. After lengthy deliberations the chair on which she was to sit was perched on top of two tables in the recreation hut, so that the refugees would not be able to grab her. While these preparations were being made, and Raphael was doing some interviewing on his own, she was kept waiting outside the camp. Naturally she became more and more impatient, and asked for permission to use the telephone. Permission was granted. She called F. C. Blair in Ottawa, with whom she had cordial relations, and told him that unless she was allowed into the camp right away, she would write to every newspaper in the country. Though Blair had absolutely no authority over the military, he managed to soften up the commandant. When Ann Cowan was shepherded into the mildewy old fortress and saw the "throne" she was to occupy, she became outraged. She would not have the men look up to her, but insisted on facing them on their own level.

Here is the account of her visit from the diary of Henry Kreisel:

> A certain Mrs. Cowan has come with Mr. Raphael. . . . She is small, has a doll's face and a very well-formed body. She wears a blue dress and blue shoes to match. I then go back to my work (making nets). Suddenly I am called to this Mrs. Cowan by Mr. Fischer, the camp leader. He asks her whether she can get a sponsor for me, so I might be released in Canada and she says yes. Then he mentions that I write, asks me to bring down some of my work. I gave her a copy of my poems. She said she'll have them published. I told her that I have no typewriter and need one. She makes a note.

Kreisel had already given some of his poetry and short stories to Mrs. Ben Robinson of Montreal, the wife of one of the most prominent members of the Committee. Some of them were published in the Jewish newspapers and, according to Mrs. Cowan, proved to be a magnet for sponsors, not only for Kreisel, but for several others as well.

Alexander Paterson

In September 1940 the Canadian government, unhappy about having been sent refugees instead of the promised Nazis, had asked London to send over a highly placed representative to help undo the confusion it had created. Secretary of State Herbert Morrison appointed Alexander Paterson, a man who, as His Majesty's Commissioner of Prisons in England, had become well-known for having modified the Borstal system for juvenile offenders. He was not only a polished and shrewd diplomat, but also a man with a healthy distaste for block-headed bureaucrats and brass-hats, just the kind of people who had put obstacles in the way of his prison reforms.

In Morrison's letter of appointment it had been stated that Mr. Paterson was to consider the cases of the civilian internees who had been transported to Canada, and to recommend which of them should be allowed to return to Great Britain, if they so desired. Also, he was to make necessary arrangements with the Canadian government to have the selected internees returned to England, and to facilitate their migration to other countries provided they had obtained visas authorizing their emigration. In addition, Mr. Paterson was asked to give to the Canadian government whatever information was available relating to the classification and treatment of civilian internees transported to Canada.

At least three of the internees had met Alexander Paterson before he arrived in Canada in the middle of November 1940. Ralf Hoffmann had encountered him briefly during the previous winter in Lingfield while Paterson had been active as head of an inspection team. Ralf Hoffmann recalls:

> When we met again in Canada, he recognized me at once. He asked me to tell him my story. The session took about an hour and a half. It turned out he knew some of my Quaker friends. By the time our conversation ended, we were calling each other by our Christian names. I told him I wanted to go back to England. The fact that this was a time when our shipping losses were very high was absolutely no consideration. The one thing that mattered to me was to get out of the camp as fast as possible. Nothing else mattered. So I was put on the first available transport back to England.

Ernest Borneman had had a much longer association with Paterson. He had worked for him in England in the thirties when German prison experts were visiting the United Kingdom.

> Paterson had made it a rule that, since British country hotels were dreadful and served dreadful food, we ought to put up the German officials in country houses. That was absolutely brilliant. We drove around England with these awful Nazis, from prison to prison, and at night they stayed with the British aristocracy. It was a perfect solution.

When I was ushered into his presence in Sherbrooke he looked at me and said, "Ernest, what are *you* doing here?" And I asked him, "Alec, and what are *you* doing here?" He replied, "Well, we'll have to get you out of here." I wanted to know how. "Well, *think!*" he said, "What can you do for the war effort?" "You know very well what I did before the war, Alec. I studied cultural anthropology at the London School of Economics and prehistory in Edinburgh. What the devil can I do with *that?*" "*Think!*" he repeated.

Now, I had read in the papers that John Grierson had arrived in Canada to start the National Film Board in Ottawa. I had once met Grierson in London, in connection with an anthropological film I had made for Malinowski. I was sure he wouldn't remember me. But anyway, I thought I'd just mention Grierson who, of course, was a fellow-Scot. I said, "Why don't you two Scots get together and break a bottle of Scotch and decide what you're going to do with me." I didn't think for a moment he'd do anything. But do you know what this extraordinary man did? That very same evening he took a train to Ottawa to speak to Grierson. The reason was that he'd discovered I had been classified as "unreleasable" because of the many protests I had launched against camp conditions.

That was the kind of challenge that appealed to Grierson. Like Paterson, he believed in fighting the stupid establishment on every front. So Grierson got me out. But it took him six months! On June 10, 1941, I was released, as one of the first internees who did not have first-degree relatives in Canada.

The third internee to have met Paterson previously was Walter Wallich.

I had known Paterson in Berlin, through Alec Dixon, a mutual friend of ours, who was correspondent of the *Daily Telegraph*, second to Hugh Carleton Greene. He had come to Berlin to attend a prison congress. I was fifteen or sixteen at the time and home from my English school for the holidays.

Paterson stayed in our house. We had a tennis court and he played a reasonable game. We were playing doubles; I was serving—appallingly badly. I tried to explain to him that opposite me there were trees. But at the spot where I threw up the ball there was a little bit of sky, and I couldn't

see the ball. "Ah," he said, "the little tent of blue we prisoners call the sky." I didn't react. He said, "You mean you
don't know Oscar Wilde's *Ballad of Reading Gaol?*" I said no.
He then promised to let me have a copy. That is how we
became acquainted. I saw him several times before the war,
and corresponded with him from camp.

Paterson arrived in Sherbrooke in bitter cold weather,
wearing a shirt with a butterfly collar and a Homburg hat
but no overcoat when everybody else was wrapped up in
whatever they could find. I had a two-hour talk with him in
the boiler room, about general conditions in the camp. He
often had a personal spur which led him to a much wider
field. This benefited many people.

When Paterson went to Ottawa he met all the "leading
players," including Senator Cairine Wilson and Constance Hayward. In Montreal he spent a great deal of time with Saul Hayes.
"I had the greatest admiration for him," Hayes told me. "There
weren't enough hours in the day for him. He used to stay in the
Windsor Hotel. Our office was on St. Catherine Street between
Peel and Stanley. I could see him from my window as he walked
toward us in the cold winter, without an overcoat. We became
good friends. We played bridge together. He liked to drink pink
gins."

When Paterson visited Farnham, Major Kippen sometimes
had breakfast with him at the hotel, before driving him to the
camp. He too remembers him enjoying a pink gin for breakfast.

On his visits to the camps, Paterson was appalled by the
anti-Semitism rampant among some of the military personnel.
After his return to England in the summer of 1941, he wrote
about it in his Report to the British government.[25]

Sitting day after day in a small cell through the open
window came the shouts of the guards and sometimes of
the officers, alluding to the fact that the internees were
Jews and commenting, not infrequently, on the correctness
of their birth. This was much resented by the men but those
provoked to answer merely met with a week in a cell.
Having borne this for a while, I drafted the following order
and the General concerned was good enough to sign it and
have it communicated to the troops:

"Canada is a free country, where different races have
contrived to make a great nation, where every man is free

to worship as he pleases. It has been brought to my notice that personnel in the Prisoners of War (II) Camps have on occasion been heard referring in a contemptuous way to the fact that those in their charge are of the Jewish race and faith. This practice is unworthy of a free Canadian and will cease forthwith."

Paterson interviewed hundreds of us, visiting all the camps where Categories B and C aliens were interned. Since he had no dossiers on us, he had to decide intuitively whether we were genuine refugees or not. I doubt whether he ever made a mistake. Whenever he thought that the need to return to England was not totally justified, his advice to the particular internee was to stay put and hope that soon the Americans—in some cases the South Americans—would open their doors and allow him in.

He usually conducted interviews in a small cell. The camp leaders would issue tickets and the internees had to line up to speak to him. "The leaders," Paterson reported, "know their men and organize with skill. The only shouting is done by the guards in khaki." Usually each interviewee would start with, "My case is rather different from the rest, Sir. I don't want to waste your time, and I know there are a lot of men waiting to see you, but if I could explain. . . ."

"Your life is more important than my time," Paterson would reply. "I'm in no hurry."

He would listen patiently, very much aware that we were facing an acute crisis in our lives. If we didn't want to join the Pioneer Corps and if we didn't qualify for any of the categories in the White Paper, and if we had no relatives or friends living in the United States, we realized that we were facing the possibility of remaining behind barbed wire until the end of the war. Many frequently changed their minds about what they wanted to do. "It should be remembered," Paterson wrote in his Report, "in defence of the mind-changing habit that I tended to change the advice offered as the prospects of immigration . . . grew brighter or fainter."

I was one of those who constantly changed his mind. Paterson's visit brought to a head my agonizing dilemma: should I sign up for the Pioneer Corps? Should I wait until the doors to the United States were opened to me? At first, many of my Cambridge friends faced the same dilemma, but then most of them decided to go back to England to join the Pioneer Corps. At that time none of them knew that after about a year's service in the non-combatant Aliens' Battalion it was possible to graduate to the regular British Army, even though no one became a naturalized British subject until after the war.

I had a brother and a sister living in the United States, and my mother was in London waiting to join them. On the other hand, I felt a strong pull back to England as I was the only member of our family who had lived there for five years. But my sister and her husband advised me to wait for an American visa unless I could join the regular British Army. In the end, I decided to wait for the American doors to open.

In the course of his investigations Paterson recorded this memorable case history:

> A sensitive young Austrian of 18 years was in 1940 a student at Leeds University. Appalled by the prospect of internment, he tried to commit suicide. He recovered and was interned and sent to Canada. His elder brother, who enjoyed a much more stable personality, was fortunately in the same camp and came to see me to say how the camp was telling hard upon the youngster's nerves. It was arranged that he should be transferred to an Italian Camp near Montreal where he could apply for a visa to join his parents in South America. Unhappily, at the camp, while the Italian Army was retreating in Libya, he made some boyish boasting remark about the superiority of German over Italian soldiers. This need in no way have been taken to prove Nazi proclivities, but it excited the suspicion of the Intelligence Officer who reported the matter to the military authorities. A week or two later, when plans for the immigration of the lad to his parents were going forward, it is regrettable to find in his dossier at the camp an order from the General to the effect that this lad was a very dangerous Nazi, should be shown no leniency, treated with the greatest security, should be considered for transfer to a Nazi Camp, and all plans for his immigration should be cancelled.
>
> After visiting the Camp where he had incurred this evil reputation and hearing all that could be said against him (and also a good deal that was said for him by the Sergeant-Major and some of the Jewish refugees there) I was firmly of the opinion that he was a genuine anti-Nazi. A friendly

medical officer was found to agree that transfer to a Nazi Camp might well lead to insanity and suicide. After acquiring further information, I wrote to the General commanding the District and asked him if he would accept my assurance of the lad's loyalty, and received a kindly note saying that the minute would be expunged from the record and he could sail for Brazil.

Return to England

As the option for release in Canada was not yet open to us, Constance Hayward remembers that Paterson expected about one thousand of us to return to the United Kingdom and another thousand to emigrate to the United States.

Just before Christmas, he went to Halifax to arrange the first transport of 287 internees back to England. There were many farewell parties in the camps conducted with mock gaiety and bravado.

The returnees proceeded under heavy guard to Halifax, where the *Thysville*, a Belgian Congo steamer under Captain Powell, was waiting for them. Before the war this flat-bottomed steamer had plied its trade between the middle reaches of the African Congo and the Belgian port of Antwerp. It was one of the ships that had responded to the appeal by governments-in-exile, after the fall of Belgium, Holland, and France in June 1940, to sail to Britain to avoid falling into the hands of the Germans. It was now part of the British merchant marine, engaged in the sugar trade between the West Indies and Halifax.

The crew, consisting of Belgian Congolese and *Lascars*, i.e., East Indian sailors, had heard stories about U-boat attacks in the Atlantic and the bombing of Liverpool. True, the *Thysville* had crossed the ocean once, but it had clearly not been built for that purpose. As a result, the crew declined to sail.

A number of internees were capable of running a ship's engines. Everybody volunteered to do *something*, be a cook, a waiter, etc. The rest of the crew was picked from the pool of sailors available in Halifax Harbor at the time. Two free Frenchmen had arrived from Hong Kong to go to London in order to join General de Gaulle. They had travelled across the Pacific, then across Canada, and they depended on Captain Powell to get them back to England.

Eventually, he agreed to sail with the crew now at his disposal, and the *Thysville* left on Christmas Day, taking the northern route nearly as far as the North Pole. At the outset the ship sailed in convoy but then became separated from it. There was a plane on deck, and due to the fact that her cargo was badly distributed she developed a list. The frequent appearance on the western horizon of a plume of smoke gave rise to the speculation that the *Thysville* was being shadowed by a battleship. The voyage took about three weeks. Captain Powell was drunk much of the time. He also had his French mistress on board with him.

Among the returnees was Count Friedrich von Lingen, Hans Kahle and Klaus Fuchs. It is not clear whether Lingen had wanted to return to England; what is clear, however, is that Winston Churchill wanted him back, though Lingen may not have known that. Whether there ever was any intention of exchanging him for British prisoners in German hands is not clear, but Lingen was afraid of that. The officer in charge of the returnees was Captain Godfrey Barrass, the British intelligence officer who had established contact between Lingen and the Athlones the previous summer in Quebec. Lingen was in charge of submarine watch. On New Year's Eve everyone drank champagne; he and his friends—many from Cambridge—sang popular Berlin songs.

The *Thysville* arrived in Liverpool just as an air-raid siren sounded the "all clear." On the quayside was a company of British soldiers with their bayonets fixed. Captain Powell, sober by now, asked the lieutenant in charge to come on board. The lieutenant advised him that he and his men had to escort the internees back to Huyton. "Not like that!" Captain Powell replied. "Sheath your bayonets. These lads have worked hard and do not deserve such indignity."

They were taken back to Huyton to be processed. All those who were not required for the war effort in other capacities immediately joined the Pioneer Corps.

The circumstances under which the various transports returned to Britain differed widely, as did the ways in which our boys were told that they were on the list.

Max Perutz had just spent three days in solitary confinement in the Sherbrooke police station for swapping identities with a non-Catholic (Perutz was a Catholic of Jewish origin) in order to remain with his Jewish friends. This happened at the time when the first camp at Quebec had been split, when there seemed a chance to cross the U.S. border. "Soon after that episode," he told me, "the camp commandant called me in to tell me that the Home Office had ordered my release and that I had been offered a professorship in the United States. He seemed a little embarrassed, having just sent me to prison. He then asked me if I wanted to return to England or remain in Canada until my release to the United States could be arranged. I replied that I wanted to return to England, which drew the comment, 'You will make a fine soldier,' something nobody has said to me before or since. Holding a British passport, I was back in Canada in 1943 on an Admiralty mission. I was accommodated at the Château Laurier in Ottawa; nobody searched me for lice."

Walter Josephy was treated royally when he returned to England on the luxury liner *Strathmore* as a first-class passenger. At Liverpool he was once again received with machine guns— "the whole bit"—but was released to join the Pioneer Corps after spending about a month on the Isle of Man. Rolf James, on the other hand, went back on a different ship and slept "in the luggage hold for fourth-class passengers on top of ammunition boxes." Karl Kruger arrived in Liverpool in the middle of an air-raid. He did not have to go to the Isle of Man, but was escorted to Edinburgh, the place where he had been interned, to rejoin the Scottish-Presbyterian family with whom he had been staying before. He had converted to Catholicism in the camp and the family was *not* pleased. Alfons Rosenberg won his freedom the moment he stepped on British soil.

By April 1941, 17,745 out of a total of close to thirty thousand internees had been released in England under the government's White Paper, and by August 28 only two internment camps were left on the Isle of Man, in contrast to nine the previous November. Only thirteen hundred *refugees* remained in internment. This acceleration in the release process was partly due to Churchill's change of attitude.

On May 15, 1940, he had thought it "important that there should be a very large round-up of enemy aliens and suspect persons in the country." As early as January 25, 1941, he wrote to the Foreign and Home Secretaries: "I have no doubt that there is a certain amount of risk that some bad people may get loose, but our dangers are much less now than they were in May and June. The whole organization of the country, the Home Guard and so forth, is so much more efficient against fifth column activities that I am sure a more rapid and general process of release from internment should be adopted."

On March 31, 1941, Sir Andrew McFadyan, one of the tribunal chairmen, made a speech at a political meeting. As a prospective Liberal candidate for Hampstead—the home base of many Jewish refugees—he referred to Alexander Paterson as the man "who had swept through the Canadian camps like a cleansing breeze." Sir Andrew spoke to some of the returnees and came to the conclusion that "they are ready to make every allowance for what they were charitable enough to regard as the kind of blunder liable to occur in war, eager to be employed in any work which furthered our common purpose. This attitude," he said, "does them honour—and should cause us some little shame. . . . We are not a cruel people, but we sometimes are— though our enemies rarely believe it—a stupid one. . . . That our *ersatz* Gestapo lost their heads is no excuse for the ill-treatment of Hitler's earlier enemies."

Knocking at the Gates

In Sherbrooke, Freddy Grant, the composer of "You'll Get Used to It," wrote another song:

> Knocking at the gates of the States
> To shelter from the rain;
> Hoping that soon out of the dark
> The sun will rise again.

> Knocking at the gates of the States
> To find a home at last;
> Waiting for a new day to dawn
> When stormclouds and night have passed.

>> I can see your blue-hilled horizon
>> Down where the rainbow ends;
>> But I can see no sun arisin'
>> If you don't know your foe from your friends.

> Isn't there a ghost of a chance
> Or will it be in vain?
> Knocking at the gates of the States;
> I'm dying to live again.

Almost 80 percent of those interned in Sherbrooke who had not volunteered to go back to England had made applications in 1938–1939 for visas to enter the United States. The figures must have been similar in the other camps. There still was not yet the slightest evidence that Canada was anxious to have us, but a large number of us had relatives in the United States who were making frantic efforts through the National Refugee Service in New York to get us there.

What was the difficulty? Generally speaking, it was the suspicion on the part of powerful interests in the United States that Washington was being asked to admit people who were neither wanted by England nor by Canada, and it was therefore concluded that these countries must have good reason for this. The specific difficulty was that we were in captivity, and that captives normally cannot enter the United States. As Alexander Paterson phrased it in his Report:

> The practice of parading them singly or in small groups under an armed guard at American consulates was not a solution that could be expected to work smoothly. . . . The American Consular authorities not unnaturally disliked the attendance of uniformed guards with fixed bayonets at their Offices, and normally refused to grant a visa to a man who was still in captivity.

In Hermann Bondi's case the news came through one day in Sherbrooke that he was to be taken to Camp S on St. Helen's Island in Montreal, and to wait there until his family's lawyer had completed arrangements for an interview with the American consul. Unlike most of the other internees who had merely applied for a visa, Bondi already had a valid one. The consul was willing to conduct the interview, but was not at first prepared to see Bondi in the custody of an officer in uniform. But somehow the lawyer persuaded the officer to stay out of the room, while the consul was examining Bondi. The visa was duly stamped. However, the U.S. Immigration Branch of the Department of Justice reversed this decision under the regulation which did not permit the entry of aliens from territories contiguous to the United States unless they had themselves paid the passage to that territory. An immigrant had to land as an ordinary civilian passenger at a United States port.

Bondi's parents in New York appealed. On February 3

Paterson called on the head of the Visa Department in Washington. He was told that a favorable decision had been reached, and that the Immigration Department had been overruled. On March 10 *that* decision was reversed once more by the Department of Justice.

But Bondi told me, "I didn't mind. I had never been anything but lukewarm about going to the States and happily returned to England in June."

The challenge facing Paterson and our other friends was, first, to convince the Americans that we were "rather nice people," and secondly, to construct a "scheme" whereby, when "knocking at the gates" of the United States, we were not captive but free men. Since the Canadian government would not consider our release in Canada, Saul Hayes and his associates devised a "scheme" whereby we would be shipped to Newfoundland first, released there, then appear before the American consul in St. John's as free men, and subsequently sail from there to New York.

Every little detail of the "scheme" was worked out, including travel and housing arrangements while in St. John's, and assurances were given that the American consul there would cooperate once the State Department had given official approval. Ottawa and London enthusiastically supported the "scheme," and Paterson had every reason to believe that Washington, too, would agree to it. For three or four months it looked as though it might work, and we in the camps received regular bulletins from relatives in the States, assuring us that it was only a matter of weeks, if not days, that we would receive the green light.

Paterson had to be in Washington on December 23 to begin serious negotiations. Accompanied by British and Canadian officials, he first saw Mr. Coulter from the Visa Department. That conversation went well. On Christmas morning he went to church. When he came back to his hotel he found in the lobby "little groups of parents awaiting me to ask when I was going to send the children back to them." He assured them he was optimistic. On December 26 he went to see the Attorney-General, Robert H. Jackson, who told him there were no legal difficulties at all, but there may be a political problem. So, together with the acting British ambassador, N. M. Butler, and the Canadian chargé d'affaires, M. M. Mahoney, Paterson went to see the Under-Secretary of State, Sumner Welles, who sympathetically asked for particulars on each individual case. All this looked hopeful. Paterson then returned to Montreal and the Committee was mobilized to compile a provisional list of one hundred names. Dossiers were transferred to the American consulate in Montreal. However, after a few weeks it became increasingly evident that the State Department was procrastinating.

Throughout the winter and early spring, negotiations continued, while Saul Hayes, Charles Raphael and their colleagues tried to cope with mountains of correspondence. In the meantime, Lord Halifax had become British ambassador to Washington, and on April 18 he and Paterson called on Secretary of State Cordell Hull. He, too, was sympathetic and promised to look into the matter.

The reasons for the delay of the "scheme" soon became clear. The American Legion had got wind of it. According to Saul Hayes, the word "scheme" had sinister, conspiratorial overtones in American usage which it did not have in Canada and England. "I wish we had never used it," he told me. In any case the American Legion had a bill introduced into Congress providing that nobody who had been in an internment camp could be admitted to the United States until one year had elapsed, during which time that person had enjoyed complete liberty in the country from which he came. That would have meant that we would have to be free in Canada for at least one year before being allowed to enter the United States. According to Alexander Paterson, "this was not a practical proposal to put before the Canadian authorities."

Dozens of letters and memoranda were sent to influential Americans. On May 30 Paterson lunched at the Mayflower Hotel in Washington with Colonel Taylor, "the *fons et origo* of the whole movement," as he described him, to try to persuade him that the men and boys who were supposed to enter the United States were by no means dangerous enemy aliens. "The conversation lasted for three hours," Paterson reported, "but I was not privileged to take a large part in it, as the patriotism of the Colonel is of a voluble and excitable nature."

To all intents and purposes, the Newfoundland "scheme" was dead. One of the reasons for its collapse was that, in

Paterson's words, "it was a cast-iron scheme which was being foisted on to the American public by a British official. . . . Latent but potent was an anti-Semitic bias, rarely admitted, as rarely missing."

All this was discouraging enough, but then another blow was struck. The question arose whether those of us who held visas for Latin American countries could travel across U.S. territory. Besides, new regulations had been issued prohibiting the granting of visas to any aliens with first-degree relatives in German-occupied territories. Eight months before Pearl Harbor, on May 15, 1941, the Canadian minister in the United States, Leighton McCarthy, conveyed to Ottawa a note from the State Department which illustrated to what extent the American government was willing to yield to isolationist and xenophobic pressure. Expressing sympathy with the refugees, the note stated that "the fact cannot be ignored that it has been found necessary to maintain these refugees in confinement under military supervision. It would be unwise, particularly at this time, to sanction the entry into the United States of any person whose presence might conflict in any way with our national defense program."

The note also suggested to the Canadian government that in its own interest and that of "any countries on this hemisphere" it should do nothing to facilitate entry into these countries, because such a move might "interfere with efforts now in progress to strengthen hemispheric defense."

The Canadian government was unimpressed by these arguments and did nothing to prevent an attempt initiated by some of our relatives in the States to circumvent the American Legion by entering the United States via Cuba.

The project (it was not a "scheme") was taken sufficiently seriously for six men to leave camp on May 12 and proceed via Halifax to Cuba. For each of them their relatives had deposited with the Cuban government a bond of $500, together with a return fare of $150 and a maintenance credit of $2,000. Ernest Eliel was one of the six; several others left on a later transport.

The ship sailed via Boston and Bermuda to Port-of-Spain, Trinidad, where the six disembarked on May 28. (It was known that on July 1 regulations would change. From that date on, only Washington and no longer the U.S. consul in Havana would have discretion in the granting of visas. The idea was to fly to Cuba via Venezuela, in the hope of reaching Havana around June 1, which would have given them one whole month to obtain their American visas.)

However, no one remembered to reserve space on the plane from Port-of-Spain to Havana. Everything was fully booked for weeks ahead and the six men did not reach Havana until July 5. Ernest Eliel stayed in Havana and finished his university studies there. He says his years in Cuba were not pleasant and he now takes the view that it would have been better had he waited patiently in the Canadian camp. A friend with whom he had travelled to Cuba managed to enter the United States in November 1941, because he had a Dutch wife who had preceded him. Two others also entered the United States in 1941; the rest had to stay in Cuba from between two and five years.

In spite of American concerns for hemispheric defense, at least two of our men went from the camp to Brazil and one to Venezuela. A few had visas for Mexico and other Latin American countries. Moreover, thanks to Dr. Jerome Davies of the Y.M.C.A., who somehow conjured up the fare, one of our boys joined his family in Shanghai. But that was in someone else's hemisphere.

A Man Called Blair
When the director of immigration in Ottawa heard that the Americans were unwilling to issue visas to refugees while they were in custody, he could not understand what the fuss was all about. "What we have to do," he wrote in an internal memo dated January 13, 1941, "is protect Canada against the release of these people here. Since there are probably about fifteen hundred who will want to go to the United States, we would create a very undesirable situation by having them released in Canada."

F. C. Blair had joined the Immigration Department in Ottawa in 1903, at the age of twenty-nine. In 1924 he was appointed assistant deputy minister and in 1936 he became director of the department, with the status of a deputy minister. His dedication to his job was so strong that, when he finally retired in 1944, he had accumulated two years' sick leave.

James Gibson, who in 1940 was private secretary to Mackenzie King, remembers him well. "All Blair's experience had been in Ottawa," he told me. "I think the record will show that he had been to fewer international meetings on immigration than some juniors in his department. In a curious way Mackenzie King had a kind of institutional loyalty to him as 'old Ottawa,' literally from the turn of the century. . . . If Blair wanted to slow down the wheels or put a stop to things, Mr. King wasn't going to bring any pressure to bear to change that. . . . There was almost a kind of legend about Blair: if you wanted to cite an example of obstructionism, he would have been the Number One candidate. . . . He was the most difficult individual I had to deal with the whole time I was a public servant. He was a holy terror!"

Constance Hayward thought of him as an honest man who did his duty as he saw it. She never quarrelled with him; it would have been useless. Saul Hayes observed that he was always "correct" with him, and never made an anti-Semitic remark in his presence. According to Hayes, Blair's successor, A. L. Jolliffe, was far more brusque than Blair, less righteous but more humane.

F. C. Blair was a major force in Ottawa. It was universally known that his minister, Thomas Crerar, was not particularly interested in the immigration department and allowed Blair to make policy rather than merely administer it. If he had wanted to, he could have made certain distinctions between ordinary immigrants and refugees from Hitlerism. The fact that he didn't do so made him the perfect servant of Mackenzie King's government.

Not that the prime minister was insensitive to Jewish suffering. After the Crystal Night in November 1938 he wrote in his diary, "The sorrows which the Jews have to bear at this time are almost beyond comprehension. Something will have to be done by our country." Three days after the Crystal Night, he attended the funeral of the wife of a man he deeply respected, the Jewish Member of Parliament A. A. Heaps. He then wrote that although it would be "politically difficult" to fight for the admission of some Jewish refugees, he felt it was "right and just, and Christian."

The remarkable thing about Mackenzie King was that, while his intentions were honorable, he always managed to justify his inability to carry them out by telling himself that to do so would endanger the delicate balance of political forces in the country. No one was better equipped than F. C. Blair to prevent upsetting this delicate balance.

On October 1938 he wrote that he was not in favor of persecuting Jews. "It would be far better if we more often told them frankly why many of them are so unpopular. If they would divest themselves of certain of their habits, I am sure they could be just as popular as our Scandinavians." When he received enquiries from Jewish refugees in England or France regarding possible immigration, he wrote, a month after war broke out: "When the Empire is fighting the battles for the liberty of these people, they at least ought to have enough red blood in their veins to find out before running away from the area of conflict whether their services will be of any value to the country which has given them shelter."

Soon after our arrival in Quebec, F. C. Blair was informed that there were some Jews among the prisoners from England. Blair was involved from the beginning. He sat on the committee Mackenzie King had appointed to consider internment matters. Sir Frederick Banting, the discoverer of insulin, and J. M. Macdonnell, president of the National Trust Company in Toronto, approached Blair "in the hope that it might be possible to have the case of these unfortunates dealt with in some way."

"I told Mr. Macdonnell," Blair wrote in an internal memo on August 7, 1940, "that evidently some mistake had been made in moving certain camps." Referring to some people "changing places in the transfer of enemy aliens to overseas places," he wrote, "It appears that all they had to do was switch numbers and we may find that in the end the presence here of so many Jewish people is merely another illustration of their ability to beat others to it."

In response to a query whether some of us might be allowed to remain in Canada, Blair wrote to O. D. Skelton, "It would be impossible to justify before public opinion in Canada the release of these internees in Canada and it would also open up again the matter of making Canada a waiting room for people who want to get into the United States."

Very soon a test case came up. Professor Peter Brieger of the University of Toronto had a seventeen-year-old nephew who was interned with us. (Ernest had gone to Leys School in

Cambridge.) Professor Brieger asked Leonard Brockington, who had been the first chairman of the C.B.C. Board of Governors from 1936 to 1939 and was now special assistant to the prime minister, to introduce him to Blair and others in Ottawa. He wished to discuss the possibility of his nephew's release. As a result of these meetings, Blair wrote to his minister:

> I am sure that once the door is opened the news will be put on the grapevine and we will be immediately confronted with appeals from all quarters. . . . I am sorry to trouble you with this, but it is necessary to face the ultimate issue and consider the general question of how far we can go, before the door is opened even to one. No doubt there are numbers of these people in internment camps who are quite friendly to the British cause whose cases must appeal to our sympathy. I have wondered sometimes whether the "mistake" in sending them here was not intentional on the part of some person overseas. Having gone through several experiences of getting an open door for a Jewish movement, I foresee a determined and concentrated effort to have all these people released in Canada, and if that is approved as a matter of policy we will try to work it out with as little delay as possible. But if it is not intended to release these people generally, then we must have some well-defined policy as to what cases are to be given favorable consideration.

The Brieger intercession failed, and the boy returned to England on the *Thysville.*

Blair was among those in Ottawa who took exception to the assumption prevalent in Westminster that the United Kingdom government had a say in who was to be released in Canada and who was not. In response to queries from our families in England, the Home Office often replied that it had no objection to releasing those internees in Canada whom it had cleared.

In an internal memo of September 24, Blair wrote: "I asked the Minister whether he thought the Home Office was playing the game with Canada in suggesting to private individuals the release of interned prisoners of war without first consulting the Dominion Government. It all looks to me like a well laid plan."

On the following day the minister, T. A. Crerar, reported to Blair that there had been discussion in the cabinet about the situation of anti-Nazi internees.

As you are aware, arrangements have been made, or are being made, to segregate internees of this class. The opinion of Council was that until the British government officially proposed to us that these persons should be released we should continue to treat them as internees. In other words, we will not assume the responsibility for releasing them. Should the British government formally request that some of these persons, or all of them, be released, the matter would be again dealt with by Council in the light of the circumstances that may exist at the time and with a view to determining whether or not, if released, they should be required to return to Britain or be permitted to remain here.

As an experienced civil servant Blair would never openly question the government's decisions. But sometimes, when he disagreed, he found it hard to conceal his views. In a letter dated December 21, 1940, to Colonel Stethem, he went as far as he ever did to unburden himself:

A couple of days ago Mr. Crerar said he thought we should take some steps now to deal with a few of the more pressing cases. The moment this is done, there will be, figuratively, a rush to the door and a determined effort to get the release of the whole lot, including those destined for the United States. Some people profess not to be able to understand why there should be any objection to admitting any number of Jewish people to Canada to wait here until they can get into the United States. We take a determined stand against anything of that sort because in no case should we have any assurance of their admission to the United States, and none of them could be sent back to where they came from. Further than this, it puts us into a very awkward position with residents of Canada whose requests for the admission of their relatives or friends have been refused. These residents cannot appreciate why we give favors to people in the United States which are refused residents of Canada. I am puzzled how to make a distinction, so far as admission to Canada goes, between the various cases that come up. The Government, as we are both aware, does not want any wholesale delivery of these internees to Canada.

During 1941 a number of decisions were made in Ottawa enabling the release of certain categories of refugees: those with first-degree relatives, students, skilled and agricultural workers.

Ernest Tobias, a Czech farmer in Wales, Ontario, wrote to Ottawa on September 23, 1941, asking for the release of "one H. S. Abrahamson to work on the farm at $20.00 per month plus board and clothes." In his reply to Mr. Tobias, F. C. Blair stated: "I observe . . . that you gave your citizenship as Czechoslovakian and your race as Czech. Mr. Abrahamson is of Jewish race and German citizenship. If, as I suppose, he is an Orthodox Jew, I wonder how you can expect him to board in your home if, as you declared on entry, you are of Czech race. In case you may think this question of race is unimportant, I may say that not once but scores of times we have been told by Jewish young men admitted to Canada to work on farms that they cannot remain on the farm because they cannot eat Gentile food. . . . There is really no object in releasing a Jewish young man expecting that he will be satisfied to work and live in a Gentile home."

However, F. C. Blair was less biased when he received letters from Professor Albert Einstein in Princeton recommending the release of Helmut Blume and Hans Reiche. Blair was an ardent collector of autographs.

The First Releases
On October 10, 1940, F. C. Blair received a lawyer sent to him by Mrs. Swinton, who lived in Vancouver. Her son's name had appeared on the short list of those who had first-degree relatives in Canada. Kurt Swinton was Heckscher's energetic right-hand man in running the Farnham camp school, and a popular lecturer on science. He held a Master's degree in radio engineering from the Technical University of Vienna.

The director of immigration conveyed to the lawyer that Ottawa had no jurisdiction over enemy aliens sent from the United Kingdom. "I also informed him," he later wrote, "that we were not favorably disposed to the liberation in Canada of aliens sent here for safekeeping by the British Authorities." But once the decision had been made to permit the release of internees with close relatives in Canada, nothing really stood in the way of Swinton's liberation. His sponsor was Howard Ferguson, a former premier of Ontario.

On February 18, 1941, Kurt Swinton was called to the commandant's office in Farnham. He had already heard from the family's lawyer that his release was imminent, so he was not surprised. "I took him to the station." Kippen recalls. "I had told him to put on civilian clothes. I didn't want the village to know about this release." As Swinton said goodbye to Major Kippen he clicked his heels. "I said to him, 'Kurt, cut that out. You don't click your heels in this country. Remember that!'"

Immediately upon arrival in Montreal, Swinton offered his services to the war effort. "I went from pillar to post," he told me, "to Northern Electric, to R.C.A., to Marconi, all to no avail. Then on to Ottawa, to the National Research Council and finally to the Assistant Commissioner for Internal Security of the R.C.M.P. He never blinked," Swinton recalls. "He treated me the way a snake treats a canary just before swallowing it. I told him, 'If you think I am a spy, re-intern me. If you don't, let me help the war effort.' One morning I woke up to discover that I was a commissioned officer in the Canadian Army."

The *Commandant's Journal* of Farnham for Monday, October 15, 1941, reads:

> Kurt Swinton, who was released from this camp as an internee on February 18, visited the camp today. He is now second lieutenant in the Royal Canadian Signal Corps. This visit caused some considerable excitement and comment. He saw some of his old friends who are interned here and lunched at the Officers' Mess as a guest of the Commandant. So the turn of the wheel within eight short months flips. Internee Swinton into Second Lieutenant Swinton and he remarked that this could not happen under any other flag than the Union Jack, and it is true.

Major Kippen made sure the guard officers were present at the luncheon. "They took a dim view of this," Kippen recounts.

> "How can we be sure of this fellow?" they said. I told them, "You be pleasant to him! I know this man's all right." So they were pleasant to him.
>
> Then, after lunch, I took him to the enclosure and handed him over to Sergeant-Major Breslin, a very good sergeant-major but a little bit narrow-minded. He looked as though to say "What *is* this!" Anyway, he took Swinton to his old hut where all his friends were. They all stood up when they came in; their eyes popped out of their heads when they saw him. The sergeant-major left him alone in there, on my orders, for half an hour or so. Then he

brought Swinton back to my office. He was so moved by the whole thing that he wept. Later I heard he was promoted to Captain, and then to Major, and then to Lieutenant-Colonel.

I did not see Kurt Swinton again until after the war. One day, by golly, I discovered that he was the speaker at the Canadian Club. So I went to hear him. He made a very good speech, too. I saw him afterwards; I wanted to take him home but he had a very tight schedule. And so did I. . . .

Charles Wasserman's mother was a psychoanalyst in Ottawa. She went to see Mackenzie King, and her son also was one of the first to be released. Two Camp B inmates who had escaped from Holland after the German invasion had only one contact (if that is the word) in Ottawa: Her Royal Highness, Princess Juliana. She had arrived in Canada with her children a week or so before us. In fact, rumors had circulated on the *Sobieski* that she was in the same convoy, but she had actually arrived a little earlier.

The two internees wrote a letter to the princess asking her to intercede on their behalf so that they could be re-united with their families. This is how they concluded their request:

> In daring to write this letter we trust that Your Royal Highness will help us to be free again, aware of the fact that the House of Orange has always given refuge to all those in distress, and particularly to the Jews fleeing from Spain and Portugal in the past centuries. Twice we fled from Nazi Oppression and we hope for a victorious end of this war, thus to be able to return to Holland and live again among the Dutch people which we learned to esteem so very much.
>
> With the deepest wish that the Almighty which gives salvation unto kings and dominion unto princes may give Your Royal Highness and all the Royal Family peace and rest and help you to return to your country for an everlasting kingdom of the House of Orange, we are, yours, . . .

In a short story entitled "The First Kiss," published in the *New Yorker* on January 12, 1963, Arturo Vivante wrote about "a camp on a small island on the St. Lawrence, in full sight of Montreal. Week after week I proclaimed my anti-fascism and hoped to be let out. At last, after a year, an American actress— a friend of my family—came to Canada for a Red Cross Tour. In Ottawa, she met Prime Minister Mackenzie King and asked him if I couldn't be released. The next morning I was free."

In 1940 Arturo Vivante was a sixteen-year-old Jewish boy whose family had fled from Italy to England in 1938 after Mussolini had introduced anti-Semitic laws. When Italy declared war, Arturo was interned and sent to the "Italian" camp on St. Helen's Island in Montreal. The American actress to whom he referred in his short story was the great Ruth Draper, whose dramatic monologues—*The Italian Lesson* and *The Children's Party*, for example—will never be forgotten by those who had seen her deliver them. She was a friend of Charles Raphael, and when she had heard that he was in Canada doing work for refugees, she wrote asking him whether he could help a protégé of hers. Ruth Draper had known Arturo Vivante since infancy. Allegedly, she had had a love affair in Italy with Vivante's uncle.

Instead of replying to the letter, Raphael called on Ruth Draper in New York.[26] They spent a lovely evening together; she wanted to hear all about the bombings in London. After supper she took out a letter from her London dresser, a cockney, and read it aloud. It was about "a funny thing that happened to Bert, Polly's second boy—the one with the red hair—who was knocked off his bike by an explosion on his paper round." It was a great performance.

Then she raised the subject of Arturo Vivante. She told Raphael that in her innocence she had assumed that it would be enough to tell the authorities that she was ready to take full responsibility for the boy if he could come to New York. She was baffled when she discovered that red tape prevented it. Charles Raphael recalls:

> Moving swiftly into high gear, she had spoken to some personal friends in high places—Mrs. Roosevelt, Cordell Hull, Justice Frankfurter, Governor Lehmann of New York, and others—but nothing, it seemed, could be done. Now she was not only baffled but enraged.

They both discussed possible strategies to get Arturo released.

> I had practically given up hope. . . . Each side was too committed and too obstinate. But if one refugee could somehow be released, it might loosen the whole log jam. "Then it isn't selfish of me to press just for Arturo," Ruth Draper said. "On the contrary," I told her. "If we could treat him as a special case it might start everything." She had a

tremendously strong, handsome face; one could hardly imagine anyone resisting her will. "I'm going up to Ottawa next week," she said, "to give a performance in aid of the Red Cross."

Prime Minister Mackenzie King attended Ruth Draper's performance and during the party he gave for her afterwards, he said, "Ruth, you have done so much for Canada; is there anything Canada can do for you?" So she said, "There is a young innocent boy, whom I've known since he was a baby, being held in one of your internment camps behind barbed wire. . . ." He turned to one of his aides and said, "Why is this being done?" The man turned red and said, "Oh, unfortunately there is some regulation. . . ." Mackenzie King got very angry and said, "This is outrageous! Release the boy tomorrow into Miss Draper's care and get rid of the regulation."

There is another version of this story: Alexander Paterson in his Report does not mention any performance, nor does he suggest that Mackenzie King ever met Ruth Draper personally. According to him, she and Paterson had a cup of tea together in Ottawa during her Canadian Red Cross benefit tour. On that occasion she told him about Arturo Vivante. He advised her that, for the time being, immigration to the United States was very difficult. Apparently, Ruth Draper wrote to Mackenzie King when she got back in New York. King replied immediately promising that in return for her services to the Red Cross Society of Canada, "he would use his prerogative to procure the boy's release."

Whichever version one wishes to accept, Mackenzie King did promise to obtain Vivante's release. In Vivante's own recollections he took poetic license when he said he was freed the next morning. King made his promise to Ruth Draper early in May; Vivante was released on July 10.

When Paterson heard about King's pledge he was delighted because, since Vivante was England's and not Canada's prisoner, it clearly would have been iniquitous to release the protégé of an American citizen when protégés of Canadian citizens (unless they were first-degree relatives) were still unreleased. He therefore decided to use Vivante's case in the manner Charles Raphael had suggested to Ruth Draper. To break the deadlock,

Paterson told Minister Crerar that he was unable, "in conformity with the principles governing the administration of British justice, to cable home advising anxious parents that they could secure the release of their boys in Canada if they would contribute ten thousand dollars to the Canadian Red Cross."

Paterson then wrote to the Under-Secretary of State, Dr. E. H. Coleman, that if the proposal to release Vivante in Canada could be accompanied by an assurance from the Immigration Department "that a considerable number of schoolboys and students shall similarly be released in this country," then Vivante's admission "will be welcomed as a liberal gesture on the part of the Canadian Government in helping to atone for some of the mistakes of my Government."

The minutes of a Canadian war cabinet meeting held on May 13, 1941, refer to "an internee from the United Kingdom on behalf of whose request for permission to remain in Canada upon release by U.K. authorities strong representations had been made." The prime minister expressed his views as to the governing principles when considering such requests, stating that cases should be dealt with sympathetically, "provided that the *bona fides* of applicants were established, and reasonable guarantees forthcoming as to maintenance." The cases should be investigated individually, with a view to reaching just and humane decisions. This was a monumental breakthrough, but except for a trickle of exceptional cases, bureaucratic inertia and lack of interest by a sufficiently large number of influential people in Ottawa prevented large-scale positive results.

One of these exceptional cases was Ernest Borneman. He did not have blood relatives in Canada, but thanks to Paterson's enterprising spirit and John Grierson's ability to cut the red tape and engineer his release, Borneman joined the National Film Board in Ottawa. The date of his release was June 10, one week before the second transport of 330 refugees returned to England, and the day his friend Heinz Meyerhof was buried in Sherbrooke.

Meyerhof was a brilliant medical researcher who had studied in Cambridge. He taught immunology at the camp university and had correctly diagnosed his own illness, which, I believe, was a perforated ulcer. The camp's medical officer had disagreed with him; had he concurred, Meyerhof's life would have been saved. Max Perutz, another friend of his, who by then was back in Cambridge, had to break the dreadful news to his mother. Borneman accompanied his friend's coffin to the burial ceremony at the Sherbrooke cemetery. Then a kind man from the Canadian Red Cross took him to the station and saw him off. This was the sad beginning of Borneman's happy and productive years at the National Film Board.

ELEVEN

The New Status

The breakthrough of May 13, 1941, was not merely the result of Mackenzie King's sense of obligation toward Ruth Draper; the groundwork had been carefully laid before by Alexander Paterson, Senator Wilson, Constance Hayward and Saul Hayes. They all agreed that, apart from the few special cases, releases on a large scale were unlikely unless our status was changed from prisoner of war, Class 2, to that of refugees, and that the running of the camps was taken out of the exclusive hands of Stethem, i.e. the Department of National Defence, and administered separately, though jointly with National Defence, and by the Secretary of State. A similar change had taken place in England during the previous summer, when control of internment camps was transferred from the War Office to the Home Office. This was the change Norman Robertson of External Affairs had had in mind the previous October.

Paterson had an active role to play in bringing about these changes. He had spent a good deal of time inspecting the camps. He had this to say when he recorded his impressions after returning to England in the summer of 1941:

> For some months I forbore from making any official comments on the conditions obtaining in the camps. It was not one of the primary objects of my coming and, as the Home Government had forced the custody of these refugees on Canada and failed to distinguish them very clearly from definite and dangerous Nazis, I was in rather a poor position to offer a very outspoken criticism. But the easy,

comfortable policy of silence and appeasement could not be maintained after a visit to a very lonely camp towards the end of winter. They brought into the cell a shy German of seventeen years, whom I asked to read one of the categories in the White Paper. He replied he could not read it as he had broken his spectacles five months ago and, although he had the money, was unable to get them mended. On enquiry it appeared that his story was true. For five months he had been unable to read books or newspapers, and even his mother's letters had to be read aloud to him by another refugee. . . . I should have forfeited much of my little self-respect if I had left Canada without making comment on such callous negligence.

On April 26, he presented his Report to Dr. E. H. Coleman, the Under-Secretary of State. He recommended that a Commissioner of Refugee Camps be appointed. "Preferably he should be a civilian, but if a suitable one cannot be found, there are at least two commandants of internment camps who have the vision and the tolerance to inaugurate a new administration. . . ." He stated that there was "something incongruous in the spectacle of some hundreds of professional men, mingled with baffled schoolboys and mid-European peasants, all being counted and kept by uniformed soldiers of every rank. It seems so odd that in many cases the better brains should be inside the wire."

Paterson recommended that welfare officers be appointed for each camp, "civilians of not too advanced an age." Radios and newspapers should be provided as a matter of course, because "innocent men interned for innumerable months suffer from 'internitis' and therefore overly indulge in 'grievance-chatter.'" He suggested the director should work closely with the Central Committee without there being any "feeling of suspicion and mistrust on one side or fear and reluctance on the other;" rules as to punishment should clearly be laid down, and it should be understood that punishment outside these rules would carry grave risks to those who inflicted them.

Paterson found it "very disturbing to find distinguished university professors dressed as circus clowns; the uniforms are both degrading and unworthy of a civilization that believed in encouraging the individual." He suggested that the uniforms be abolished altogether. Finally, visitors should be allowed, even "if there was an occasional letter or illicit comfort smuggled through the wire." He concluded that this was not "too high a price to pay for the inrush of fresh air that such friendly contact with the outer world would bring to the camps."

Most of his recommendations were accepted by the Canadian government. He now was very much involved in the search for a director. When no suitable civilian could be found in Ottawa, Montreal or Toronto, Paterson proposed Colonel R. W. S. Fordham, the commandant of one of the Nazi camps, who had impressed him "as a man of wide sympathy, strong character and a most charming personality." This recommendation also was accepted, and Colonel Fordham's appointment became effective on July 1, 1941.

Colonel Fordham was a man of forty-four who had had a distinguished career in the First World War when, at the age of twenty, he was made a captain. He was wounded, captured by the Germans and made a prisoner of war. Between the wars he had built a lucrative law practice in Niagara Falls, Ontario, and until 1939 when he joined the army, one of his clients was Sir Harry Oakes, the Canadian millionaire who was murdered in the Bahamas in 1943.

Sherbrooke, Farnham, and the Ile aux Noix were designated as Refugee Camps following our status change to "Refugee," effective July 1, 1941. (Camp B in Fredericton, New Brunswick, had been dissolved on June 21.) Our new status was duly announced. However, except for the abolition of uniforms and the establishment of visitors' huts, we did not notice any visible changes for the better. On the contrary, its primary effect was not to make us feel more satisfied with our lot, but less so, since it accentuated the absurdity of our imprisonment.

If a civilian commissioner had been found who understood us the way Paterson did, the new arrangements might have been given some meaning. However, Colonel Fordham was no Paterson. In spite of accepting Paterson's recommendations, he substantially retained the military character of the camps, notwithstanding the attitudes of commandants such as Major B. B. W. Minard (Ellwood's successor in Sherbrooke) and Major B. R. Racey on the Ile aux Noix, who put as human a face as possible on Fordham's military government.

On June 24, Ellwood met with the hut-leaders in Sherbrooke

to explain the new situation. The *Commandant's Journal* notes that "bitter disappointment was registered," because only minor changes were contemplated, and this came "as a distinct shock." The next day there was a mass meeting. "Address was well-taken," the *Journal* reports, "and a number of good-natured laughs were forthcoming ... because the Commandant accidentally opened his address by reference of 'this change from Refugee to Internment Camp.' The reversion of the order amused them intensely and put all in a good frame of mind to accept what he said."

On July 12 I wrote a letter to my sister in New York. When she received it certain passages (here italicized) had been underlined in red ink.

> One reason I write today is to show off the first privilege our new status has brought us, the fifty-line limit and this lovely notepaper ...
>
> Goldner was here yesterday and declared that emigration, even from Cuba, was now "practically hopeless." I feel the time is ripe for a decision. At the moment I'm strongly inclined to a return to England. ... As for the status, there is no definite information, but lots of very plausible rumors. In any case, as there is no chance for release here, these things are irrelevant as I am unwilling to wait literally for years for such an uncertain event. But in the balance of factors, it is important to realize that the privileges which we may get will *very probably not balance the curtailment of spare time by an extension of working hours*, and by the fact that, while up to now the Canadians have provided us very generously with food and clothing, *we will in future have to pay—in accordance with these reliable rumors—for our upkeep out of increased wages, the balance, rumors say, being paid by some Canadian Jewish organization, which will probably be less generous.*

On July 30 Colonel R. S. W. Fordham wrote a personal letter to my sister, adding it to mine:

Dear Madam:
The accompanying letter was referred to this office by the censor on account of part of its contents. The writer has underlined in red ink several statements that are either untrue or improper or unfair. It is sometimes extremely difficult to make certain Refugees comfortable and happy in

any sense of the words, as instances occur where they seem anxious to find fault and complain. It is feared that the present example is such a case. Actually, many changes have been made of late for the benefit of Refugees, and it is probably correct to say that nowhere are they treated better than in Canada. When Mr. Koch writes a letter of this character, he incurs the risk of having the question of his allegiance adversely viewed.

Nevertheless, the letter is being forwarded to you rather than withheld, and the writer is being asked to be more careful in future about what he puts on paper.

Yours very truly,
(R. S. W. Fordham)
Commissioner of Refugee Camps

I have been much more careful ever since.

If my letter had irritated Fordham, it was nothing compared to those Dr. Bruno Weinberg sent from Farnham. He was an experienced international lawyer who repeatedly wrote to Senator Cairine Wilson and Constance Hayward, as well as to others, asking for help in preparing a legal paper about our new status. He wanted to know, for example, whether Canadian law recognized the right of sanctuary; he requested copies of various orders-in-council and the War Measures Act; Dr. Weinberg was anxious to find out how much legal authority the League of Nations High Commissioner for Refugees, Sir Herbert Emerson, had in Canada. He also was curious about Emerson's legal relationship to Senator Wilson, the chairman of the Central Committee for Interned Refugees. (The Canadian government had approved her appointment as his representative.)

As Dr. Weinberg had received his legal training on the Continent, and not in England, many of his requests must have seemed somewhat outlandish. It may have been all right to ask for a copy of the Immigration Act, but why did he want to study the laws on foreign exchange? Why did he want to see the order-in-council giving Norwegian fishermen the right to fish in Canadian waters? Besides, Dr. Weinberg was less than discreet in some of his references to the legal competence of Stanley Goldner. He also questioned the wisdom of putting various committees together under the umbrella of the Central Committee for Interned Refugees.

Fordham was exceedingly troubled by all this. In a letter to

Constance Hayward dated September 20, 1941, he complained about Dr. Weinberg, who was "continually writing letters to addresses outside the camp containing unfair and often scandalous statements about the Canadian authorities, and the Government generally. He has been cautioned about this several times, but seems unable to control his pen. Weinberg's behavior in the camp has been such that he is not one whose release I could genuinely recommend, if I were asked for an opinion. One hesitates to think what kind of scurrilous trash he would write if we were at complete liberty."

On October 3 Fordham wrote to her again pointing out that would-be publishers of Weinberg's letters should be told that publicity of any kind about the camp "is frowned on at these offices." He added the following postscript: "I am going to consider re-interning any released refugee who publishes such material in defiance of the policy of these offices."

In a special letter addressed to the camp, Fordham noted that he had been appointed primarily for the purpose of bringing about improvements in the living conditions of refugees, but not to facilitate their release.

On one of his early visits to Farnham, Fordham granted an interview to the committee of hut-leaders. Here are excerpts from the minutes:

> *Question:* May we expect that further developments will bring about a status like that of the Kitchener Camp where walks and short trips were allowed without any restriction for C cases nine months after the outbreak of the war?
>
> *Answer:* In arranging for the granting of privileges the Commissioner of Refugee Camps has little interest in what may have been done elsewhere. What the future may bring forth will depend on how the present privileges are observed.
>
> *Question:* Similarly, may we expect self-administration like that of the Kitchener Camp? One roll call a day ought to be sufficient. Leave might be granted under certain conditions.
>
> *Answer:* Refugees will not be expected to say how Camps should be administered unless invited to do so.

These minutes do not accurately reflect the flavor of Fordham's relationship with us. On many occasions he listened carefully to what was said and seemed truly sympathetic. No doubt he tried hard to do his job but, being a lawyer, he was skeptical about our repeated protestations of innocence and loyalty. In another letter of November 29 to Constance Hayward, who had asked him for his response to a bulletin the Committee had written, he had this to say:

> Both Captain Kemble and I went over it and several points caught our attention. One is that not all the refugees sent to Canada were innocent, by any means. My list of those whose release may not be granted is mounting steadily. Doubtless very many were apparently free of complicity in any wrong-doing, but there were some who were by no means innocent. Another point is that it seems desirable to avoid stressing the suggestion that England committed a "wrong" in sending these refugees to Canada. That unfortunate country was in a desperate position in the summer of 1940 and expediency was a first consideration. There was really no time in which to consider the right or wrong of the plight of various groups in the country. When this fact is considered, the policy followed in respect of the numerous refugees is quite understandable.

This is not quite how Paterson had described the way the British had coped with their problem. Just as one had to be fair to the British, Fordham thought one should be fair to the Canadians. The following is taken from a summary of discussions with the Farnham camp leadership on September 7:

> *Situation in Canada.* It has been ascertained by the authorities that we are not dangerous. However, the Immigration Laws of this country are an obstacle to our release. Upon inquiry why it is necessary to keep us under severe military guard, in view of our not being dangerous, Colonel Fordham replied that this is done for our protection. The Canadian soldiers and population hate everything German and do not know the difference between Nazis and us. We pointed out that the facts should be published and full publicity be given to our fate. Colonel Fordham was of the opinion that this would be useless as 90 percent of the population were not interested in the refugee problem.

I believe Fordham often had the feeling we were too eager to enter the Canadian labor market and was worried that, unless this matter was handled carefully, we might take away jobs from Canadians who had joined up. On this point he and F. C. Blair saw eye to eye. He also tried to convey to us that, instead of constantly pressing for our release, we should increase the productivity of the Works Program.

As mentioned previously, the first workshop was installed in Sherbrooke in January, 1941, followed by many more in the other camps, at the instigation of Major D. J. O'Donahoe (Major Balls). The Ordinance Branch of the Department of National Defence was very pleased with them, and by June 1941 approximately nine hundred men in four camps were making nets, doing woodwork, sewing, knitting, farming, drafting, shoe-repairing, and manufacturing various wood products including ammunition boxes, kit bags, hold-alls and pillow cases. Profit on sales was $8,036.41. The entire initial investment in these workshops had been written off. In the second half of 1941 the program was so lucrative that it was decided to resume it the following year, with increased emphasis on farming on the Ile aux Noix. By then Camp Farnham—where throughout 1941 three hundred tons of vegetables had been harvested—had closed down.

At first, the daily wage per worker was twenty cents for a four-hour day. Effective September 1, 1941, the rate of pay was raised to thirty cents, partly as an incentive and partly to distinguish the refugees from the prisoners of war who were not permitted to make more than twenty cents a day. The foremen who worked two short daily shifts received fifty cents a day. Some efforts were paid on a piece-work basis. A few industrious internees thereby managed to earn the equivalent of a week's wage for one day's work.

While many of us worked hard in these workshops and enjoyed the fruits of our labors, everyone recognized that as the project was highly profitable to the government, there was a certain danger in making the operation too lucrative. After all, the British were paying for our upkeep, and when the initial Canadian investment had been amortized, Ottawa might not be quite as enthusiastic about releasing us. This may have been an unworthy thought, but it was not entirely unrealistic.

Therefore, on February 21, 1942, the leadership of Camp N in Sherbrooke dispatched a memorandum to Major Balls, pointing out that "our willing cooperation in the Works Program for more than a year has secured for us the prospect of being permanently penalized, by our internment becoming a permanent institution. We, on the contrary, wish to express our firm belief that most of the activities of the Works Program could reach their real significance only if we were able to work eight hours a day as free men."

Trouble in Farnham

The following is an excerpt from the *Commandant's Journal*:

July 28: Very busy day concerning new status. The amount of work has increased and will increase considerably owing to this change.

July 29: Arrangements made to sell beer in the compound canteen. This announcement caused a considerable amount of excitement to the Internees and it is a privilege that will be appreciated. . . .

July 30: The compound sewing shop busy taking the red circle off the jackets and the red stripe off the trousers of the Refugees. The Refugees are not permitted to have any red on their uniforms on or after August 1, 1941.

July 31: The camp is now more or less settled down to the new Refugee basis. It will take some little time to make all the adjustments as the new status has apparently proved disappointing in scope for Refugees.

This month of July has been an eventful one in the camp. The change of status from an Internment Camp to a Refugee Camp was quite momentous. It will require a little time for the staff, for instance, to readjust themselves to the new status; the Internees now Refugees are the same people as before, but a stroke of the pen (an order in council) has given them many of the things they have demanded. It is thought that they will be very disappointed with what they have got and will agitate for more.

The various elements and factions in the compound are probably reacting in different ways and it will be interesting to know the outcome. Some of the more cynical Refugees say that nothing has changed at all except that "the illegitimate child has been rechristened." A high degree of man-management is required to run a show of this kind.

August 2: There seems to be from seven to twelve professional politicians in there whose main interest is politics, especially of the radical kind. Now that the Refugee status is established, these people are likely to agitate for more and more privileges and rights. In any case, it is a phase that has to be passed through and the transfer period from Internee to Refugee is likely to be a troublesome and stormy one from the camp administration standpoint.

August 8: This was the last day allowed for wearing of the old Prisoner of War uniforms. It has been a difficult job to have all the uniforms altered, as it was necessary to have the large red circle on the back of the jackets covered up with blue denim. The red stripe on the trousers was also covered up with a piece of material sewn over it. Refugees are not allowed to wear the Prisoner of War uniform under any circumstances, and of course they are delighted not to have to wear it, although, strange as it may seem, quite a few are not in any hurry to part with it.

August 10: There was quite a commotion in the compound today at approximately 1500 hours. Apparently a good number of Refugees, led by someone who is at present unknown, conceived the idea of painting a large sign on the roof of the dining hall which faces the west and the road that runs north from the Farnham–St. Brigide highway to the . . . A-12 training camp. It was noticed immediately they started to work and it was taken down. Three Refugees were taken in the detention cells for not complying with an order given by an N.C.O. [The sign was to read *Refugee Camp.*]

August 11: Five Refugees up today for orderly room and sentenced to detention varying from 3 to 7 days. This was in connection with the trouble yesterday in the compound and these 5 Refugees were guilty of non-compliance with orders.

August 19: More grumbling in the compound stirred up by the communistic element there. Apparently . . . the communist leaders work with indirect and undercover methods. Someday their efforts will probably blossom forth in some kind of riot or trouble.

A small number of Nazis were still left in Farnham, some painfully known from pre-war encounters in Germany or

Austria. In the summer and early fall of 1941 those of us who had been in contact with relatives in Europe through the Red Cross had their letters returned with the notation "addressee unknown." The conclusions we came to were obvious: the deportations to the east had begun. Understandably, the presence of Nazis in our midst, however "well behaved," had become unbearable, especially since the camp had been officially renamed "Refugee Camp." Our camp leadership sent a cable to the British Home Secretary, Herbert Morrison, to advise him of a resolution passed "by the whole camp community," asking for the removal of all those who were not anti-Nazi. The cable was intercepted by the censors.

Consequently, on August 13 and again on September 14, our camp speaker wrote letters to Fordham asking for the removal of those who were not refugees. At the same time, the speaker complained to him that the right to communicate directly with the Home Office had been denied to us; this, the letter pointed out, was in contravention of the White Paper.

Fordham did not respond to the request. Among those who did not wish to be labelled "refugee" was Dr. E. R. Winkler, our camp doctor, who had the confidence of the Canadian medical officer, Captain F. W. Gilday, and his orderly, W. Kiefer. Dr. Winkler was a tall, thin, taciturn man who kept his views to himself, in contrast to his talkative orderly.

On September 14 at 10:30 p.m., half an hour after lights-out, Kiefer was in the washroom of Hut A, together with another man, a merchant seaman named Ehricke. Addressing Kiefer in German with the familiar *Du*, Ehricke asked him with some emotion in his voice whether it was true that he considered all those who had applied for enlistment in the Pioneer Corps as traitors to the Fatherland. Kiefer brusquely replied: "Don't say *Du* to me. We are not on such terms. I don't want to talk to you." This enraged Ehricke. "If you're not a refugee," he shouted, "why don't you talk to the Swiss consul?" Kiefer replied, "I haven't needed the Swiss consul yet. But whenever I need him I will see him. I'm not a refugee. Everybody knows that." At this point the merchant seaman grabbed Kiefer and beat him up.

An internal Board of Inquiry was immediately set up to decide how best to deal with this breach of law and order. Five days later, Leo Inslicht, the newly elected camp speaker, wrote to Captain Gilday requesting Kiefer's dismissal, because "the camp as a whole regards him as a person under suspicion of owing allegiance to the present German government, and that he may be using his position and the information accessible to him by his activity in the hospital in a way detrimental to the interests of the refugees." Inslicht enclosed a copy of a report in which Kiefer was quoted as saying, "We are in possession of the names of all the men who have applied for the Pioneer Corps, since we examine everybody. Some day it might be an advantage."

Captain Gilday replied:

> Your insolent letter received. I am in charge of the hospital and any interference from without . . . will be dealt with by me and not to your advantage. Kiefer will not be dismissed as long as he discharges his duties to my satisfaction.
> This is purely and simply a medical and hospital matter.
> F. W. Gilday, (RCAMC)
> Medical Officer, Camp A.

The camp leadership published this correspondence together with similar letters exchanged between them and the authorities.

The camp was in a state of high tension. The dispute had brought to a head a confrontation between the inmates and the military authorities. We had pressed for the removal of Nazis, but nothing had been done, and we realized that unless they were removed there were bound to be more ugly incidents. It was completely incomprehensible why the authorities had not responded to a request which seemed perfectly reasonable to us.

However, the camp was not entirely united on this issue. The inhabitants of the Priests' Hut, who had always kept aloof from camp politics and were preoccupied with their own concerns, did not associate themselves with the majority. Some of them may have thought that the camp was unduly influenced by communist agitators, while others may have felt the Nazis were not doing anybody any harm. In any case, this was not *their* problem.

As for the majority, this was a highly emotional issue touching on a fundamental principle, namely our status as refugees. To most of us it was irrelevant that a small number of communists were making the most of the confrontation. Jews and gentiles felt equally strongly about this principle.

On September 25 the commandant took action. Without

notice, seven men were removed to the "Italian" camp on St. Helen's Island in Montreal. They were in his and Fordham's eyes the ringleaders. Some of them were communists, such as Wilhelm Koenen and the actor Gerhard Hintze, who in highly dramatic fashion had to be carried out of the camp while declaiming to his "Kameraden" that "this is fascist-capitalist democracy in action!" Others were by no means communists, such as camp speaker Leo Inslicht, a quiet, thoughtful man. He had written a long, careful document in Camp B some months earlier pleading for a change of status. But Inslicht had caused displeasure in Fordham's eyes for "inaugurating a spirit of resistance among sections of the refugees that had not been favoured by the previous leader." This also gave Fordham the opportunity to act against Bruno Weinberg, the fervent social-democrat, who had been the debating champion *against* the communists in Camp B. After Weinberg's release, Fordham had several meetings with him in Ottawa. He began to respect Weinberg's superior legal mind and at one point even offered him a job in the Civil Service. Weinberg declined.

As a result of the "seizure" of the seven men, hundreds of internees rushed out of their huts, streamed into the compound shouting protests, and demanding the return of the seven. The response of the authorities was to place a machine gun near the front gate.

The camp leaders implored everyone to return to his hut. They were deathly afraid that things might get out of hand and that some of the guards would start shooting. A meeting was called. It was decided to go on a hunger strike immediately until the seven were returned. When the trucks tried to enter the camp with the food rations, pickets blocked the entrance. Some of our boys quickly sneaked into the kitchen to steal bread and smuggle it into their huts. During the following day much of the anger, which up to then had been focussed on the military *outside*, was deflected to the strike-breakers *inside*, i.e., those living in the Priests' Hut.

Here is an extract from the diary of Father Anton Ummenhofer:

> The camp was at a boiling point: it was like being inside a
> swarm of bees. . . . At around two o'clock the seven men
> were taken away. With Hintze they had to use force which

got the mob even more excited. The mob shouted at the soldiers "Fascists! Traitors!" The soldiers took it with patience and calmness. The machine guns at the gate fired two shots into the air. In the uproar the men shouted, "Why don't you shoot us!"

We in the Priests' Hut demanded our food from the adjutant. Our rations arrived in the evening. . . . Some of our people went to the kitchen and prepared the meal. We were breaking the strike. Some of us were spat at. A few dozen people from other huts also came to eat. On Saturday morning there were about eighty of us at breakfast. The picketers stood in front of the dining hut and wrote down the names of everyone who came to eat. When we left, we nearly came to blows. Excitement continued to increase; the boys moved around in gangs. They plundered the kitchen's wood supply; then they assaulted the kitchen. People inside were beaten up and literally thrown out. A "raiding party" (like in the SA) went from hut to hut and took out the beds. There was serious physical abuse which could have ended in deaths. Some men fled to the detention hut. The rations truck was kept away by force. Finally the "raiding party" came to our hut; we turned them away calmly, whereupon their leader called them back. Then we contacted the adjutant and demanded more protection. He promised it to us and asked us to pray that he need not shed any blood. We received our rations in the hut and ate our meals there. Gradually people came to their senses. Colonel Fordham set an ultimatum and the strike broke down.

From the *Commandant's Journal:*

September 28: At 1000 today the camp leader, deputy camp leader and hut leaders were paraded before Col. R. S. W. Fordham. After a full discussion the camp leaders were told that the hunger strike must stop immediately, and until it did, nothing could be discussed. The hunger strike ended at 1430 hours and the situation quited [sic] down. Col. Fordham left the camp at 1800 hours for Ottawa being satisfied that the situation was well on its way to normal again.

September 30: . . . The whole dust-up was more of a tempest in a teacup than anything else. The political agitators had got the atmosphere to such a point that all that was needed was something to touch off a riot. The removal of the seven men to another camp . . . was exploited to the full. . . . If it had not been this incident it would have been something else.

The officers had done everything they could to end the hunger strike. One of their methods had been to invite acting camp leader George Liebel to the officers' mess and confront him repeatedly with a variety of dishes he had not seen since before internment—roast chicken, etc. They wanted to tempt him to eat, so that they could announce to the camp that the leader himself had broken the strike. Liebel stood firm.

The medical officer's methods were a little more straight-forward. A refugee who had gone to see Dr. Winkler in the hospital for treatment of a painful right hip was present when the M.O. asked Dr. Winkler, "Who is this man?" Dr. Winkler replied, "He's the fellow on hunger strike." "Chuck that bastard out; we're not going to treat him," said the M.O.

In the end, the camp leadership had to call off the strike. It had proved impossible to maintain adequate discipline. A series of other ugly incidents, many of them involving the guards, had occurred.

When the strike was over, twenty-eight camp leaders, including hut leaders and other office-holders, put their signatures to a letter addressed to the commandant:

> We deeply regret certain events which have taken place during the last few days. . . . We wish to emphasize that disparaging expressions directed against Canadian officials and guards by some inmates are strongly disapproved of by us. . . . We feel shocked at certain incidents. . . . We wish to regard these outbursts as a temporary loss of self-control. . . . We herewith undertake to make it our personal task to exert all our influence to bring about a spirit of mutual tolerance as long as we belong to one community, involuntary though it may be.

Major Kippen accepted the apology.

The trouble that had occurred in Farnham soon became known in England. Two M.P.s, D. N. Pritt and Eleanor Rathbone, raised the matter in the House of Commons; the Home Office asked Ottawa to explain what had happened. Fordham had to write so many letters that when he was asked one more time— six months after the event—he noted testily that the matter crops up "with the same frequency and regularity as the moon changes." Yet, he remained convinced to the end that he had done the right thing. "The camp returned to normal as soon as the trouble-makers had been removed," he wrote. "Productivity in the Works Program increased." Although he would have been justified in keeping the seven men on St. Helen's Island, Fordham did allow four of them to be sent back to England, and the remaining three were returned to Farnham at the end of the year.

As to the attitude of the "trouble-makers" vis-à-vis Dr. Winkler and Kiefer, Fordham stated that a number of the refugees, headed by Inslicht, "saw fit to take a violent dislike to these two men, *for no logical reason* [italics mine], with the result that Dr. Winkler had a heart attack and Kiefer feared for his personal safety." Eventually both men appealed to Fordham to be transferred to a place "that would give them freedom from persecution by Jews. Each virtually became a refugee from refugees."

One wonders how it was possible for Fordham to write *"for no logical reason."* He had been the recipient of a number of specific and emphatic requests to have Dr. Winkler, Kiefer, and a few others, removed for reasons he could not have forgotten. Alexander Paterson, a shrewd and discriminating observer of human nature, had called him "a man of wide sympathy, strong character, and most charming personality." He was not a professional soldier, inexperienced in civilian and political affairs, but a successful lawyer of some sophistication. Those who remember him would not call him insensitive to the sufferings of individuals. Did he really believe that this was a matter of civil rights, that the civil rights of a few Nazis had to be protected from a mob of refugees?

I have only one answer. Like Blair, he was a man of his time who reflected prevailing attitudes. No doubt he hated the Nazis in Germany, but the presence of a few Nazis in a refugee camp was not as serious as the far more weighty issue of "communist trouble-makers." To him we bore the image of a group of hysterical, self-pitying and chronic complainers who had been induced through cunning communist tactics to invent a phony issue to force a confrontation. The presence of a few Nazis was not "a logical reason"; in his view our real purpose was to make trouble for trouble's sake.

Two months later, a similar situation arose in the Sherbrooke camp. It was a far less emotional affair, but worth mentioning because it illuminates the strength of Fordham's convictions and his attitude toward us.

On June 6, Commandant Major B. B. W. Minard called to his office camp speaker Franz Kraemer to ask him to see a seventy-year-old man named Meyerhofer, who was about to be transferred to Sherbrooke from another camp. His release had been authorized by the Home Office and he was free to return to England. But he didn't want to go there; he wanted to go to Mexico instead. Although his chances to get a visa were negligible, he was quite prepared to wait for it in a Canadian internment camp. So far, so good. But there was one problem: Mr. Meyerhofer, you may recall, was the man who, two years earlier in Trois Rivières, had left the ranks of the refugees to join the Nazis. Not only that, but he had declared in public that he was a German and would rather belong to "these people than to the Jews."

Of course Kraemer did not know this at first. But Major Minard and his adjutant, Captain A. P. Cameron, did. The meeting had been arranged outside the compound and the sad old man made quite a good impression on Kraemer, "until he suddenly made a few casual remarks on the side, indicating that he was neither a refugee nor well disposed towards the Jews." (I am quoting from the subsequent exchange of letters with Fordham.)

Franz Kraemer returned to the camp and soon discovered that at least forty men remembered old Meyerhofer from Trois Rivières. On June 14 he and the other camp leaders sent a letter to Fordham:

> We certainly respect the old age of this man, but we cannot be expected to respect a man who, in the presence of Captain Cameron, has openly shown by his general attitude all but disrespect for us. Naturally, this man was neither persecuted nor attacked during his stay in the camp. It has been put to us that motives of intolerance underlie our attitude. If there is any question of intolerance, it comes from the Authorities who force this man into the camp against his own will.... We insist that men who openly expressed their sympathy with the Axis powers should be taken out of our midst.... We refuse to be mixed up with Nazi sympathizers or converted Nazis.

On June 18 Fordham sent this reply:

Some of the expressions used in the letter struck me as being highly improper to come from interned refugees and indicate very clearly that many of those at Sherbrooke Camp do not realize their position.

The use of the word "refuse" and "insist" . . . is very irregular and no more letters containing such expressions will be tolerated. The writer is entirely familiar with the various types of men who are at Sherbrooke and will send thereto whoever should go there. Interned refugees who see fit to object to any such transfers will be moved elsewhere, if necessary. In the event of any similar letters being sent to these offices and signed by camp representatives, they will be removed from office peremptorily.

There is no intention whatsoever of sending Meyerhofer to another camp and he must be accorded the tolerance and fair treatment due him. . . .

TWELVE

The Final Phase

On May 13, 1941, the Canadian cabinet had decided to consider individual releases if sponsors could be found to guarantee our maintenance. Mainly thanks to the work of the Central Committee for Interned Refugees, by April 1942 sponsors and employers had been found for more than two hundred and fifty of us; in the following months the process was considerably speeded up. Three categories received priority: students, men qualified for war work (which was gradually diluted to mean *any* employment in industry or business), and work in agriculture.

The releases began in earnest in October and November of 1941. The sovereign authority in matters of release, once authorization had been obtained from the Home Office, was Blair. He discharged his duties with customary, if not excessive, conscientiousness. Admittedly, he was right to be suspicious of some of our more imaginative claims. If anyone said he had seventeen years of experience as an *animal raw produce sorter* he only may have had sixteen years. If Blair found out, that was the end of it and the man was declared unreleasable. If anyone wrote down that he was a farm laborer with considerable experience, Blair's immigration officers would inspect his hands to see whether they showed traces of manual labor. A reckless friend of mine, who has since become a millionaire, had told them he was a toolmaker. When he was released it was quickly discovered that he did not know the difference between a hammer and a screwdriver. He was promptly reinterned. One rabbinical student, who was barely eighteen years old, declared he had eighteen months' experience as a plumber. Blair raised his eyebrows; how could such a young boy have acquired such extensive know-how? The boy's explanation was that he had learned plumbing while he was in camp.

Fortunately, Saul Hayes and Constance Hayward were often on hand to soften the stern old man. His power to hold up things was formidable, and his immigration officers, who had to conduct the long interviews in the camps, occasionally, but not always, reflected their boss's caution. This caution was, of course, magnified if there was the slightest taint on the applicant's record. This happened to our two musical superstars, Helmut Blume and John Newmark.

The Home Office had already authorized Blume's release, but his dossier contained a confusing reference to his tribunal hearing in England during the winter 1939–40, when he had told the judge that he had a Jewish mother, but had been drafted into the German Army in 1938. His gentile father had been a psychiatrist in charge of a large mental institution and, consequently, from early childhood on, Blume had been familiar with the various symptoms of mental illnesses. In order to obtain his discharge from the German Army he had simulated incipient schizophrenia. It was a highly dangerous life-and-death game. In the end he was successful and able to make his way to England.

When the story of this ploy came up at the tribunal hearing, the judge never doubted Blume's statements. He was certified as a genuine refugee, but his record contained an unexplained reference to a "nervous breakdown." For two or three months Blume sweated blood while many of his friends were released. He was in despair after the immigration officer had said to him, "Either you really did suffer a nervous breakdown, in which case you are disqualified from entering Canada, or you made up the whole thing, in which case you are a fifth columnist and will blow up bridges." In the end, one of his friends was visited by a woman from Ottawa who knew Blair. She came to see Blume, and when she later reported to Blair that the young man did not look like a fifth columnist, he ordered his release forthwith.

A few months later Blume gave his first piano recital in Ottawa. He paid Blair a visit to thank him, and although the old man was cordial he seemed a little confused because he said,

"My dear Mr. Blume, if we had as little trouble with other refugees as we've had to get you released, everything would be fine."

John Newmark's difficulties were slightly different. The camp doctor in Camp B was an ardent theatre buff from Berlin; he had been so delighted with Newmark's staging of *Androcles and the Lion* that he decided to reward him with a week's stay in the camp hospital. "It was heaven," Newmark recalls. "No roll calls, unlimited amounts of jam for breakfast, linen on the bed, and complete privacy."

When it came to his interview the immigration officer asked Newmark, "Have you ever been ill?" Newmark said no.

"You've never had a nervous breakdown?" the officer continued.

"Never," Newmark insisted.

"Then you're a liar!" the man exclaimed triumphantly.

It soon dawned on Newmark that the stage-struck doctor had entered "nervous breakdown" in his medical records to account for his hospital "holiday." However, justice prevailed in the end.

Blair's approval was required for any change of occupation once release had been granted. (At the time, selective service regulations did not permit a Canadian employee to change jobs without permission either.) Moreover, while he did not actually have the power of veto over marriages, it was made known to us that the Immigration Department frowned on our getting married while our status, "friendly aliens enjoying temporary liberty in Canada," was still open-ended. I remember one of our impatient young lovers who had to sign a statement to the effect that he would defer his intended wedding until it had been determined whether or not he could stay in the country.

There was no clear distinction between Blair and Fordham's authority over us. Fordham was responsible for us whether we were behind barbed wire or not. For example, it was he who informed us that we were ineligible for service in the Canadian Armed Forces and that we should keep our personal belongings to below one hundred and fifty pounds.

For those whose liberation went smoothly, the pattern was very much the same: initial exhilaration, enchantment with Montreal, sometimes disappointment with Toronto, especially because on Sundays practically everything was closed. Add to that the close contacts evolving into friendships with Saul Hayes, Constance Hayward, Ann Cowan, and Stanley Goldner and the other men and women of the Committee who worked so hard to introduce us to Canadians, find sponsors for those left behind in the camps, and give us moral support. Charlotte Whitton, later mayor of Ottawa, was also among those who took an interest in the Committee's work; she had been active in the refugees' cause since the late thirties.

Yet, for many, release was a bittersweet experience: they felt lonely and confused at first, having become accustomed to camp life where all decisions were made for them and everything was predictable and safe. Now, suddenly, crossing a street in a busy city was an unnerving experience; sleeping alone in a room without hearing the comforting sound of a hundred men snoring was like being exiled to some distant, unfamiliar and boring island. I was surprised to learn from a well-adjusted friend that for months after his release he avoided traffic and busy streets; he couldn't stand the people, the cars and the noise. There were even some who preferred Toronto to Montreal. This is an extract from a letter from Hans F. to his old friends in camp:

> To tell the truth I didn't enjoy my short stay in Montreal. I was so excited about the sudden change of atmosphere that I simply could not believe I was a free man. I felt awful and had a splitting headache throughout my stay. . . . I was only too glad when I jumped on the Ottawa train last Sunday morning. . . . It was raining hard all the way from Montreal to Ottawa, and the dark and dusky morning somehow corresponded with my inner sadness. . . . I felt so terribly lonely without you boys; you cannot imagine my feelings. Once you have left the camp you realize for the first time how much you miss the boys with whom you have been living these last two years. And while I am writing these lines I feel that I am among you in Hut 6B or in the Canteen Hall. . . .
>
> Well, travelling in a railway coach you meet all kinds of people. . . . "It is a rainy morning," said an army officer who was also going to Ottawa. "Rainy morning is right," I replied. . . . "Are you a Norwegian?" he asked. "No." He: "Are you coming from Belgium, then?" I: "No." He: "I like your European accent. It's swell. Are you an Austrian?" I: "My God, can't you stop asking questions? The government

would not like me to talk about my country of origin." He: "If that's the case, I'm sorry to have asked you."

And from another letter, written by Henry G.:

When we ten had passed the gates, everybody felt somehow funny and during our journey in a not too crowded C.P.R. train to Montreal everybody was quiet. At Windsor Station a girl from the Committee awaited us, and a few minutes' walk found us at their offices. . . . I left quickly to have a short glance at Montreal, together with R. We both felt rather dumbfounded and out of place. The crowded streets, the dense traffic, the strongly painted girls dressed in bright colors—but men wear bright colors, too—the difficult street crossings, and so on. At 3 o'clock I left Montreal again, this time alone, in a marvelous air-conditioned train with magnificent seats. I felt very tired, but I could not sleep as the engine made a terrific noise before passing the frequent unguarded crossings. Punctually at 9:45 I was in Toronto where I was met by E. with whom naturally I speak only English. . . .

Toronto is a modern town with many skyscrapers, and I like it better than Montreal. The streetcars—you do not call them trams here—are mostly very modern, and, as each line goes straight along one street only, you soon find your way through the city easily. . . . It is amazing how quickly you make acquaintances. It is a custom here—naturally not done by me—to whistle when passing nice girls who might then stop and you can talk with them. I have never seen anything like it; you can get to know a lot of people without difficulty. Yesterday a nice friend of E's was driving us around in his car, and then suddenly he stopped in front of a house of relatives of his without saying a word to us. We had to go in and after having introduced us to various people with the words, "Meet my friend Henry" I was considered one of them. Funny, how simple all this is.

Most sponsors had no reason to regret their generosity toward the internees, but no doubt there were also cases of frustration and disappointment by both sides. In a curious way our cause became fashionable. Apparently it did not harm the social prestige of many good citizens to be patrons of refugees, and the Committee people in all likelihood appealed to individual vanities when they tried to persuade someone to "take" a boy. We were lucky. Many young "native" Canadians who wanted to attend university did not have sponsors to underwrite their studies, nor did they have kind Committee ladies to invite them to Sunday afternoon tea.

On Monday, October 27, I was called out of the compound to see the commandant. My first thought was that I was in some sort of trouble. I was told two people were waiting to see me in the visitors' hut. I had no idea who they might be, since I had received no advance notice. My heart was beating furiously; this *has* to be good news, I thought. There they were: a tall gentleman of about seventy and his wife who was much younger, handsome and beautifully dressed. From the way he thanked and dismissed the guard I had the impression—which turned out to be correct—that he was a retired military man.

They told me they had received a letter about me from England. I immediately remembered that my mother had written to me about some friends of friends who had been told about me. In order not to build up my hopes, she had added that she didn't expect anything to come of it: this had been one of several such approaches.

"Well, how are they treating you?" the lady asked.

"Not bad," I smiled.

"How about the camp school?" he enquired.

"It's great," I replied. It turned out he knew a good deal about it. He and H. M. Tory had worked together during the First World War organizing the Khaki University.

"Well now," he continued, "I think we should try and get you out under the students' scheme. That should not be too difficult. Then we'll see about the Army. I understand you're prepared to enlist?"

I swallowed hard. "Yes, of course," I said. "But I understand they won't accept me."

"We'll see about that," he said. "I think I'll be able to get you into a decent regiment."

I attended a number of camp farewell parties in my honor. Since I was by no means the first to be released under the student scheme, a certain routine had evolved at these parties. Whoever was leaving had to pledge to find sponsors for his as yet unliberated friends.

On Sunday afternoon, November 9, while listening to the Mozart *Requiem* on the radio, I was once again summoned. This time the immigration officer wanted to ask me a few questions.

"I understand you already have a degree," he said. "Why would you want to get another one?"

I told him it was true that I had been prevented from taking my final exams, but that Cambridge University had given me my B.A. as though I had been absent for reasons of health.

"How old are you?" he then asked, his nose stuck in the dossier which contained my birthdate.

"Twenty-two."

"Did you know that you have to be under twenty-one to benefit from the student scheme?"

"Yes, I've heard that, but I understand that Toronto has some interesting postgraduate programs for law students. Surely . . ."

He was a kind man and did not hold up my release. Together with two others I left the compound the next morning, the first time since our traumatic arrival in Sherbrooke on October 15, 1940, thirteen months earlier.

Before we were allowed to board the train our luggage was searched. After that, everything went well. I was just at the right age to savor all the joys of my new-found freedom. My sponsors met me at Windsor Station and I said goodbye to my two colleagues.

The first thing I was offered at my sponsor's house in Westmount was a glass of scotch. Never has scotch tasted better. During dinner I tried to be amusing about camp life; after dinner I phoned a friend who had arrived in Montreal a couple of weeks earlier. He too had family in the United States and told me that, the American Legion notwithstanding, it might be possible, after all, to cross the border. Once more I was faced with a dilemma; should I join the army in Canada, or go to the States, where sooner or later I would no doubt enlist in the American army? (This was three weeks before Pearl Harbor.)

The next morning I took a bath in a real bathtub. Then I phoned my sister in New York, who confirmed that the American doors seemed to have opened again. This was corroborated by the Committee people whom I had gone to see at 1121 St. Catherine Street West.

In the end I was spared any decision-making. I found out that the Americans had no intention of letting us in, and the

Canadian Army was as yet disinclined to accept enemy aliens. After ten luxurious days at my sponsor's house I registered at the School of Law at the University of Toronto. While life on and around the campus was highly agreeable, Toronto, in contrast to Montreal, struck me as shabby and provincial.

The total enrolment for the LL.B. course I had decided to take consisted of only two students—Carl Morawetz from Camp I and myself from Camp N. In a report about the students' scheme written on February 26, 1943, and sent to the Secretary of State from Fordham's office, I recently found the following paragraph which modesty will not prevent me from quoting:

> The plan was put into effect in the late summer of 1941 and has worked successfully ever since. The students involved have given neither the Commissioner of Refugee Camps nor the Director of Immigration any trouble at all and in most cases have done exceedingly well in their studies. There are two such students in the School of Law, University of Toronto, who are said by Professor W. P. M. Kennedy to be two of the most brilliant he has ever had.

The General and the Rabbi
A Contemporary Legend

One morning, late in 1941, Major-General Leo R. La Flèche, D.S.O., Légion d'Honneur, P.C. (C), LL.D, sat at his desk in Ottawa waiting for someone who had requested an appointment with him. As a matter of fact, London had asked him to receive the man, a rabbi, but he had no idea why, although he had been told that the call had come to Canada House directly from Mr. Churchill's office, having originated with the Chief Rabbi of all England.

The general had a crippled arm and only one eye as a result of severe wounds suffered in 1916, at which time he had been left for dead on a battlefield in France. He now was Deputy Minister of National War Services, having served as Canadian representative with the French Armies under General Weygand until the collapse of France in June 1940.

There was a knock at the door and Rabbi Abraham Price was ushered into the general's office. He was a man in his forties sporting a red beard. Considered to be one of the most learned talmudic scholars in Canada, he was highly respected in the Jewish community for his piety. Although his English was far from perfect—he needed help when composing letters to high officials—he was interested in modern ideas and by no means inexperienced in the ways of the world. Having come to Toronto from Warsaw via Paris a few years before the war, he had founded the Yeshiva Torath Chaim, at the corner of Ulster and Markham Streets in Toronto. Although the college had a few students who in due course were ordained rabbis, it needed more.

The general rose as Rabbi Price was shown in. Courteously he was offered a chair, but the rabbi declined, preferring to pace slowly and with dignity to the corner of the general's office that faced east. There, with quiet deliberation, he slipped a prayer shawl over his shoulders and, performing a ritual orthodox Jews observe during morning prayers, he strapped onto his left arm and his forehead the phylacteries (leather straps and small cubes containing parchments with biblical verses). He then began to recite his prayers in Hebrew.

The general watched him with amazement. At the appropriate moment, Rabbi Price took three steps backwards, satisfied, judging by the expression on the general's face, that the right atmosphere had been created for the sermon he was about to deliver. Calmly and leisurely he then removed his prayer shawl and packed away his phylacteries.

"The Jewish people have a long history," he began in halting English, "which started when Abraham assumed his faith from God and which the sons of Abraham have preserved through the ages, with fidelity and devotion. Until now the burden of this divine transmission has rested largely on the shoulders of European, and more specifically, Polish Jewry who had become the curators of the complex and subtle refinements of the faith.

"As you, General, no doubt know, this great tradition is now mortally threatened by the New Barbarians. Fortunately," the rabbi continued, "some dozens of young custodians of that tradition now find themselves on Canadian soil. They were placed there by chance, though 'chance' may not be the right word to describe intentions the human mind cannot readily comprehend. These young men have been imprisoned by a strange quirk of the law, a law which provides that you, General, now have complete authority over their future. What I mean to say is that you have the power to fulfil God's will and ensure the continuation and perpetual life of God's promise."

The general scratched the back of his head. "Please sit down, Rabbi Price," he said, "I'm not quite sure I follow you."

The rabbi sat down. "Let me explain, General," he proceeded. "On the Ile aux Noix, in Refugee Camp I, there are a large number of rabbinical students whose release I wish to request so that they can join my college in Toronto."

"But my dear Rabbi," the general exclaimed, "there has been a grave misunderstanding! I have absolutely nothing to do with them. I hardly know anything about this business. The man to see is Mr. F. C. Blair, the Director of Immigration."

"Are you sure, General? I've been told . . ."

The general interrupted, "I'm afraid you've been misguided, Rabbi. Let me telephone Mr. Blair."

Rabbi Price knew all about F. C. Blair. He bit his lip as the general summoned his secretary. "Get me Blair on the line," he said.

"All right," the rabbi then heard La Flèche say, "in your office at three this afternoon. I'll come along, too, if you don't mind. Thank you." The general hung up. Rabbi Price left the general's office, and they agreed to meet again at the appointed hour.

During a lonely lunch the rabbi wondered what course of action to take. He decided to appeal to F. C. Blair's patriotism; he also knew that Blair was an elder in the Baptist church. Besides, he had the feeling that General La Flèche would support him.

Once the three met in Blair's office the rabbi stated his case. "This is a great opportunity for Canada," he pleaded, "if these students are released, Canada will become what Poland had been for many centuries—the home of the continuing Revelation and the Flame of the Jewish Faith."

"This may well be so," Blair replied politely. "But we face a serious difficulty. Any one of these students might turn out to be a spy for Hitler."

"My dear Mr. Blair," Rabbi Price retorted with a trembling voice, "if any one of them would be revealed to be anything other than a most loyal friend of Canada, you can have my head."

Blair looked at La Flèche, La Flèche gave a slight nod. Soon thereafter the students were released.

Rabbi Price's high ambitions were not fully realized. Although three of the camp boys—Albert Pappenheim, Erwin Schild and Julius Litke—emerged from his college as rabbis and he remains a revered figure to all his former students, the school went into sad decline after the war. This was partly due to the secession of a group of students for whom Rabbi Price was too worldly. They did not quite approve of his ideas which encouraged them to complement their Jewish studies with junior matric, or with degrees from the University of Toronto, including some experience in the world of business. These students went to Montreal where they found a more congenial environment. The decline of the college was due to the rise of the day-school movement. Parents who wanted to give their children an intensive Jewish education no longer relished sending them to a live-in establishment, not even one headed by a great and enterprising talmudic scholar.

The Toolmakers and the Censors

Our rabbinical students were released in groups, and so were our toolmakers. But it was Fordham's view that Canadian employers were reluctant to hire Germans, even if they were refugees. Therefore he inspired Major Balls to conceive a Crown Corporation which could make use of the considerable toolmaking skills found in the camps. The primary purpose of Machinery Services Limited—according to the official description—was "to ease the tension of the new machine-tool market by rebuilding used equipment to such a degree that machines could be qualified 'as good as new.'" The project was an unqualified success, giving employment to about fifty or sixty of our men. In the mid-forties most of them, their German accents notwithstanding, were easily absorbed into Canadian industry.

In 1941 a workshop had been built in a hut in Farnham outside the compound, equipped by the shipbuilding firm of Sorel Industries Limited, employing fifteen of our highly professional draftsmen. It demonstrated their skills, as well as the leadership qualities of Hellmut H. Pokorny, the man who had been the driving force behind both projects. Pokorny had succeeded Lingen as camp speaker. He was a Berliner, formerly employed as production engineer for Siemens in Germany, who had emigrated to London in 1936 where he opened his own electroplating plant.

The Farnham workshop, legitimized by a special order in council, was a praiseworthy example of the Canadian genius for the profitable coupling of private and public enterprise. Our draftsmen received ten dollars a week from the private sector which was credited to their accounts by the public sector.

No private enterprise was involved in Machinery Services Limited: it was run by the government alone, with Pokorny as its superintendent. Located in two factory halls, seven miles west of the center of Montreal in Ville LaSalle, the plant was close to a railway siding of a C.P.R. branchline that led directly into the main building.

When the first recruits arrived toward the end of January 1942, nothing was ready for them. They had to live in drafty railway cars during the freezing cold winter; tending the stove at night was practically a full-time job. After two months they moved to a hostel. The plant itself was an old dilapidated marble mill, but with the passage of time and the application of caustic humor and Central European ingenuity they turned the place into a well-run and profitable operation.

In later phases, "native" Canadians joined the work schemes. The government had every reason to be pleased with our performance, and we had every reason to be pleased to be located next to Seagram's Distilleries, not because it gave us easy access to its products, but because Allan Bronfman, the brother of Sam, arranged for cheap meals to be served to our toolmakers at his newly opened cafeteria across the tracks from the factory. There they were treated as if they were Seagram employees.

Considerable pressure was brought to bear on those whom Major Balls considered qualified to volunteer. In Sherbrooke we had a highly skilled toolmaker, Alexander Horak, who cherished the well-founded hope that he might soon find employment with a Hungarian manufacturer in Toronto. He was therefore unwilling to sign up for a government project which, rightly or wrongly, seemed to him another form of internment. Sergeant-Major Macintosh, a special patron of his, introduced Horak to Major Balls. "Sonny boy," Balls said, slapping him on the shoulder, "this is your great chance. You'll make lots of money. You can take a bus any time you like to downtown Montreal. There are lots of pretty girls there." Horak was adamant. The next time around he was told that arrangements had been made for him to board in a private house in Lachine. Horak still stood firm. After a few more attempts Major Balls gave up, but announced gleefully, "I'll fix you." This caused Horak some concern. By chance he found out that Major Balls had written to Dr. E. H. Coleman, the Under-Secretary of State, recommending that Horak remain behind barbed wire until he had changed his mind. Wasting no time, Horak brought this matter to the commandant's attention. It was raised in Ottawa, and within a few weeks Horak was allowed to go to Toronto, where he began making tools for the Hungarian.

As to Hellmut Pokorny, he went into partnership in 1945 with the French-Canadian manager with whom he had worked at Ville LaSalle. The four pressure die casting machines he had designed and built became the nucleus of a three-man operation in 1946. When Pokorny retired in 1970, the plant was giving employment to four hundred men.

The thirty men who joined a large group of censorship examiners for the Department of National War Services in 1943 were not released collectively, but individually. They worked in Temporary Building 8 near the Experimental Farm in Ottawa.

Some of them had gained their freedom in other capacities and then joined the Civil Service in Ottawa—with Blair's blessing—to improve their living and working conditions. Their job was to censor the letters written by and to prisoners of war and civilian internees (Category A).

It must have been a bizarre experience for them to censor prisoners' mail, now as free men. They had been chosen because their integrity was beyond doubt, because they were knowledgeable about Germany and Austria, and fluent in the language. They were also able to detect hidden messages in innocently sounding phrases, an indispensable qualification for such work. They had acquired these skills in Germany and Austria when they tried to dupe the Nazi censors. Those who did not find the work boring became good detectors of suspicious characters; they relished the undoing of their nefarious fun and games. The censors' work was invaluable to the Canadian authorities, who up to then had had to recruit such personnel mainly from the ranks of the German departments of universities, and in England. In fact, much of the supervisory personnel came from the United Kingdom.

Release of a V.I.P.

Ernest (Putzi) Hanfstaengl had been transferred to Fort Henry in Kingston, Ontario, from Camp R in Red Rock early in 1942. Once the Americans were in the war, he no longer had any doubts about Germany's ultimate defeat. He had held back when the British had suggested, in the late winter of 1939–1940, that he might "write himself free" by putting his inside knowledge of the Nazi leadership at the disposal of British propaganda. He would not do this while in captivity, he said, but what he conceivably may have meant—and what the British may have understood him to mean—was that it might be imprudent for him to cast his lot with the Allies while the outcome of the war was very much in doubt. Now that was no longer a consideration. He was prepared to work for the Allies as a German patriot, to prevent them from "pulverizing" *all* Germans, the good *and* the bad.

It is not clear why Hanfstaengl did not approach the American government directly offering his services. Perhaps he thought any such offer might be stopped by the censors. In any case, one day a man from the Hearst Press visited the Fort and spent a few minutes talking with him in a corner. "Fortunately," Hanfstaengl reported, "he recognized my name." He gave the man a letter addressed to the Secretary of State, Cordell Hull, but it was actually meant for F.D.R., his old Harvard friend.

High-level diplomacy between the Americans, the British and the Canadians ensued, and soon afterwards an adviser to the president arrived in Fort Henry in a large black limousine; he was accompanied by his wife. His name was John Franklin Carter, and Hanfstaengl had known the couple in Berlin. Carter told him that the president had reacted favorably to his letter, accepting his offer in principle. "Well, first let me see how things are with you here," Carter said. Hanfstaengl then described life in the camp in such lurid terms that Mrs. Carter burst into tears.

Carter then told him that a number of difficulties would have to be resolved.

This took several months. On June 30, 1942, the eighth anniversary of the Roehm purge, which Hanfstaengl may have survived only because he was in the United States at the time, an American agent arrived at Fort Henry. He drove Hanfstaengl directly to Carter's house in Washington, explaining in the car that the Americans had "borrowed" him from the British, but that he had to remain in some form of custody. Carter and his wife welcomed him warmly, "thereby wiping out the misery of nearly three years." Here is his own account of what happened next:[27]

> "Before we have lunch, Dr. Hanfstaengl," Carter said, "I must introduce you to the guard the President has selected in accordance with our arrangement with the British Government." It was something of a cold douche, but I thought the sooner I met the fellow, the better. Carter ushered me into the next room, and there stood Sergeant Egon Hanfstaengl of the United States Army. [Egon is Hanfstaengl's son.] We gave each other a bear-hug and I burst unashamedly into tears.
>
> My first interview almost brought the mission to an end there and then. I was to be accommodated in an officer's bungalow in Fort Belvoir. I was introduced to the commanding general and we talked about this and that and the course of the war. During this conversation I got up and walked over to the big wall map of the Atlantic. "There is only one place for you to start the invasion of Europe, General, and that is here," I said, putting my finger on Casablanca. "It is the nearest point for your depots and you will be able to take possession of North Africa and roll up Italy in no time." Now I know nothing about military strategy and was just making what I hoped was an intelligent comment. If I had let off a bomb the general could not have been more appalled. He broke off the conversation without comment, left the bungalow, where the guards were quietly tripled and Egon promptly removed. I heard afterwards that the general had thundered that I was a spy and obviously knew all about Operation Torch. The matter went right up to the President who, I am told, laughed heartily, but suggested that it might be better if I was accommodated elsewhere.

Soon afterward a villa was found for Hanfstaengl in Bush Hill, Virginia, about twenty-five miles south of Washington. His son Egon was allowed to join him there. It was a run-down place which, according to him, had not received any repairs "since the boom of 1850." In the living room ancient brocade was peeling from the decaying walls, drooping over the portraits of early Americans.

Thanks to a powerful radio receiving set, Hanfstaengl was able to listen to German broadcasts. Every week six or seven typewritten sheets went to the president and to other American and British officials. A stream of military and civilian visitors called on him. Roosevelt saw to it that a Steinway grand piano was installed, but once arrangements had been completed to have a piano tuner come in to make it playable (negotiations had taken nine months), it was discovered "that the unfortunate gentleman in question was tuning angels' harps in heaven."

Listening to the radio, Hanfstaengl obtained a good idea of what was going on in Germany. Basing his reports on what he heard and what he knew, the main theme he constantly repeated in his reports was that there were important elements in the *Wehrmacht* who were non- (if not anti-) Nazi and who should receive Allied encouragement so that they could effectively resist Hitler. To him the communist danger was in the long run far more serious than the Nazi danger, and he felt that the Allied war aim should be the establishment of a constitutional monarchy after the war, perhaps under the regency of Lingen's aunt, Princess Viktoria Luise, with Hjalmar Schacht as its chancellor. He emphatically warned against what he considered the disastrous policy of unconditional surrender which would merely prolong the war by stiffening the determination of nearly all Germans.

Six weeks before the presidential election of 1944 it was feared that news of his presence in the United States might leak out and become an issue that might hurt Roosevelt's chances. (By then his son Egon was with the United States Army in the Pacific, at his own request.) Hanfstaengl left Bush Hill, Virginia, in September 1944 and was transported back to the Isle of Man in a state of deep depression; at times he felt suicidal. Once more he had failed to influence the course of events, and foresaw the destruction of Germany, "good and bad alike."

On September 14, 1945, he read in the *Daily Mail* that one of its correspondents had unearthed at Gestapo headquarters in Berlin a list of all those who were supposed to have been liquidated in the spring of 1940 after a successful invasion of Great Britain had taken place. "There were many illustrious names on the roster," Hanfstaengl recounts, "but figuring modestly half way down was that of Dr. Ernst Hanfstaengl." Although his lawyer drew this matter to the attention of the British authorities, he remained in internment.

He returned to Germany in the spring of 1946 and was kept in a camp in Recklinghausen for another six months. His blood pressure had dropped from one hundred and sixty to forty-five, and he had lost a lot of weight. With fifteen marks in his pocket, and a third-class railway ticket to Munich, he was finally released on September 3, 1946.

The Rear Guard

By September 25, 1942, 602 refugees had been released in Canada. Farnham was the first camp to be liquidated and on January 23, 1942, 445 of our men were transferred to Sherbrooke, where they remained until November 25, 1942. On that day 294 refugees were transported from Sherbrooke to Camp I on the Ile aux Noix. Their place was taken by 594 Category A merchant seamen who found Camp N in Sherbrooke considerably more fit for human habitation than it had been when we arrived there more than two years earlier. By December 1942, 341 refugees were still interned, of whom 113 were scheduled to return to the United Kingdom. That left a dwindling number of 228 at Fort Lennox on the Ile aux Noix.

For those who were left behind, the final phase was desperately demoralizing. It was heartbreaking for them to watch their more fortunate friends leave, promising to do their best to find sponsors or employers for them. Some were left behind, not because they were less smart or less enterprising, but because their gifts or interests were too specialized to attract sponsors. One of them was Helmut Kallmann; he was a music historian, and sponsors who loved music preferred performers such as Blume, Kander or Newmark, and considered Kallmann's talents a dubious investment. He stayed, patiently keeping himself busy as the camp librarian, but he became more and more despondent as he watched the intellectual and social quality of camp life deteriorate.

If morale was low then, it touched bottom one year later. One of the men, the Austrian "aristocrat" Berger-Voesendorf, suffered from acute depression. He had always kept himself aloof, looking down upon the "common people," and dreaming of a return to his homeland where he hoped to resume a pre-Hitlerian, if not a Hapsburgian, existence after the war. Occasionally, while in the throes of happy euphoria, he would offer to a few of his chosen acquaintances—he had no friends—the position of chancellor in his cabinet. He had nothing but disdain for the "rabble." Of course he was mercilessly teased.

During the night of May 2, 1943, Berger-Voesendorf slashed both his wrists. Fortunately the camp dentist, Dr. George Borchardt, arrived in time to save his life. He was taken to the Military Hospital at Ste. Anne de Bellevue. . . .

Nothing illustrates better the depths to which camp life had sunk than the appointment of S.S.G. as camp leader. (I am withholding his full name out of charity.) A man in his early forties who looked much older, he was of medium height with a flabby, milk-white complexion. He was an extremely intelligent person and a skilled politician whose particular genius lay in the manipulation of financial affairs. He claimed to be a disciple of the financial "wizard" of the pre-Nazi and Nazi period, Hjalmar Schacht. According to police records, he had been convicted in France in 1927 and in 1935 for uttering worthless checks. When he arrived in England in 1938 with a Danish passport under a false name, he posed as a German-Jewish banker who had suffered terrible privations at the hands of the Nazis in Dachau. (Later he told the commandant of the Seaton Internment Camp in England that he had escaped the brutalities at Dachau by acting as clerk for the commandant.) Soon after S.S.G. landed in England, British Intelligence discovered that he was a German agent, amply financed by a bank in Amsterdam, and was "charged with organizing German Intelligence or activities of some subversive nature." He was arrested, sentenced to six months of hard labor and on January 19, 1939, recommended for deportation for making a false statement to a police officer.

In Seaton S.S.G. had told the commandant that he was

impotent as a result of an airplane crash in the First World War. (He was fifteen years old in 1914.) Yet he was being pressed by solicitors to contribute to the support of a child by a German girl resident in England. He regularly received money from a lady in Devon whom he addressed in his letters as "Dearest Darling," telling her that he was seeking a divorce from his wife and stating that he was willing to become a Roman Catholic "to please her."

In Seaton he also whiled away his time writing a paper on castration as practiced under Hitlerism, dedicating it to the "Officer Commanding, 14th General Hospital, in token of his appreciation of kindness and expert treatment received."

The Seaton report closes with this sentence: "S.S.G. is an expert liar, an unmitigated scoundrel, and probably a black-mailer."

This was the scene as the final curtain descended on the last refugee camp on the Ile aux Noix, with unreleasables such as camp leader S.S.G. being shipped back to England, and releasables released.

But it was not all over for Walter Loevinsohn whom in Sherbrooke we used to call "The General" because of his expert knowledge of military matters. In Germany he had been a member of the Jewish Boy Scouts, and in England he was an instructor with the Jewish Volunteer Committee which provided training without weapons for refugees hoping to join a Jewish Brigade as part of the British Army. Loevinsohn was accordingly labelled a "militant Zionist, dangerous trouble-maker."

However, that was not the reason why, at the end of 1943, he was not yet released; suffering from TB of the hip-joint, after spending three months in Ste. Anne's Military Hospital, he had been sent back to Sherbrooke in November, 1941 and remained there for over one year, without getting better.

During that year he repeatedly tried to be transferred to a proper hospital or a sanitorium. His efforts were supported by Senator Cairine Wilson and the camp administration, but to no avail. Eventually he was taken to the hospital in Sherbrooke, X-rayed, and told his hip was just fine and he could walk again—"right now." As he received no satisfactory answers to his questions, he refused to walk. The doctor warned him that if he did not walk now, he would never walk again in his life. Loevinsohn said he was prepared to take that risk. The doctor was furious and sent him back to the camp. Had he not refused so stubbornly, he was later told at Ste. Anne's, the damage to his hip would have been enormous.

A letter Loevinsohn had sent to relatives in England was returned by Fordham with the following note:

> To the Commandant,
> Refugee Camp Sherbrooke
> 2 July, 1942:
> Attached letter is rejected as its writer has been definitely informed that his transfer to a sanitorium is not in contemplation, as it is entirely unnecessary and would not be warranted. He is becoming a nuisance.
> signed: Fordham

During that year Fordham resisted all attempts by Jewish organizations to have him moved to a proper hospital. When Sherbrooke was dissolved in November 1942, the question arose what should be done with him. He had been flat on his back for seventeen months and it seemed inadvisable to return him to England as a stretcher-case.

Camp leader S.S.G., despite his police-record or character flaws, behaved admirably and persuaded the medical officer that there were no proper facilities to look after him in his camp. Therefore, he had to be sent back to Ste. Anne's. To this day Loevinsohn is grateful to S.S.G. for "doing the right thing by me."

At Ste. Anne's, he was put in a forty-eight-pound body plaster cast and all he could move was his head. Whenever any one of the Nazis started to talk, he would say, "Shut up, you Nazi!" This attitude did not make him very popular with his roommates, and on one occasion several of them attacked him as he lay immobile. He was saved by the guards who came in and brandished their Sten guns. On another occasion a nurse accidentally came across a butcher's knife hidden in the drawer of a night table; it was obvious to her that it was to have been used to kill Loevinsohn. She immediately reported her discovery to the hospital authorities; a search was conducted, the knife was found, and within minutes Loevinsohn was moved to a room without daylight and full of garbage cans (which, however, were soon cleared out). He complained bitterly and so did his guards: one sergeant, two corporals and five men. He was there for a few weeks and repeatedly tried through the mails to be taken out. Consequently, his visiting privileges were cancelled.

Towards the end of his stay his conditions improved somewhat and he was given a comfortable and sunny room. In January 1944 he was moved to Mount Sinai Sanitorium in Ste. Agathe in the Laurentians, where he slowly learned to walk again. He was released in April 1946, having been in Canadian hospitals for five years.

After the war, the British insisted that he be sent back to England. They were afraid he might proceed to Palestine from Canada once he was able to walk again. Senator Wilson intervened on his behalf with Canadian High Commissioner Vincent Massey in London, who spent two and a half hours arguing with an official at the Home Office. The official sighed and finally said, "If you want him that badly, you can have him."

Loevinsohn remained in Canada. When he got married, he sent Fordham a wedding announcement on which he wrote: *Post tenebras venit lux.* (After darkness comes the light.) Fordham sent him a pleasant reply.

Friendly Aliens
As Rabbi Price had told General La Flèche, our presence in Canada was due to a quirk of the law. According to that law we were enemy aliens. Although the English tribunals had turned us into *friendly* enemy aliens, we had been interned and shipped to Canada.

On November 11, 1942 Colonel Fordham sent a circular letter to all of us telling us that we were "regarded as *friendly* aliens enjoying temporary liberty in Canada." As such we were not eligible for enlistment in the Canadian Army, unless by special order-in-council or authorized by the cabinet and the R.C.M.P. To join the army, another quirk of the law prescribed that our status had to revert to that of *enemy aliens,* or rather "enemy aliens who voluntarily accept an obligation to military service," but in order to do so, we had to declare our intention to become British subjects.

The order-in-council was passed on December 10, 1943. But there was an important qualification; a directive issued on

May 29, 1944 stated that we could enlist for active service, but would "probably not be sent overseas at the present time." Only at the very end of the war were some of the men who had enlisted sent overseas, and I have heard of no one who was in combat.

Still, the order-in-council was a tremendous step forward. A list of 952 names of refugees who now were eligible for naturalization after the war was compiled by the Immigration Department. The editors of the Quebec newspaper *Le Bloc* got hold of the list and affixed after each name the word *Juif* (Jew), printing it in that form on May 6, 1944. (*Le Bloc* had attacked the Mackenzie King government for making Canada the "dumping ground" of England).

Many of us enlisted, but only a few were told that we could not serve overseas. Gideon Rosenbluth was among those who was told. In fact the recruiting officer showed him a mimeographed directive to that effect. By then Rosenbluth was an economist working for the Wartime Prices and Trade Board, and it was felt that he would be more useful if he stayed in his present job. Gerry Kahn was asked whether he would volunteer to serve in the Pacific. He declined because he wanted to fight in Europe. So he stayed in Camp Petawawa, Ontario, for the duration of the war, censoring prisoners of war mail, especially in Italian. George Brandt enlisted after having joined the National Film Board. He volunteered for overseas service, was trained in military intelligence, but never went overseas. He returned to the Film Board in uniform, by agreement with the army, to make German-lauguage films. Another volunteer was Günther Bardeleben, who by the fall of 1944 was working as a laboratory assistant at the National Research Council in Ottawa. He found himself in the Medical Corps, was dispatched to Belgium and then proceeded to Germany with the Army of Occupation. So did Max Freilich who, wearing a Canadian uniform, attended two sessions of the Nuremberg War Crimes Trial in 1946.

Carl Froehling had been anxious to join up. He was working at the time in a junkyard in Kingston under conditions he found unbearable. After having paid his rent, he had $2.50 a week to live on; therefore, $1.30 a day as a private in the Canadian Army seemed to him a considerable improvement. In March 1944 he went to the recruiting station to be sworn in. After the ceremony, his employer phoned the commanding officer to tell him that Froehling was ineligible for military service, and that if they would let him go he would give him a raise. They looked up the regulations and were totally confused. In the end they decided Froehling's employer was probably right. After fifteen days in the depot he became an honorably discharged veteran. He received his discharge button and eighty dollars with which to buy civilian clothes. He used the clothing allowance to pay his fare to Ottawa to see Senator Wilson. Now more determined than ever to get into the army, he at last managed on April 4 and received his battle training. Just as he was about to be posted overseas, someone remembered that he wasn't allowed to go. After a stint defending the coast of Labrador, he was eventually sent overseas, and soon found himself in a reinforcement camp in Ghent, Belgium, where a great experience awaited him.

The man to decide whether Froehling was to reinforce the First Division in Italy or the Third Division in Germany was none other than Sergeant-Major Macintosh, who meanwhile had become a major. Since Froehling had been a stoker in Sherbrooke Camp, Macintosh recognized him immediately. When names were read out, it appeared that there had been thirty-five casualties in Italy; therefore thirty-five men had to be chosen to reinforce the Canadian troops there—Froehling's name was the thirty-fifth. Macintosh thought it was wrong to send a German to Italy; Germans, he thought, would be more useful in Germany. With characteristic finesse, he asked, "Have we got a Wop in the house?" Since an Italian shoemaker was present, he went to Italy, and Froehling was sent to Germany.

The week after the war ended Steven Stadthagen went with an advance party from England to Holland. He was in the Intelligence Section of a Highland regiment. They flew over the battlefields in a small plane. About a week later the question of leave came up. He asked the company commander whether he could go to Hamburg; he had a hunch, he said, that he might find his mother there, whom he had not seen since he had left Berlin before the war. He had no idea whether she was still alive, and since she was Jewish the chances were not promising. The company commander offered to drive him to Hamburg, which had been levelled by Allied bombing. It was said that in certain parts of town forty thousand corpses were still under rubble. The reason for Stadthagen's hunch was that his mother (who had been divorced from his father) had a friend in Hamburg who was a director of Shell Oil Company. The Shell Oil building, by a miracle, was still standing. He went to the main entrance and asked a guard whether he had ever heard of his mother's friend. The guard smiled and told him he was upstairs. Stadthagen rushed up and, all out of breath, asked the Shell executive whether he knew anything about his mother. "She's in the next room," his step-father announced. "We got married last week."

My own encounter with the Canadian Army was considerably less colorful, though it had its memorable moments. In the fall of 1942 I was among the students who flocked westward to help with the wheat harvest, since many farmers were away on active service. Soon after our return a crisis shook the campus of the University of Toronto. As all Canadian students were subject to compulsory military training, the question had arisen whether we, the released refugees who were considered ineligible for overseas duties, were not in a preferred position enjoying the privileges of a state-financed education without being allowed to assume the normal obligations of citizenship.

By a tie-vote the university's Board of Governors decided on November 16, 1942, not to admit some twenty more students whose applications already had been accepted. This decision triggered a highly emotional debate which forced everyone to take sides. The members of the Board had been appointed by the province of Ontario. George Drew, the premier of the province, accused the federal government of incompetence. On the one hand, he said, you tell us that these boys are perfectly all right and anti-Nazi to the core, eager and willing to join up, while on the other, you don't allow them to enlist. The pro-Drew newspapers—the *Globe and Mail* and the *Toronto Telegram*—backed the Governors. The *Toronto Star* defended the right of the refugees to be admitted, regardless of whether they could enlist or not. The student paper *Varsity* came out on our side, and so did, most effectively, *Saturday Night*, whose editor, B. K. Sandwell, had been one of the signatories of the telegram sent to Mackenzie King in 1939 appealing to him to admit the refugees from the ship *St. Louis*.

For many professors the moral aspects of the whole question assumed major proportions. C. B. Sissons, professor of ancient history at Victoria College, had sponsored David Hoeniger; he had been admitted in February—in November his registration was cancelled. Professor Sissons, supported by the president of the college, advised Hoeniger to carry on with his studies. At the height of the crisis Hoeniger was playing soccer for Victoria College against the medical students' team. He made a pass which allowed his team to beat the medics 1 to 0, but the losers protested and the Victoria team was disqualified because they said it included a player who had no right to be on it.

In the end the admissions crisis was resolved very simply. Ottawa decided to allow universities to enroll us for compulsory military training without the requirement of taking the oath of allegiance, thus placing us almost in the same position as all native Canadian students. The thirty-five refugees on campus who had been released from internment, including myself, happily joined the Canadian Officers' Training Corps. Once a month I had to report to the Royal Canadian Mounted Police, as all enemy aliens were required to do, occasionally proudly wearing my uniform.

In the summer of 1943 we spent two weeks in a training camp at Niagara-on-the-Lake. But when I tried to enlist in the regular army on April 18, 1944, I failed the medical examination for the most trivial of reasons: they didn't like my feet. This, however, did not prevent me eight months later from being accepted at the C.B.C., nor from the satisfaction of a full and happy life as a broadcaster for nearly thirty-five years.

Epilogue

Forty Years Later

It is sometimes said about us that we are the most successful group of immigrants who ever entered Canada. This is flattering, but what is success?

Some do substantially the same work they did when they were released and have not "advanced" at all. They live inconspicuously and modestly, yet think of themselves as successful. I understand one of us who went back to England became a bum who searches for treasures in garbage cans in the back streets of Soho. He, too, may think of his life as a success.

I am concluding this book with a *Who's Who*. This will give the reader a concrete idea of who we are, leaving him or her to decide who is and who is not successful by his or her own definition.

My wife started work on the *Who's Who* on the basis of the list of 952 names which the Immigration Department had compiled at the time the order-in-council of December 10, 1943, was passed. These were the men who had been declared eligible for naturalization after the war. I have seen references to another list containing 972 names, but haven't seen the list itself. Indeed, I have discovered one or two people who were released in Canada but whose names do not appear on my basic list. I attribute this discrepancy to the same factors which cast doubt on all the statistics relating to us, from the numbers on the ships bringing us here to the population figures in the different camps at various times. Whenever I examined them closely, I discovered some inaccuracies, possibly for the same reasons why our sergeant-major had such a difficult time counting heads during roll calls, particularly when he ended up with too many.

With the basic list of names in my wife's hand, I began sending form letters to one or two dozen people I remembered and whose addresses I had or could easily discover, requesting each of them to give me more names. I then wrote, requesting diaries, pictures and memorabilia. Replies began to accumulate on my desk. Many of my correspondents were kind enough to send me much valuable material, and I followed up every name that had been mentioned to me of people who had remained in Canada or had arrived from England after the war. Some addresses my wife discovered in phone books of various cities, always using the basic list to supplement the names sent to me. I was considerably less systematic in my search for people who now live in the United States, and only haphazardly pursued those who returned to England or now reside in other parts of the world. I approached them only if I could remember them or if they were of special interest to me.

While I was writing this book, my wife and I were able to locate altogether 478 ex-internees. In the *Who's Who* following this chapter, I listed: 283 in Canada; 80 in the United States; 18 in the United Kingdom; 17 in other countries.

Not everyone consented to have his name included in the *Who's Who*. Eighty preferred to remain anonymous, for various reasons which reflect the special character of our group and the nature of our experience.

We have no group feeling—we do not belong to Old Boys' Clubs, nor do we have associations, or annual camp reunions where we all get together to drink beer and sing "You'll Get Used to It," telling each other stories about the sergeant-major.

A few friendships have endured, but once we were released most of us did not feel the need to keep in touch. Although we may now say that the years behind barbed wire were invaluable to our development or that internment was a key event in our lives, and although we may even enjoy exchanging reminiscences once in a while, we tried in the years that followed our release to forget camp as quickly as possible. Very often, when we met in the street, we remembered the face but had forgotten the name. We wanted to be Canadians, not refugees.

Now that the youngest among us are fifty-six, internment has become synonymous with our lost youth; to think of it has become an exercise in nostalgia. But for those who did not wish to be included in the *Who's Who*, it was a painful period of which they do not wish to be reminded.

There were other reasons for their reluctance to be named. Some saw no point in being associated with a project they did not consider worthwhile; others had deliberately concealed the fact that they had once been arrested and interned for being "enemy aliens." They felt that the same stigma that was attached to having been incarcerated still exists today. One man who was born in East Germany asked me not to mention his name, because in case of another war he may be arrested again if it became known that he had been arrested before. It is not entirely inconceivable that a few declined to be mentioned because they did not wish to disclose their Jewish backgrounds.

Many have done well in business, and some have done very well. But more characteristic of our group is the number who went into the professions, into academic life, and the arts. This has to do with the nature of our group.

Mordecai Richler described the impression we created on the Jewish community when we emerged from the camps.[28] What is true of the Jewish community also applied to Canadian society as a whole. Richler was born in 1931, so he was about eleven when he first met some of us while he was hanging around Tansky's Cigar and Soda Store on St. Urbain Street in the working-class ghetto of east-end Montreal.

> The war in Europe brought about considerable changes within the Jewish community in Montreal. To begin with, there was the coming of the refugees. These men, interned in England as enemy aliens and sent to Canada where they were eventually released, were to make a profound impact on us. I think we had conjured up a picture of the refugees as penurious *hassidim* with packs on their backs. We were eager to be helpful, our gestures were large, but in return we expected more than a little gratitude. As it turned out, the refugees, mostly German and Austrian Jews, were far more sophisticated and better educated than we were. They had not, like our immigrant grandparents, come from *shtetls* in Galicia or Russia. Neither did they despise Europe. On the contrary, they found our culture thin, the city provincial, and the Jews narrow. This bewildered and stung us. But what cut deepest, I suppose, was that the refugees spoke English better than many of us did and, among themselves,

had the effrontery to talk in the abhorred German language. Many of them also made it clear that Canada was no more than a frozen place to stop over until a U.S. visa was forthcoming. So for a while we real Canadians were hostile.

There was a happy relationship between the qualities derived from our backgrounds and from the maturing process of the camp experience itself *and* of Canada at the time. The war had transformed the country from a colonial backwater of the British Empire into a modern nation. We came in at just the right time, at the beginning of the cultural and economic postwar boom, and most of us were at just the right age. There we were, rejected by Europe and unwanted by the United States, anxious to adopt Canada as our new home and eager to do well in it. There had hardly been any immigration to Canada since the nineteen-twenties, and we did not have to compete with other groups, as the postwar immigrants have had to do. As immigrants we had, as it were, a monopoly. Once the war was over, not many of us had to overcome serious obstacles imposed by anti-German or anti-Semitic prejudice. The war had turned Canada into a far more open and receptive society.

Everything was there to help our integration. Many of us married Canadian-born girls; to make friends, we knocked at Canadian doors and they were generously opened.

The universities were at the beginning of their great expansion, and so was Canada's cultural life. In 1940 only four fully professional orchestras existed. Their seasons lasted seven months out of twelve, so that the musicians had to supplement their incomes by teaching or doing supplementary work of one kind or another. Today there are eleven symphony orchestras playing all year round.

It did not take us long to feel at home in Canada. Having been burned in youth by the excesses of European chauvinism, Canada's relaxed attitude toward its nationhood suited us perfectly. Not many of us have any sympathy with Quebec's aspirations, which remind us too often of what we had escaped in the thirties.

For all these many reasons most of us chose to remain in Canada after the war, even if we could have gone to the United States or returned to Europe; we quickly grew roots in

Canadian society. Many of us even passed the ultimate test of true Canadianism: a passionate interest in hockey.

While traditionally the United Kingdom is less inclined to assimilate foreigners than Canada, in one respect it accepted the refugees more quickly; a sizeable number who graduated into the British Armed Forces from the Pioneer Corps were actually in combat. Some joined the Navy, others the commandos and other regiments. At the time of the invasion of the Continent these men were encouraged to change their names in case they were taken prisoners. One of them participated in the D-Day landing as a sergeant and had gone on patrol with another soldier; he stayed with his comrade when he was injured, was captured by the Germans and interrogated for several days. Had they found out who he really was, they most certainly would have shot him.

Those who went to the United States also have done well; Henry Kissinger wasn't one of us. Had he emigrated to England in 1938 instead of the United States, he might have been. In that case he would have received top marks in the camp school and the Canadian sky would have been his limit.

As it has been ours.

Notes

[1]Martin Gilbert and Richard Gott, *The Appeasers*. London: Weidenfeld and Nicholson, 1963.

[2]Bruce Hutchison, *The Incredible Canadian*. Toronto: Longman's, 1953.

[3]M. J. Proudfoot, *European Refugees, 1939–52*. Evanston, Illinois: Northwestern University Press, 1956.

[4]Irving Abella and Harold Troper, "The Line Must be Drawn Somewhere: Canada and Jewish Refugees, 1933–1939," in *Canadian Historical Review*, June 1979.

[5]Arthur D. Morse, *While Six Millions Died*. New York: Random House, 1968.

[6]Ken Adachi, *The Enemy That Never Was*. Toronto: McClelland and Stewart, 1976.

[7]Norman Bentwich, *They Found Refuge*. London: The Cresset Press, 1956.

[8]Max Beloff, "The Anti-Semitic Persuasion," in *Encounter*, August 1979.

[9]Louis de Jong, *The German Fifth Column in the Second World War*. Chicago: University of Chicago Press, 1956.

[10]Andreas Hillgruber, *Hitler's Strategie, Politik und Kriegsführung, 1940–41*. Bernard & Graefe Verlag für Wehrwesen, Frankfurt am Main.

[11]Reprinted from F. Lafitte, *The Internment of Aliens* (Penguin 1940) by kind permission of the Policy Studies Institute (previously Political and Economic Planning).

[12]Keith Feiling, *Neville Chamberlain*. London: Macmillan's, 1970.

[13]Charles Ritchie, *The Siren Years*. Toronto: Macmillan's, 1974.

[14]Martha Dodd, *Through Embassy Eyes*. New York: Harcourt Brace, 1939.

[15]Joachim Fest, *Hitler*. New York: Harcourt Brace Jovanovich, 1974.

[16]Ernst Hanfstaengl, *Unheard Witness*. Philadelphia-New York: Lippincott, 1957.

[17]Eugen Spier, *The Protecting Power*. London: Skeffington, 1951.

[18]François Lafitte, *The Internment of Aliens*. Penguin Books, 1940, pp. 141, 142.

[19]Benjamin Patkin, *Dunera Internees*. Australia: Cassel's, 1979.

[20]Carlos Baker, *Hemingway*. New Jersey: Princeton University Press, 1952.

[21]Carl Weiselberger was an inmate of Camp B. "The Rabbi With the Axe" was originally published in German under the title *Der Rabbi mit der Axt*. Translation by Monica Koch. Reprinted by special permission of Dr. Herta Hartmanshenn and Professor Frederick Kriegel, University of Victoria, British Columbia.

[22]Ronald Stent, *This Bespattered Page?* London: André Deutsch, 1980.

[23]Erhard Ingwersen, *Berliner Originale*. Arani Verlag, 1958.

[24]Interview in Oral History Project, Imperial War Museum, London.

[25]Paterson Report, 1941, PRO DO/996/41P/00147.

[26]Chaim (Charles) Raphael, *Memoirs of a Special Case*. London: Chatto and Windus, 1962.

[27]Ernst Hanfstaengl, *Unheard Witness*. Philadelphia-New York: Lippincott, 1957.

[28]Mordecai Richler, *The Street*. Penguin Books, 1969.

Appendices

The Prison Ships and their Cargo

Name of Ship	Date of Departure	Port of Embarkation	Description of load (based on diplomatic records)	Date of Arrival in Quebec
Duchess of York	June 20	Liverpool	2112 Category A internees 535 Prisoners of War	June 29
Arandora Star	July 1 sunk, July 2	Liverpool	473 Category A internees (146 drowned) 717 Italian internees (453 drowned)	——
Ettrick	July 3	Liverpool	1308 Category B, C internees 405 Italian internees 785 Prisoners of War	July 13
Sobieski	July 4	Greenock	982 Category B, C internees 548 Prisoners of War	July 15

Between June 29, 1940 and July 15, 1940
the following persons arrived in Quebec:

2112 Category A internees (including 178 refugees)
2290 Category B, C internees
405 Italian internees
1868 Prisoners of War
6675

The Internment Camps

Prison Ship	Name of Internment Camp	Camp Population at time of arrivals (based on camp records)	Dates
Ettrick	L (Quebec City, Quebec)	793 (Category B, C)	July 13 – Oct. 15, 1940
Ettrick	Q (Monteith, Ontario)	501 "	July 14 – Oct. 15, 1940
Sobieski	T (Trois Rivières, Quebec)	715 "	July 15 – Aug. 12, 1940
Sobieski	B (Little River, New Brunswick)	711 "	Aug. 13, 1940 – June 21, 1941
Sobieski	I (Ile aux Noix, Quebec)	273 "	July 15, 1940 – end of 1943
Ettrick/Sobieski	N (Sherbrooke, Quebec)	736 "	Oct. 15, 1940 – Nov. 25, 1942
Ettrick/Sobieski	A (Farnham, Quebec)	523 "	Oct. 15, 1940 – Jan. 23, 1942
Duchess of York	R (Red Rock, Ontario)	1,150 (Category A)	July 1, 1940 – Oct. 31, 1941

Who's Who

ABUSH, Max—upholsterer; Toronto; p. 170
ADAM, Hans—manufacturer's agent (retired); active community worker; Montreal
ADLER, Hans—senior advisor on integration, Statistics Canada; Ottawa
ADLER, Rudolf—rabbi, Ohev Shalom Congregation; Orlando, Florida
ALBERSHEIM, Eugene—manufacturer of sportswear; Winnipeg
ALSBERG, Henry—manager of research and development in a chemical company; Northbrook, Illinois
ALTMAN, Alfred—designer and renovator of homes; Toronto
AMBERG, Carl—chairman, Department of Chemistry, Carleton University; Ottawa; p. 155
AMTMANN, Wilhelm—violinist, teacher and author (retired); Ottawa; pp. 93, 155
ANSBACHER, Solomon—rabbi, Shaar Zion Congregation; Montreal. Deceased, 1978
ARNHOLD, Gerard—major shareholder in several companies involved in the manufacture, distribution and export of photographic and cinematographic equipment; Sao Paolo, Brazil; pp. 140-142
ASCHER, Gerald—electrical engineer, formerly with NASA, now in solar research; Alexandria, Virginia
ASHERMAN, William—import-export business; Montreal

BACHRACH, Joseph—chairman, Department of Chemistry, Northeastern Illinois University; Lincolnwood, Illinois
BADER, Alfred—president, Aldrich Chemical Company; distinguished art collector; Milwaukee, Wisconsin
BAER, Doctor Charles G.—dentist; Montreal
BAER, H. Albert—manufacturers' agent for children's clothes; Toronto
BALL, Jack—shoe wholesaler; Toronto
BARDACH, John—marine biologist; professor and research affiliate, University of Hawaii; Honolulu, Hawaii
BARDELEBEN, Gunter—clinical chemist, Toronto General Hospital; Toronto; p. 251
BARRASS, Godfrey—freelance writer for advertising and private business; also worked for the Ontario government. Deceased 1979, Toronto; pp. 48, 49, 79, 80, 82, 83, 193
BARTH, Henry—insurance agent; Montreal
BAUER, Gustav—credit salesman; Montreal; pp. 120, 121
BAUM, Gregory—professor of religious studies, St. Michael's College, University of Toronto; pp. 5, 146, 150, 151, 169, 170
BAUM, Robert—project coordinator, International Packings Corporation; New Hampton, New Hampshire
BAUMGARTEN, Willi—hotel and restaurant manager (retired); Toronto
BAYREUTHER, Willi—employee, plumbing and heating manufacturer (retired); Montreal
BEIFUS, Arthur—silver-plater; Toronto
BELITZER, Alvin—performer and teacher of popular music; Toronto
BENDER, Fritz—research chemist, forest products research laboratory, (retired); Ottawa
BERENBLUM, Bernard—retail salesman of men's wear; Toronto
BERGÉ, Len—pianist-conductor of popular music; musical director on cruise ships; New York City; p. 155
BERGMAN, Ken—sales representative. Deceased 1955, Toronto
BERGMAN, Ralph—sales representative. Deceased 1979, Toronto
BERGMANN, Frederick—bookkeeper and computer operator; New York City
BERKOWITZ, Leo—traffic manager, import company; Montreal
BERNHARD, H.D.—barrister; Toronto
BEVERSTEIN, Doctor Jacob—physician; Toronto
BEVERSTEIN, Lothar—furniture manufacturer; Toronto
BIBERFELD, Henry—lecturer, Beth Jacob Teachers' College; consulting chemist; Montreal
BIBERFELD, Julius—fur manufacturer; Montreal
BICK, Bernard L.—production superintendent, Industrial Home for the Blind; Brooklyn, New York
BINDER, William—bookkeeper for Zionist organization. Deceased 1965, Toronto
BLAIR, F.C.—director of immigration. Deceased mid-forties; pp. xii, 183, 186, 200-205, 219, 227, 230, 232, 239, 240, 242
BLOCH, Arthur—wholesale meat merchant; Montreal
BLOCK, Victor—professor of German, McGill University, Montreal (retired); Ithaca, New York
BLUETH, John—consultant, mechanical engineer in aircraft industry; Montreal
BLUGER, Walter—statistician, Government of Canada (retired); Ottawa
BLUME, Helmut—former dean and professor emeritus, Faculty of Music, McGill University; Montreal; pp. 21, 39, 138, 155, 156, 205, 231, 232, 246
BODENHEIMER, Doctor E.L.—physician; New York City
BOLDES, Heinz—manager, retail store; Toronto
BONDI, Sir Hermann—physicist and mathematician; Chief Scientist, Department of Energy; London, England; Director-General of European Space Research Organization, Paris, 1967-1971; London, England; pp. 24, 196, 197
BORCHARD, Doctor George—dentist (retired); Montreal; p. 247

BORNEMAN, Ernest—professor of social and cultural psychopathology, Psychological Institute, University of Salzburg, Austria; author; Scharten, Austria; pp. 5, 72, 92, 139, 140, 187, 188, 210, 211
BRAMSON, Henry—bookkeeper and comptroller (semi-retired); Montreal
BRANDT, George—professor of drama, University of Bristol; Bristol, England; pp. 38, 139, 171, 251
BRAUN, Wilhelm—professor, former chairman, Department of Foreign Languages, Literature and Linguistics, University of Rochester; Rochester, New York
BRIAN, Walter—travel agent; New York City
BROOKS, Vernon—professor of physiology, University of Western Ontario; London, Ontario
BUCHHOLZ, Werner—senior engineer, IBM Corporation; Poughkeepsie, New York
BURGGRAF, Father Joseph—member of the Pallottine Community in the United States. Deceased in the early seventies

CAHEN, Oscar—artist; guiding spirit of *Painters Eleven*, a pioneer group of Modern Art in Canada; Represented in the National Gallery in Ottawa, the Art Gallery of Ontario, and in the Public Library and Art Gallery of London, Ontario; killed in a car accident, 1956; pp. 156, 157
CAHN, Arno—director of development, Household Products Division, Lever Brothers; New York City
CAHN, Doctor Charles—psychiatrist, Douglas Hospital; Montreal
CAHN, Fritz—department store manager (retired); Ottawa
CAHN, Peter—consulting broadcast engineer; Montreal
CARLEBACH, Ephraim—rabbi, House of Israel Congregation; Ste. Agathe, Quebec
CASSIRER, Thomas—professor of French, University of Massachusetts; Amherst, Massachusetts
CHARY, Henry—aircraft component designer and engineer; Los Angeles, California
CLEMENT, Erich—engineer; Liverpool, England
COHEN, Rudy—chartered accountant; Montreal
COLEMAN, Harry W.—controller, construction supplies company; Toronto
COOPER, John—controller; Toronto
CUMMINGS, John—businessman (aluminum) (semi-retired); Montreal
CURTIN, Walter—photographer; Toronto

DAHL, Kurt—real estate investor; Toronto
DALTROP, Werner—businessman (scrap metal); Toronto
DAMMERS, Francis S.—marketing director, aluminum company; Morristown, New Jersey
DEMUTH, Armand—business executive (retired); Montreal
DEUTSCH, Ernst—professor of physics, Memorial University; St. John's, Newfoundland
DE WATH, Edward—cost engineer in his own consulting firm; San Francisco, California
DIESS, John—owner of travel agency; Merrick, New York
DOERR, Heinrich—shipping department, DeHavilland Aircraft of Canada (semi-retired); Toronto; pp. 116, 117
DRESNER, Erwin—vice president and general manager, McGregor Hosiery Mills; Toronto
DRUCKER, Fred—research promoter of renewable sources of energy; Toronto
DUSCHENES, Lutz—teacher. Deceased 1952, in France
DUSCHENES, Rolf—architect; Saint John, New Brunswick

EBNER, Hugo—lawyer; Vienna, Austria
ECKERS, Hans—architectural designer; Beloeuil, Quebec
ECKSTEIN, Felix—accountant and author (semi-retired); Toronto
EDELMAN, Franz—vice president, Radio Corporation of America; Princeton, New Jersey
EDMISON, J.A.—assistant to the Principal of Queen's University, Kingston, Ontario (1950-1959); member of the National Parole Board; taught criminology at the University of Ottawa (1967-1973); also, director of John Howard Society and co-founder of Trent University, Peterborough, Ontario. Deceased 1980, Peterborough; pp. 127-129; 142
EGAN, George—owner of printing company; Montreal
EGGERT, Reverend M.—priest; formerly active in Quebec where he was known as Père Onésime; Boettingen, West Germany
EHRLICH, Gunter—president, air-conditioning company; Montreal
EHRLICH, Phil—electronic engineer; Toronto
EISENHAMMER, Kurt—post office employee; Toronto
EISINGER, Josef T.—physicist, biologist and historian, Bell Laboratories; Murray Hill, New Jersey; p. 152
EISINGER, Kurt—agency and interline manager for North and Central America, Lufthansa; New York City
ELIAS, Joseph—rabbi, principal of Beth Jacob High School of the Yeshiva Rabbi S. R. Kirsch and of the Rika Breuer Teachers' Seminary in New York; Monsey, New York
ELIEL, Ernest L.—professor of chemistry, University of North Carolina; Chapel Hill; North Carolina; pp. 199, 200
EPSTEIN, John H.—printer; Bowie, Maryland
EXTON, Eric—president, Seel Enterprises Limited; active in Jewish and non-Jewish philanthropies; Toronto

GURAU, Henry—general manager of auto aerials manufacturing company; Toronto
GUTER, Ernest—professor of accounting and business administration, Dawson College; Montreal; pp. 140-142
GUTTER, Leo—employee; Montreal
GUTTMAN, Werner—secretary treasurer and assistant to the president of chemicals import company; Montreal

HAAS, Gerhard—research scientist, General Foods Corporation; Tarrytown, New York
HAHN, Ben—businessman (retired); Toronto
HAHN, Jack—planner, designer and supervisor of major engineering projects; vice-president and director, SNC Group; Toronto and Montreal
HAIN, Max—butcher; Toronto
HANFSTAENGL, ("Putzi") Ernest—deceased 1975 Munich; pp. 50-55, 58, 59, 112-114, 117, 243-246
HARIDGE, Peter—patent examiner; Ottawa
HARTOGSON, Naphtoli Hartog—journalist and educator; Montreal
HAYES, Saul—until his retirement in 1974, Executive Vice-President of Canadian Jewish Congress. Deceased 1980, Montreal; pp. 129, 181-185, 189, 198, 199, 201, 212, 231, 233
HAYWARD, Constance—member of Board of Governors, Acadia University; worked for the Citizenship Branch in the Department of the Secretary of State in Ottawa until 1958; Wolfville, Nova Scotia; pp. 181-182, 184, 189, 192, 201, 212, 216, 217, 218, 231, 233
HECKLER, Walter—director of scrap metal company; Montreal
HECKSCHER, William S.—art historian; consultant, Department of Rare Books, Princeton University Library; Kress Professor at National Gallery of Art, Washington, D.C.; former member of Institute for Advanced Study; Princeton, New Jersey; pp. 5, 40, 41, 93, 147-153, 166
HEIDENHEIM, Dieter—product designer for plumbing manufacturer; London, Ontario
HELLER, Peter—professor of German and comparative literature, State University of New York, Buffalo; Williamsville, New York; pp. 21, 39, 87-91, 122-124, 130
HELLER, Peter (Fritz)—systems engineer and consultant; Bromley, Kent, England
HELLMANN, Joe—development officer (retired); Ottawa
HELLMAN, Doctor Kurt—anaesthetist; Mount Sinai Hospital, Toronto; assistant professor, University of Toronto
HERALD, Bob—graphic design consultant; corporate art director for medical publishing house; New York City
HERRMANN, Manfred—United States Merchant Marine; New Orleans, Louisiana
HILLER, Erwin—accountant; Toronto
HINDS, Gerald—Canada Council; Ottawa
HIRSCHFELD, Fred—horologist; New York City
HIRSCHFELD, Henry—partner, electrical contracting company; Montreal
HIRSCHLAND, Joe—accountant; Toronto
HIRSHFELD, Otto—department store buyer; Montreal
HITSCHFELD, Walter—atmospheric physicist; Dean of Graduate Studies and Vice-Principal (Research), McGill University; Montreal; p. 46
HOENIGER, F. David—professor of English literature, Victoria College, University of Toronto; Toronto; p. 254
HOFF, Richard   translator (semi-retired); Ottawa
HOFFMAN, Peter—owner of Manitou Sports College, Ivry-sur-le-lac, Quebec; Montreal
HOFFMANN, Ralf L.—chairman, Hoechst Canada (retired); Montreal; pp. 40, 187
HOLTFRETER, Johannes—professor emeritus of Zoology, University of Rochester; member, National Academy of Sciences; Rochester, New York; pp. 146, 147
HOLZ, Willi—employee, electrical instrument company; Ajax, Ontario. Deceased 1979
HOMBURGER, Walter—managing director, Toronto Symphony Orchestra; Toronto
HORAK, Alex—hotel manager (retired); Vienna, Austria; pp. 241, 242
HORN, Alfred—merchant, leather and giftware; Montreal. Deceased 1980
HORN, Warren—exporter; Montreal
HUEPEDEN, Marten—chief of engineering/architectural division, Training System Headquarters, Canadian Forces Base, Trenton, Ontario

INSLEY (Inslicht), Leo—owner of cutting tool distribution company; London, England; pp. 222-224, 227

JACOB, Kurt—actor, editor, translator; Toronto
JACOBSON, Garry—industrial merchant; Montreal
JAFFE, Doctor Fred—pathologist, director of laboratories at Queensway General Hospital; Toronto
JAKEROV, Alex—project manager, air pollution control devices manufacturing company; Ottawa
JAMES, Rolf—project manager, Association of Canadian Advertisers; Toronto; p. 194
JONASSOHN, Kurt—professor of sociology, Concordia University; Montreal
JOSEPHSON, Rudi—employee, Department of Trade and Commerce (retired); Ottawa
JOSEPHY, Walter—teacher of electronics communications at a community college; Ottawa; p. 194

KAHAN, Heinz—employee, Canadian National Railway (retired); Montreal

KAHLE, Hans—released in England in 1941; active as a military journalist for the *Daily Worker, Time Magazine*, and other publications; returned to East Germany in 1946; made Chief of Police of the Land Mecklenburg-Vorpommern. Died in 1947 of heart failure; pp. 84-87, 131, 164, 193

KAHN, Alex—butcher; London, Ontario

KAHN, Gerry—salesman, artifacts and giftware; Victoria, British Columbia; p. 251

KALLMANN, Helmut—chief, Music Division, National Library of Canada; Ottawa; pp. 39, 246, 247

KAMERMAN, Fritz—lens grinder (retired); Los Angeles, California

KAMNITZER, Heinz—historian and essayist; television and film writer; translator; East Berlin, East Germany

KANDER, Gerhard—stockbroker, Toronto; pp. 155, 246

KANTOROWICZ, Aaron—net manufacturer; Montreal. Deceased 1979

KAPELLER, Lawrence—sales manager; Ottawa

KASSNER, Doctor Edward—general practitioner (retired); Southport, Prince Edward Island

KATES, Josef—chancellor, University of Waterloo, Kitchener, Ontario; consultant, management science, operations research, computers and systems analysis; Toronto

KATZ, Paul—manager of giftware business; Montreal

KATZENBERG, Teddy—baker, Montreal. Deceased 1979

KAUFMAN, Hon. Mr. Justice Fred—Quebec Court of Appeal; Montreal; p. 49

KAUFMAN, Hans—violinist and musical entrepreneur; Toronto; p. 155

KENTON, Egon—owner of wholesale giftware business; Toronto

KENTON, Rolf—chartered accountant; Toronto

KESTLER, Heini—employee, Montreal. Deceased 1976

KESTLER, Rudy—editor of English publications at OECD; Paris, France

KIEWE, Henry—sewing machine mechanic; Montreal

KIPPER, Bernard—owner of industrial packaging business; Toronto

KLAG, Leo—owner of graphic art company; Montreal

KLEIN, Doctor Edmund—physician, skin cancer specialist; associate chief, Department of Dermatology, Roswell Park Memorial Institute; Buffalo, New York; pp. 39, 170

KLEINER, Kurt—sales manager of gift importing company; Toronto

KLINKHOFF, Walter—owner of art gallery; Montreal

KNEPLER, Henry—authority on the role of the social sciences and humanities in engineering education; consultant to UNESCO; former chairman, Department of Humanities, Illinois Institute of Technology, Chicago, Illinois

KNOLL, Bert—purchasing manager for a diesel company; Montreal

KOBER, Walter—window dresser; Montreal

KOCH, Eric—writer; Toronto; pp. 2, 3, 36, 40, 63, 77, 147, 190, 191, 215, 216, 235-237, 253, 254

KOCH, Doctor Paul—assistant director, Chemical Laboratories, Montreal General Hospital; Montreal

KOENIG, Bert—salesman; Ottawa

KOENIG, Willi—partner in electrical company; Montreal

KOHN, Fred—shirt cutter (retired); Toronto

KOHN, Walter—shoe manufacturer (retired); Toronto

KOHN, Walter—professor of physics, University of California, San Diego; director, United States National Institute for Theoretical Physics; La Jolla, California

KOKISH, Hugo—real estate broker (retired); Montreal

KOLLER, Philip—economist; Ottawa. Deceased 1961

KRAEMER, Franz—head of Music Section, Canada Council; Ottawa; pp. 39, 155, 169, 170, 228, 229

KREISEL, Henry—professor of comparative literature, University of Alberta; novelist; Edmonton; pp. 17, 18, 37, 47, 48, 168, 186

KRIEGER, Rudy—(retired); Montreal

KRUGER, Karl H.—parish priest; Grangemouth, Stirlingshire, Scotland; pp. 56, 57, 114, 115, 194

KUNSTLER, Peter—consulting engineer; Cleveland, Ohio

KUTNER, Hans—manager of lumberyard (retired); Ottawa

LAKS, Jacques—consulting engineer; Montreal

LAMBEK, Joachim—professor of mathematics, McGill University; Montreal

LANDECK, Bernard—part-time worker in nursing home; formerly, employee of mail order company; Chicago, Illinois

LANDMANN, Henry—sales representative of display materials manufacturing company; Montreal

LANG, Herbert—salesman (retired); Toronto

LANGSTADT, Robert—professor of fine art, Concordia University; Montreal; pp. 37, 40, 157, 170

LASSMAN, Saul—consulting engineer; Montreal

LAZAR, Joseph—owner of industrial diamond tool company; Montreal

LEHMAN, Peter D.—owner of food service company; Burlington, Ontario

LEPPMANN, Wolfgang—professor of German, University of Oregon; Eugene, Oregon

LEVI, Guiseppe—owner of travel agency; Montreal

LEVI, Leo—chartered accountant; Toronto

LEVIN, Fritz—killed in action in Israel in 1948 in defence of the Kfar Etzion settlement in the Hebron Hills. Buried in the Military Cemetery of Jerusalem

LEVY, Kurt—professor of Hispanic studies, University of Toronto

LIEBEL, George—vice-president and general manager of company producing flavors and fragrances; Toronto; p. 226

LINGEN, Fritz—studied agriculture in England after his release; changed name to George Mansfield; set up a model farm in Hertfordshire; married Lady Brigid Guinness, youngest daughter of Lord Iveagh, in 1945; became a British subject in 1947; was readmitted as a German subject in 1953; adopted the title Prince Friedrich of Prussia; chairman of a German cultural center in London; marriage ended in 1966; before the date for the final divorce hearing could be fixed, he disappeared near Bingen, West Germany—ten days later his body was found in the Rhine River; pp. 43–46, 81–83, 124, 125, 141, 169, 193, 241

LION, Edgar—urban planning expert; Montreal

LIPNOWSKY, Harry—(retired); Winnipeg

LISSAUER, H.A.—businessman; Clarks Summit, Pennsylvania

LISSMANN, Hans—zoologist; Fellow of Trinity College, Cambridge, England; retired but still active in biological research; Cambridge, England

LITKE, Joel—rabbi, Beth Jacob Congregation; Oakland, California; p. 240

LITTAUR, Eric—pharmacist (retired); Montreal

LOEB, Justin—manufacturer of bathroom accessories; Toronto

LOEBENBERG, Leo—consulting engineer; Montreal

LOEVINSOHN, Walter—senior engineering industry executive and industrial consultant; Montreal; pp. 19, 20, 22, 41, 42, 71, 248–250

LOEWENTHAL, Julius—professor of pharmacology, McGill University; Montreal

LOW, Zeev—rector, Jerusalem College of Technology; Jerusalem, Israel

LOWE, Herbert W.—stockbroker; Toronto

LOWENSTEIN, Rudi—headwear manufacturer; Winnipeg

LUWISCH, Charles K.—chartered accountant (retired); Montreal; pp. 50, 73

MAHLER, Max—owner of cigar store; Montreal

MAHLERMAN, Hermann—Hebrew teacher (retired); Winnipeg

MANDL, Paul—professor of mathematics, Carleton University; Ottawa

MANDL, Willi—businessman (retired); Toronto

MANNES, Joseph—employee; Montreal

MARCUSE, Hans H.—restaurant owner; Miami, Florida

MARCZAK, Walter—(retired); Gabriola Island, British Columbia

MARKEL, Simon—consulting electrical engineer; Montreal

MARX, Ernst—businessman, Marx Metals, Ltd., Toronto. Deceased 1975; p. 40

MARX, Karl A.—owner, Marx Metals Limited; Toronto; p. 40

MASSEY, Vincent—Canada's first Canadian-born Governor-General, from 1952–1959. Deceased 1967, London; pp. 29–32, 65, 74–76, 176

MAUTNER, Doctor Lawrence—chief of Department of Pathology, St. Joseph's Hospital, Toronto; assistant professor, Department of Pathology, University of Toronto; Toronto

MEIER, K.R.—engineer, attached to World Health Organization, Rome, Italy. Deceased 1976

MEISSNER, Doctor Georg—associate pathologist in chief, Rhode Island Hospital; professor of Pathology, Brown University's Program in Medicine; Providence, R.I.

MEYER, Ernie—newspaperman; Jerusalem, Israel

MEYER, Paul Hugo—professor of French and comparative literature, University of Connecticut; Storrs, Connecticut

MICHEL, Walter—engineer, Bell Laboratories, Holmdel, New Jersey; author (arts and literature), Rumson, New Jersey

MODDEL, Martin—tailor (retired); Toronto

MORAWETZ, Carl H.—barrister; Toronto; p. 237

MUELLER, Adolf—furniture manufacturer; Montreal

MUENTZ, Sigmund—controller and office manager; Montreal

NAEGELE, Kaspar—obtained Ph.D. in sociology from Harvard University in 1952; visiting professor at the Institute for Sociology, University of Oslo; returned to Canada in 1954 and joined department of anthropology and sociology at the University of British Columbia, Vancouver, where he later became Dean of Arts; fell to his death at Vancouver General Hospital in 1965; pp. 46, 47, 101

NAGELBERG, Leo—psychologist; graduated from the University of Montreal; worked with Jewish Board of Guardians in New York City where he also was in private practice as a psychoanalyst. Deceased 1969

NASHMAN, Gerald L.—president of presses and air compressors manufacturing company; Montreal

NATHAN, Hermann A.—translator (retired), National Research Council; Ottawa

NELKEN, Abraham—teacher at rabbinical college; Montreal

NEUBERGER, Ernest—owner of shoe business; Hamilton, Ontario

NEWMAN, Eric—company secretary and director (retired); Wokingham, Berkshire, England

NEWMARK, John—pianist; Doctor of Law (honoris causa), McGill University; Montreal; pp. 5, 121, 154–156, 231, 232, 246

NOERZ, S.D.S., Brother Reimar—St. Gregory's Church; St. Nazianz, Wisconsin

NUSSBAUM, Samuel—lamp and lighting manufacturer; Toronto; pp. 4, 5, 49
NUSSBAUM, Walter—owner of travel bureau; Ramat Gan, Israel

OBERLANDER, Peter—professor of regional planning and director of Center for Human Settlements, University of British Columbia; landscape architect; Vancouver
OBERT, Toni—criminologist (retired); Montreal
OELBERG, Henry—director of finance, Allied Jewish Services; Montreal
OESTREICHER, Ernest A.—senior economist, Department of Finance, Ottawa; (1977-1979); Director for Canada, the Netherlands and the Scandinavian countries at the Asian Development Bank in Manila; Ottawa
OPPENHEIMER, E.M.—professor of German, Carleton University; Ottawa; p. 73
ORGEL, Stephan—lawyer, Ottawa. Deceased 1955
OSTWALD, Martin—professor of Greek and Latin, Swarthmore College; Swarthmore, Pennsylvania

PAPPENHEIM, Albert—rabbi, Beth David B'nai Israel Beth Am; Toronto; pp. 49, 50, 240
PERUTZ, Max—molecular biologist; received Nobel Prize for Chemistry in 1962, jointly with J.C. Kendrew, for preparing a three-dimensional model of the protein *myoglobin*; until 1979 Head of Medical Research Council's Molecular Biology; Cambridge, England; pp. 24, 193, 194, 211
PFALZNER, Paul—medical physicist, Ontario Cancer Foundation; Ottawa
PFEIFFER, Julius—chartered accountant; Montreal; p. 103
PFUNDT, Bernard—writer, businessman (retired); Hull, Quebec; pp. 18, 19, 55
POKORNY, Hans Hellmut—engineer; Perth, Ontario; pp. 240-242
POLLACK, Willi—photographer at Karsh Studio, Ottawa. Deceased in the late fifties
POLLAK, Dolfi—upholsterer; Toronto
POSER, Ernest—professor of psychology, McGill University; Montreal
PRICE, Rabbi Abraham—rabbi, Yeshiva Torath Chaim College, Toronto; author of *Mishnath Abraham* (two volumes), *Sefer Chassidim* (three volumes) and *Imri Abraham*; pp. 237-240, 250
PROPP, Max—chartered accountant; Vancouver

RAPHAEL, Charles (Chaim)—since 1969, Research Fellow, University of Sussex; Head (HM Treasury) of the British Information Services in New York City (1959-1968); well-known biblical scholar and author; writes fiction under the pseudonym Jocelyn Davey; pp. 181, 184-186, 198, 208, 209
RAPPOPORT, W.M.—chartered accountant; Toronto
RATTNER, William—salesman; Montreal
REICHE, Hans—weapons systems advisor, Department of Defence, Ottawa; author of books on philately; Ottawa; p. 205
REINHOLD, Ernst—professor of German, University of Alberta; Edmonton
RENNER, Karl D.—C.B.C. administrator (retired); pp. vii, 39
RITCHIE, Charles S.A.—former Canadian ambassador in Bonn, West Germany; permanent U.N. Representative; ambassador to NATO and ECM; appointed Canadian High Commissioner in London in 1967; Ottawa; pp. 31-33, 68
ROSE, George—optometrist; Ensino, California
ROSENBERG, Alfons—B.B.C. Overseas Service (German Section) (retired); London, England; pp. 147, 165, 194
ROSENBERG, Hans—salesman; Montreal
ROSENBLUTH, Gideon—professor of economics, University of British Columbia; Vancouver; p. 251
ROSENMEYER, Tom—professor of Greek and comparative literature, University of California; Berkeley, California; p. 39
ROSENTHAL, Henry—mechanical engineer; Montreal
ROSENTHAL, Martin—lumber business (semi-retired); New York City
ROSS, Victor—managing director and Chairman of the Board, Readers' Digest; London, England; pp. 21, 23, 45, 83, 84, 169
ROTHFELS, Horst A.—director of education, South Shore Protestant School Board; Montreal
ROTHFELS, Klaus—professor of biology, University of Toronto; Toronto
ROTHSCHILD, Kurt—president of electrical contracting company; active in Jewish communal affairs; Toronto
RUCKERSBERG, Walter—hardware business (retired); San Diego, California; p. 114
RUSSEL, James B.—life insurance agent; Toronto

SAALHEIMER, Manfred—legal consultant on human rights legislation. Member of national staff, Canadian Jewish Congress; active in numerous educational and rescue programs, as well as in post-war restitution matters. Deceased 1967, Montreal
SALTZMAN, Fred—bookkeeper; Toronto
SAMISCH, Walter—exporter of motor parts; Barnet, Hertfordshire, England
SANDER, Lothar—chemical researcher, Union Carbide Corp.; Princeton, New Jersey
SARTON, Edgar—director of European Operations, Ministry of Economic Development, Alberta House; London, England; pp. 15, 49, 73
SAXENBERG, Emanuel—partner in electrical company. Deceased 1974, Montreal

SCHEYE, Klaus—vice-president, Technical Services Division, W.R. Grace and Company; Scarsdale, New York
SCHIFFMAN, Friedel—science student, McGill University, Montreal. Deceased 1947
SCHILD, Albert—professor of mathematics, Temple University; Philadelphia, Pennsylvania
SCHILD, Erwin—rabbi, Adath Israel Congregation; Toronto; pp. 73, 240
SCHIPPER, Bernard—abducted and murdered by Arabs near Kibbutz Hasorea, Israel, in 1948
SCHMIDT, Arthur—wholesale meat merchant (retired); Montreal
SCHNITZER, Edward—manufacturer of leather goods; Montreal
SCHONHARD, Oscar—employee, Chicago branch of Tiffany's (retired); Whiting, New Jersey
SCHUSTERMAN, Leo—employee, garment industry. Deceased 1980, Montreal
SCHOTT, Werner—film editor in New York City; formerly with National Film Board, Ottawa. Deceased in the mid-sixties
SCHWARZBARTL, Kurt—designer of men's and boys' outerwear; Montreal
SCHWARZBARTL, William—employee, garment industry. Deceased 1977, Montreal
SEELIG, Doctor Gustav—physician (retired); Toronto
SEIDLER, Eric—electronics technician (retired); Montreal
SEIDLER, Harry—architect; Milsons Point, Australia
SEIDLER, Marcell—businessman, Australia. Deceased 1978
SENONER, Joseph—C.B.C. administrator; Montreal; pp. 112, 115
SERVOS, Henry—department store owner, Milton, Ontario. Deceased 1966
SHIELD, Ernest—physiotherapist (semi-retired); St. Eustache, Quebec
SHIFTON, Henry—civil servant (retired); Ottawa
SHURMAN, Fred—salesman for company manufacturing trimmings and braids; Montreal
SILBER, Bernard—furrier; Montreal
SILBER, Leo—furniture business; Montreal
SILBER, Max—furniture business; Montreal
SILZER, Fred—manager of real estate company; Toronto
SIMSON, Herbert—manager of printing plant; Toronto
SMARAC, Edward—metal plant supervisor; Toronto
SPANIER, Leonard—businessman (retired); Montreal
STADTHAGEN, Steven J.—dress designer; Montreal; pp. 252, 253
STEIN, Eric—businessman (retired); Montreal
STEIN, Theodore—senior manager, Real Estate Division, Canada Permanent Trust Company; Toronto
STEINBERG, Edgar—atomic energy, quality control technician (retired); Toronto
STEINHART, Erwin—sales and service of industrial sewing machines, Montreal (semi-retired); Ottawa
STEINHART, Gerald—sales and service of industrial sewing machines, Montreal (semi-retired); New York City
STENGER, Alfred—writer; Ottawa
STENSCH, Walter—civil engineer, concrete arch dams; Montreal
STERN, Max—owner of art gallery; Montreal
STETHAM, Colonel H.—deceased 1944; pp. 118–122, 176, 184, 204
STEUER, Ernst—employee of international paper company (retired); Montreal
STEUERMANN, Doctor Arthur—dental surgeon; assistant director, Division of Dental Services, City Hall; Toronto
STRAUSS, Edgar—accountant; Montreal
SWINTON, Kurt—president of direct mail order marketing company; chairman of mining company and financial consulting firm; Toronto; pp. 147, 205–207

TASH, Bernard—carpenter; Montreal
TAUBER, Gerald—professor of physics and astronomy, Tel Aviv University; Tel Aviv, Israel
TENGOOD, Eric Z.—municipal court clerk; Philadelphia, Pennsylvania
THEILHABER, Thola—engineer, Raytheon Laboratories; Lexington, Massachusetts. Deceased 1978
THEILHEIMER, Henry—shoe business; cantor emeritus, Temple Anshe Sholom; Hamilton, Ontario
TORRINGTON, Fred—advertising coordinator for United States Office of Tourism; chairman, Canadian Association for Applied Social Research; Ottawa
TROLLER, Bill—garage owner (retired); Ottawa
TUERKISCH, Jacob—owner of clothing store; Toronto
TURGEL, Robert—furrier; Montreal
TURKISH, Bernard—businessman (retired); Toronto

UMMENHOFER, Pater Anton—parish priest; Hintereben, West Germany; pp. 71, 157, 159–161, 224, 225

VEIT, Philipp F.—professor of German, State University of New York, Buffalo
VIVANTE, Arturo—writer; Wellfleet, Massachusetts; pp. 20, 21, 24

WAENGLER, Ernst—economics journalist; Toronto; pp. 20, 21, 24

WAGNER, Eric—processor of animal hair; Montreal
WAGNER, Max—processor of animal hair; Montreal
WALDSTON, Gerry P.—president of creative design service company; Toronto; pp. 40, 157
WALLACH, Fred—office manager (retired); Montreal
WALLICH, Walter—B.B.C. producer (semi-retired); London, England; pp. 23, 45, 73, 74, 86, 188, 189
WALTER, Gerhard—senior engineer, IBM Data Processing Product Group; Poughkeepsie, New York
WALTON, Henry—senior lecturer in German studies, Portsmouth Polytechnic; Emsworth, Hampshire, England
WANGENHEIM, Kurt—writer and legal editor; researcher for Ontario Addiction Research Foundation. Deceased 1978, Toronto
WARSCHAUER, Heinz—director of education, Holy Blossom Temple (retired); Toronto
WASSERMAN, Charles—journalist, broadcaster, novelist and film-maker, specializing in Eastern European affairs; well-known to CBC listeners for his coverage of the Hungarian uprising in 1956. Deceased 1978, Austria
WAYNE, Bruce (Weinberg, Dr. Bruno)—international lawyer, in private practice in New York City. Deceased 1978; pp. 164, 216, 217, 224
WEDELES, Herbert—wholesaler and distributor (retired); Oakville, Ontario
WEIHS, Alfred—master cabinet maker. Deceased 1971, Montreal
WEIHS, Harry—consulting engineer; Toronto
WEIHS, Walter—shoe manufacturer. Deceased 1965, Toronto
WEIL, Edward—distributor of Cuisinart food processor and housewares; Toronto
WEINBERG, Albert—magazine distributor; Toronto
WEINBERG, Berndt—chemist; researcher for Canada Packers, 1958-1964; joined Department of Industry and Commerce, Ottawa in 1964; international authority on oils and fats. Deceased 1974
WEININGER, Joseph—physical chemist, Electrochemistry Branch, Power Systems Laboratory; Schenectady, New York
WEISELBERGER, Carl—music and art critic for the Ottawa Citizen until his retirement in 1968. Deceased 1970, Victoria; pp. 104-110
WEISINGER, Arthur—display advertising (retired); Toronto
WEISS, Ernie—publishers' agent; Guelph, Ontario
WEISS, Henry—manager of textile company. Deceased 1969, Toronto
WEISSENBERG, Gunter—salesman of men's clothing; New York City
WELDON, Eric—clothing manufacturer; Montreal
WELDON, Kurt—estimator in electronic equipment company; Toronto
WIENER, Reverend Alfred—The People's Church; Toronto
WILLCOTT, Lee L.—chemist (retired); Laguna Hills, California
WILSON, Cairine, Senator—in 1956 became the first woman to preside over the Senate. Deceased 1962; pp. 181, 182, 189, 212, 216, 248, 252
WINNICKI, Ludwig—businessman; Vaduz, Liechtenstein
WISE, A. Martin—(retired); Eastbourne, England
WITTMANN, Herbert—carpenter and farmer; Ville des Laurentides, Quebec
WOLF, Henry—mathematical researcher in space technology; New York City
WOLFF, Albert—puppeteer; New York City
WOLFF, Fred W.—president of investment and trading company; Toronto; p. 93
WOLFF, Gottfried—student; emigrated to Brazil. Deceased in the mid-forties
WOLFF, Manfred—builder and developer; Toronto; p. 14
WORMANN, Bert—accountant and office manager (retired); Saskatoon, Saskatchewan
WORYMKLIN, Jonas—worker. Deceased 1980, Montreal
WRIGHT, Thomas—director of European Operations, Schenley International Company; Munich, West Germany

ZACHARIAS, Bruno—motor mechanic; service station operator; Toronto
ZADEK, Hans—importer, promotion merchandise; Montreal
ZADIK, Frank—consultant orthopaedic surgeon; Leigh, Lancashire, England
ZAHLER, S.A.—jeweller (retired); Montreal
ZANGER, Erwin—lumber company executive; Ottawa
ZIEGLER, Peter—biochemist; Assistant-Director of Research, Canada Packers; Toronto